Contents

Preface		5
Introduction		11
Chapter 1:	Kingdom Economy 1.0	27
Chapter 2:	The Foundations of Kingdom Economy	37
Chapter 3:	Kingdom Perspective on Money	61
Chapter 4:	Preparing to Prosper	83
Chapter 5:	Signs of True Prosperity	93
Chapter 6:	Your Purpose and Calling: Ultimate Keys to Kingdom Economy	101
Chapter 7:	Seed: The Secret to Your Calling and Exercising Dominion	115
Chapter 8:	Genetic Code of Your Seed	135
Chapter 9:	Your Giving Determines Your Future	143
Chapter 10:	Going to the Next Level	151
Chapter 11:	Why Our Tithing Doesn't Work?	165
Chapter 12:	Seven Kinds of Giving	179
Chapter 13:	Supernatural Millionaires	185
Chapter 14:	Two Kinds of Income: The Seed and the Bread	209
Chapter 15:	Understanding Your Inheritance	219
Chapter 16:	The Twelve Laws of Kingdom Economy	239
Chapter 17:	Prosperity and Suffering	255
Chapter 18:	Mammon and God	263
More Books & Resources		273

KINGDOM ECONOMY

Why all tithe - paying believers
do not walk in financial abundance

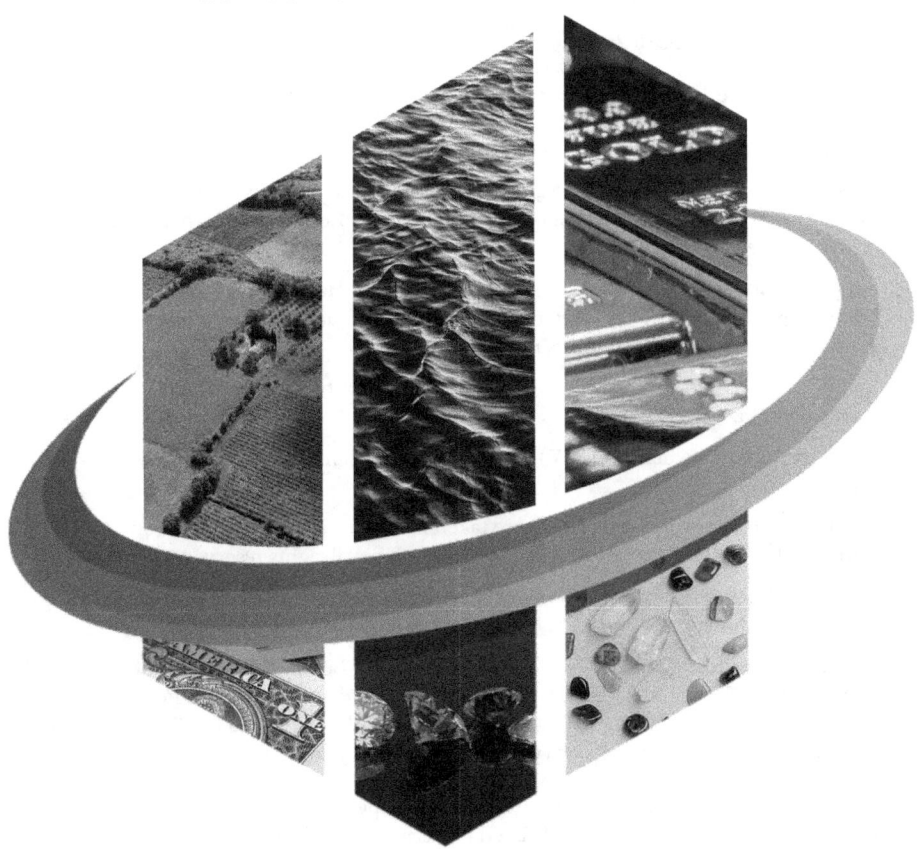

ABRAHAM JOHN

Kingdom Economy

Why All Tithe-paying Believers do not Walk in Financial Abundance

Copyright © 2019 by Abraham John

Published by Abraham John

www.TheKingdomNetwork.org
email: mim@maximpact.org
1-800-558-5020
(720)-560-4664

ISBN: 978-1-948330-26-8

Printed in the United States of America

All emphasis or additions within Scripture quotations are the author's own.

Unless otherwise indicated, all Scripture quotations are taken from the New King James Version of the Holy Bible. Copyright © 1995-2010, The Zondervan Corporation. All rights reserved.

Scripture quotations marked (NLT) are taken from the Holy Bible, New Living Translation, copyright 1996, 2004. Used by permission of Tyndale House Publishers, Inc., Wheaton, Illinois 60189. All rights reserved.

Scripture quotations marked (DARBY) are from the Darby Bible which is public domain.

Scripture quotations marked (KJV) are from the King James Version which is public domain.

Scripture quotations marked (NCV) are taken from the New Century Version®. Copyright © 2005 by Thomas Nelson. Used by permission. All rights reserved.

Scripture quotations marked (ASV) are from the American Standard Version which is in the public domain.

Scripture quotations marked (TLB) are taken from The Living Bible copyright © 1971 by Tyndale House Foundation. Used by permission of Tyndale House Publishers Inc., Carol Stream, Illinois 60188. All rights reserved. The Living Bible, TLB, and the The Living Bible logo are registered trademarks of Tyndale House Publishers.

Scripture quotations marked (NIV) are taken from the New International Version®, NIV® Copyright ©1973, 1978, 1984, 2011. Used by permission. All rights reserved worldwide.

All rights reserved. No part of this book may be reproduced or transmitted in any form or by any means, electronic or mechanical-including photocopying, recording, or by any information storage and retrieval system without permission in writing from the author. Please direct your inquiries to info@thekingdomnetwork.org.

PREFACE

"And you shall remember the Lord your God, for it is He who gives you power to get wealth, that He may establish His covenant which He swore to your fathers, as it is this day"
(Deuteronomy 8:16).

This book is not for everyone. God has given this book for the following groups of people:

- This book is for those who are willing to be transformed into the image and likeness of God.
- This book is for those who are called to fulfill an end-time purpose of God.
- This book is for those who want to be trained in managing the wealth of God's kingdom.
- This book is for those who have been faithful in giving tithes and offerings but haven't seen a financial breakthrough.
- This book is for those who are tired of religion and the regular church experience.

I believe America is going to be the last superpower on earth. There will not be another military or financial superpower on earth ever again.

God is going to raise up a different kind of spiritual and financial superpower—a kind the world has never seen before. They are going to be His people (the *ekklesia*, the true church) from every nation of the earth.

He is going to raise up whoever is willing to make themselves available to Him. He is getting ready to do a final wealth transfer to His people. Before He can transfer His wealth to His people, they need to be trained. Otherwise, if money reaches the hands of people that do not know how to manage it, money will end up destroying them.

The reason the Lord is not answering our prayers for wealth and finances is because He is trying to protect us. He wants His body to be the most productive people on earth. God never changes and His principles remain the same from generation to generation. His ways are the same but always higher than our ways—as the heavens are above the earth.

When I look at the people in the Bible to whom God transferred the wealth of the wicked, they all had one thing in common: they were all walking faithfully with God. They were not wishy-washy, fair-weather Christians. Noah, Joseph, Moses, Nehemiah, David, Daniel, Esther, and others were committed to God, even until their deaths. They had a pure heart and the fear of God in their lives. Their priorities were God and His kingdom.

They all had the same passion to please God and walk in His ways. They wanted to make their God great among the nations. Their motives were not rooted in self-preservation, personal ambition, or wealth creation. They obeyed God's Word—regardless of their circumstances. They were determined to do one thing: please God, no matter what the cost. They risked their own lives for others and for God.

This book is for those who want to please God, no matter what the cost. This is for those who are willing to stand up for their God, no matter how the world may treat them. This is for those who are willing to risk their life for the high calling of God. This is for those who want to make a difference for God in this generation and for generations to come. Dear saints, it is time for us to show the world that we are able to do what we preach. We are able to live the way we say we should.

PREFACE

I have not yet seen a person on this earth who loves to be poor. Even beggars hate it; that is why they beg. It is the desire of every human being to be financially blessed. Everyone dreams about the day when they are free to buy the things they need and not worry about money. Traveling to places where they always longed to go is another common dream.

Every minister of the gospel prays and advertises their ministry events in order to raise enough funds to cover their expenses. Money has a key place in our lives and society. Almost everything revolves around the issue of money. Most people spend the majority of their life working or doing something to make money. As long as we live on this earth, money has a role to play.

If it were not for the issue of money, the majority of the violence, murders, and wars would have never happened in the world. As the Bible says, the love of money is the root of *all* evil. The root cause of all evil on earth is the desire to have more money. People and nations lie, cheat, kill, steal, and vandalize their own kith and kin because of their greed and the desire to make more money. If money wasn't the main reason for the crimes people commit, our prisons would be half empty.

It is God's desire for us to be financially prosperous and blessed. Everyone God used in the Bible was financially prosperous. Sometimes they were the most wealthy and powerful people on earth in their day. God promised them saying, you shall be the head and not the tail. You shall be above every nation on earth and you shall lend to many nations and you shall not borrow (see Deuteronomy 15:6).

What is the key to financial prosperity? Does hard work alone lead to financial success? Will getting an education and then a job lead you to financial freedom? I don't think so. I know many hard-working people who are poor and broke. I have also seen many people with college degrees living hand to mouth.

Please don't misunderstand me. All financially prosperous people are not spiritual. We live in a world where success is measured by how much money a person possesses. If you have a billion dollars, you will be on the list of the most successful people. These people might be total failures according to God's standard. God doesn't measure a person's success based on the amount of money they have.

Financial prosperity is not the sign of God's blessing. Instead, if you are truly spiritual, you will be financially blessed as well—unless you deny that blessing by choice or because of ignorance. You don't have to be spiritual to be financially blessed. But it is impossible to be spiritual and not financially blessed. What I mean by spiritual is not someone who is always saying hallelujah or praise the Lord, or someone who is religious. Neither does spiritual refer to someone in the ministry or someone who sings in the choir.

What I mean by spiritual is someone who knows their purpose and lives in true obedience to the Lord and His Word. God promised to bless us when we seek and obey Him. The Bible says, "The young lions lack and suffer hunger; but those who seek the Lord shall not lack any good thing" (Psalm 34:10).

God didn't create man to suffer on earth. Suffering came because of the fall. He created us to have dominion and enjoy the blessings He has stored on this earth. God never expected Adam to be poor, sick or miserable. God gave the entire earth as his inheritance. Adam didn't lack anything in his life until he disobeyed God. Poverty, lack, and impoverishment came as the result of sin and the curse.

We read in 1 John 3:5 that Jesus "was manifested to take away our sins." If that is true, whatever we've lost because of sin must be restored without a doubt. Man was in God's kingdom before he committed sin; and as long as he was in the kingdom of God, he didn't lack any good thing.

Before I share with you about the kingdom economy, it is important that you have an understanding about the kingdom of God. Jesus said, "But seek first the kingdom of God and His righteousness, and all these

PREFACE

things shall be added to you" (Matthew 6:33). This book is not about the kingdom of God. Please make sure you read the other volumes on the kingdom published by this ministry. It is important to have a kingdom perspective before you learn about the kingdom economy.

At the beginning of this year we started with $600 in our bank account. In the first week of January we needed to pay our property tax, which was $1,800. What did we do? God spoke to me to sow $100 every day for the thirty-one days of January, the first month of the year as a miracle seed for the rest of the year. The first week I was at a conference in Orlando, Florida, and God said to sow. We had to believe God for the seed to sow. For the next thirty-one days my wife and I sent $3,100 to different ministries and people.

Within the first month of the year, God brought in more money than we received in six months of the previous year. I believe it was because of our obedience and faith. Keep in mind that we did that only that year because God told us to do. It was a compounded blessing and we were able to help my own people and prepare to open our fourth orphanage in India. We also helped thirty-two families who were tsunami victims to reestablish their lives. Did you exercise your faith the last time you gave? Was that part of your motive?

You will learn about giving that brings a breakthrough into your life. In this book you will learn about seven different types of giving that brings seven different kinds of blessings to your life. All giving is not the same and they don't all bring the same harvest.

If you are a faithful tithe-payer and have received many blessings from God that you do not have room enough to contain, then you do not need to read this book. If you are a tithe-payer and have not seen the blessings that the Bible promises, then this book is for you.

This book is dedicated to the precious partners of this ministry who have stood with us and sown sacrificially into this ministry. Your life is a living epistle. The commitment and the example you have shown is truly extraordinary.

I want you to know that your life and generosity has touched many lives around the world and impacted areas on this earth that otherwise would have been impossible. I believe God has given me this book to bless your life so that you can enter into the next level God has for you in your finances and be everything God intended for you to be. Thank you.

Abraham John

INTRODUCTION

THE STORY OF THE PEANUTS

I will never forget the peanuts. When I was growing up, each month the day came when my father received his salary. All the children at home waited with expectation for his return from work. We knew that when our father got paid, he would bring peanuts for us. That was the special treat we received each month for eighteen years.

When my father walked down the street to our home, we would look through the windows to see if he was carrying a packet in his hand or not. If we saw the packet, we rejoiced, knowing we would get to eat peanuts that day. From that experience, whenever I received coins from my mother or relatives, I would run to the store to buy peanuts. I used to eat them while I was walking back home. My intent was to finish eating them before I reached home because I did not want to share with anyone else.

The saddest thing was that if there were some unexpected needs or medical bills to pay for my mother's treatment, then my father did not bring any peanuts because he did not have enough money left to buy any. As children, we were sorely disappointed whenever our father came home any month, and did not bring any peanuts.

I grew up in church and in a family who believed in giving. My father believed in tithing and faithfully did that almost all his life. He worked for the government and every month when he received his salary, my father paid the tithe and all the other bills. By the fifth of the month, there was no more money left. Then we had to wait until the beginning of the next month when he got paid again. I remember my mother sending me to the neighbor's to borrow some money for bus fare or even food items to meet urgent needs of the family.

This went on for years and the financial situation did not improve. Though my father got promoted and received raises, there was still nothing left over by the end of the month. In between that, my mother became seriously ill, putting even more financial strain on the family. We had no medical insurance nor financial help, so with each visit to the doctor, more medicines were prescribed and expenses kept going higher and higher.

My father managed to send my oldest sister and brother to college. I remember as a young boy, trying to discover the reason why my mother was ill all the time. She used to cook us three meals every day for 365 days a year. There was never any break or vacation for her. People came to help her but that did not relieve her from her duties. That could have been the reason for her sickness. Whether things she needed were available or not, my mother was responsible for coming up with three meals per day. At that time, I did not have the maturity to understand things from her perspective.

By this time God put a desire in my heart to go to a Bible college in India. I did not know that I was called into ministry at that time. I did not have any dramatic encounter with God or lightning flash from heaven involved with my call. (That's what I thought God would do to call someone into ministry.) The only thing I felt was a strong desire in my heart. There were some prophetic words people spoke over my life, but I did not have any understanding about prophesy at that time either. All I knew was that I needed to leave my house and should go to this college.

When I went to my dad to ask him for permission to send me to this Bible college, he said no. I stayed around the house for another year. The

INTRODUCTION

following year I went to him again to present the idea of going to a Bible college. This time when I asked, I cried and begged him to send me. He got fed up with me, and said, "You go and do whatever you want to do." Before I went to the college, I never spoke in English. I only knew three words: *courage*, *love*, and *God*. I left my home when I was eighteen years old and went to a Bible college in the northern part of India.

After I reached there, God opened my understanding and I began to speak and preach in English within three months. God gave me English as a gift, and He told me, "You need this for your future." I had no idea what my future was at that time. I finished three years of Bible school and began to travel across India preaching the gospel.

I grew up with an irrational fear of God. I believed God was this mean, old creature, sitting in heaven with a lightning rod. He was waiting for me to make a mistake so He could strike and punish me. So, whenever I did something wrong, I could not sleep for days. Fear and anxiety would grip my heart, as I believed God would reject me and not love me any longer. I was always wondering when the lightning was going to fall from heaven on my head. I believed the reason my mother was sick was because we had done something wrong and God was punishing us for it. But I could not find a reason that made sense.

Though I came to the Lord through the Pentecostal movement and grew up as a Pentecostal, I felt in my heart there was something missing. I did not know what it was at that time. I did what everybody else did without ever asking why? The Pentecostal movement began as the result of the outpouring of the Holy Spirit in the early 1900s. It spread across the globe and missionaries went to every nook and corner of the earth and started churches with the revelation they had.

What many did not realize was that the Pentecostal movement was not complete. Their main mission was to get people born-again (saving them from hell's fire and reaching heaven), baptized, and filled with the

Holy Spirit with the initial evidence of speaking in tongues. The moment a person spoke in tongues, they thought they "arrived" spiritually and most stopped growing.

Most did not have a basic understanding of the Scriptures or the plan and purpose of God for the earth, for man, or for salvation. Their mission was—and still is—to take more people to heaven, without realizing that God never wanted any humans in heaven. He created them to manage the earth for Him. They completely neglected the biblical teachings about the earth, the very inheritance God our Father gave to us.

There is an overemphasis among Pentecostals on some of the gifts of the Holy Spirit, especially healing and prophecy. If you can prophesy, heal some headaches and backaches, then you can become a spiritual superhero. I could not figure out the reason why so many are sick in the church in the first place! If we are saved from sin, all the results of sin (poverty, curses, and sicknesses) should leave us too, right? I found out that in most cases, that was not true. Most people did not understand what salvation is. They thought it was "fire insurance" just in case hell broke loose. Their salvation was their "get out of jail free" card and nothing more.

I felt there was something missing or incomplete about the salvation people were receiving. Most of the healing that was done, was for people who had been in church for several years. I could not find any healing services that were conducted for the believers in the early church in the book of Acts. Most of the healing in the Bible was done for the unbelievers as a sign.

God sent the Pentecostal movement to lead us to something. He sent it to lead us to the person of the Holy Spirit. He was sent to earth as the Governor of the kingdom, to help us govern it and manifest the kingdom of God that is in us. Because of insecurity and the lack of proper teaching, many were attracted to His gifts for personal gratification or the need to feel significant, rather than using them for kingdom building.

INTRODUCTION

Most people never went beyond this initial stage. They got stuck with the gifts of the Holy Spirit, but neglected Him who came to help us govern the kingdom of God on earth. It is like God gave us a cow to provide us with milk. Every day we want its milk but never pay attention to the cow. What would be the end result? Either the cow would run away or it would die from neglect. In this case, the Spirit of God withdrew from us for a long time.

We didn't grow beyond speaking in tongues. We are supposed to be growing into the fullness of Christ and manifesting Him to the people and creation around us. Salvation is just the beginning of life with Christ; and speaking in tongues is the beginning of life with the Holy Spirit. They are not the destination; they are entry levels. Christ is the door to His kingdom and speaking in tongues is the entry level to everything the Holy Spirit is and what He knows. He is the Spirit of wisdom, knowledge, and understanding. He is the only Person that knows what is in the mind and heart of God (1 Corinthians 2:10-11). As I write in all of my books, *Holy Spirit is much bigger than His gifts.*

One day my mother was admitted to the hospital. My father was there in the room with her, and there was not much hope left for my mother. As a young boy, I wanted my mother and I did not want her to die. So I began to dig deeper, to find an answer for her sickness. I asked my father if he was faithful in paying tithes. He said he was. In fact, he always gave more than his tithe. Because our house was a haven for pastors and traveling ministers, at least one or two pastors visited our home every week. My mother would cook for them and at times they stayed for a few days.

I believed that if we did not pay tithes, some curse would come upon the family. I began to think the reason why my mother was ill might be because my father missed a tithe. I'd heard the old preachers say that if we do not pay God His tithe, we will end up either paying a doctor or a lawyer. I remember suggesting selling a piece of the land we owned and giving it to the Lord, so that He would heal my mother. Though he initially agreed to do it, my father did not go through with selling any of the land.

As I mentioned before, we were Spirit-filled believers, went to church or church-related activities at least four times a week and had family prayer three times a day (I am not exaggerating! We had family prayer in my home three times a day, every single day of the year!) We never went on a family vacation so we were home at least 364 days of the year. We paid tithes and gave to all those ministers who came to our house but the question remained: *Why was my mother ill and why had our financial situation not improved?*

We had a decent home. My brother and I shared a room. I slept on the concrete floor on a single mat next to my brother's bed. Besides my clothes, my only earthly possessions were that mat, a bed sheet and a pillow. My brother's wooden-framed bed was sewn with plastic strips. He had a bed but no mattress (having a bed was a luxury at that time.) We did not even know that mattresses existed. The question always remained in my heart: *Why didn't God bless us as He said in His Word?*

Every Sunday we heard the message with this focus: "Jesus is coming soon! This world is not our home, we are just passing by and once you die and cross the pearly gate you will have everything you need. The earth is going to be destroyed by fire, so don't care about it. Whatever we do is going to be wasted. So, some have to endure this life. All that matters is entering the next life." I did not understand at that time that this message was not biblical. In truth, whatever we do for God and His kingdom on earth will remain forever and ever (1 Corinthians 3:12-15).

We were living with the hope that one day things would change. Some people hoped that if they just kept doing what they were doing, then someday the situation would change. Later, I found out that the definition of insanity was to keep on doing the same thing and expecting a different result. If we want different results, we need to do something different.

First of all, we did not know what we should do differently. Secondly, we were so deeply rooted in tradition and legalism, that everything outside of our belief system was considered demonic or unholy. That is what my

INTRODUCTION

church taught me. Everyone who did not believe what we believed were not spiritual enough or worse, backslidden. That is what we were taught, so that is what we believed.

When I was twenty years old, my mother went to be with the Lord. I was in ministry by that time and got to see her and spent some time with her before she died. I was left with more questions than before, but did not know where to find the answer or whom to ask. I did not want to ask the religious circle around me, because I did not want to stir up the water and be called a rebel. So, I kept those questions in the back of my mind, thinking that one day God would give me answers.

I was taught that seeking God's kingdom meant to go and preach the gospel or to get baptized in water. I also thought that if I preached the gospel, God would be pleased with me and bless me. During that time, I joined an evangelistic organization and began to travel and preach the gospel in different states of India. We were in the northern part of India where most villagers had never heard the gospel. They were not happy that we were preaching Christ and trying to convert them from their religion.

We faced opposition; and not only that, we had to sell gospel tracts and New Testaments to these people to support ourselves. Imagine trying to sell something to someone who hates you and hates what you are selling. Whatever money we received from sales, we used to buy food. If we did not sell any materials we went hungry that day. We stayed in one city or town for two to three months and tried to reach as many people as possible with the gospel.

My belief system at that time was that if we have plenty of Christians and start enough churches in a town, the circumstances would change there over time. I went to cities and towns with hundreds of churches and discovered things weren't any different in any of them. The only difference was that instead of just the unsaved people fighting each other, the churches and believers were fighting each other too.

My team leader was a Hindu convert. He did not have any money nor anyone supporting him. Once when we had completed our outreach program in a city and were all going to go home for a break, I was going to the headquarters to receive leadership training to become a team leader. As we were departing, this brother asked me a question that changed my financial life forever. He asked me if I would support him with ten rupees per month. Ten rupees were equivalent of 20 cents USD in those days.

I did not know what to tell him. I did not have ten rupees with me and if I said yes, I did not know where the money would come from and whether I would be able to keep my word. As I thought what to answer this brother, I felt in my heart to tell him this: "If God gives me ten rupees next month, I will send it to you." We departed and went our separate ways.

I had the opportunity to go home for a few days before the leadership training started. The organization paid my way to come home. After I reached home, there was an opportunity to do some work for one of my uncles and he gave me ten rupees. I went to the post office and sent a money order to this brother. The next month God have me thirty rupees and I sent him that money. The next month He gave me sixty rupees and I sent him that money.

It multiplied every month and I began supporting him with fourteen hundred rupees per month. Something broke in the spirit in my financial life that day and God said to me "You will never lack money in your pocket again." That is still true today. God broke the spirit of poverty off my life that day. This needs to happen in every believer's life if they are serious about fulfilling their purpose. If you are interested in learning more about how to be free from the spirit of poverty, please read my book *Overcoming the Spirit of Poverty*. See the back page of this volume for more information on that.

That did not end the financial problem in my life though. God opened a door for me to come to the United States to study in a Bible school. Through a series of miracles, I reached there and joined the school. I completed another two-year degree then went back to India and started Maximum Impact Ministries. I still had a lot of unanswered questions in my heart about life and ministry.

I decided to fast and seek the Lord for the answers, so I embarked on my first forty days of fasting and prayer. When I woke up one morning I felt my heart was overflowing with revelation. I went to my desk, picked up a pen and a notebook and began to write what was in my heart before I forgot it. I kept on writing until nine thirty at night. At nine thirty the flow ended and I did not have anything left to write. I looked at my notebook to see what I wrote. I had written the answers to the questions I had been asking God. It was a chapter-by-chapter book. He told me it was not just for me; there were others who were asking the same questions and needed those answers too.

When I woke up the next morning, I felt revelation bubbling in my spirit again. I went to my desk and began writing my thoughts in a notebook a second time. I kept on writing until ten thirty at night. At ten thirty the flow of revelation stopped. I looked at what I had written and it was another book. That was the second book God gave me. It was called *Overcoming the Spirit of Poverty*. One of the questions I was asking God was, "Lord, You gave me this vision in my heart, but where is the money going to come from?" He said, "Money is not the problem. When you overcome the spirit of poverty, money will come to you."

That was the beginning of my writing experience. I never thought I could write a book, let alone in English. Now I dream in English. Ever since that fast, I never stopped writing. The rivers of living water are still flowing today. I thank God for His unspeakable gifts and grace.

After many years of waiting, God answered my question about why my mother died of sickness even though she was a believer. What killed my mother was not the devil, witchcraft, or her sins. He said, "What killed your mother was the curse of the law." As the Bible says, "For as many as are of the works of the law are under the curse" (Galatians 3:10a).

In my part of the world, the Pentecostals are extremely legalistic. They will filter a mosquito and swallow an elephant in order to obey the laws of the Old Testament. Unknowingly they bring curses upon them and others. Curses breed sickness and poverty.

They derive half of their doctrine from the books of Exodus and Leviticus. God gave the law to the Israelites through Moses. Without knowing the Old Covenant was fulfilled and done away with at the coming and establishing of the New Covenant, the religious people in my country had adopted legalistic traditions in the church. Doctrines of the New Testament church do not come from the Old Covenant. Through Jesus Christ, we are dead to the Law of Moses and free from it (Romans 7:4).

God made the Old Covenant with the people of Israel; a Gentile has nothing to do with it. If a Gentile tries to keep the Law, he or she is bringing curses upon themselves unawares. Let's discuss the Old Testament laws a little. There is nothing wrong with the Law (Romans 7:12, 16). The problem is, if we keep the Law, either we keep the entire Law or we do not touch any of it at all. If you keep part of it and break the other, you will automatically activate curses upon your life and you won't even realize it. It is like the law of gravity. If you jump from the top of a building, you will crash to the ground. You cannot blame God for not catching you. He established the law of gravity and He gave you common sense to respect that law.

If you keep nine laws and break the tenth, you are still a guilty person and curses will come upon you. *Laws are that dangerous.* Many innocent believers, because of their religious zeal, try to obey as many laws from the Old Testament as they possibly can. They think the more laws they obey, the more God will be pleased with them. That is a deception. God was already pleased with you, even before you started obeying any of His laws. They think if they keep more laws that will make them more spiritual. It will appear outwardly that they are more spiritual, but inwardly they will be a miserable wreck, because the more you try to keep the laws the more you mess up.

INTRODUCTION

One day a well-intended pastor came to see me. He asked me if I know how many commandments and laws there are in the Bible and if I kept them all. I said, "I don't know." He shared an exact number, which I don't remember now but I remember it was above six thousand. He said he made a list of all of those commandments and has been obeying them. This poor fellow was so deceived that he thought he was more spiritual than others. A couple of years later he became ill and died at a very young age.

One can never measure up to the standard of God by our own efforts. If righteousness came because of the law, then Christ did not have to come. No humans ever kept or obeyed the entire Law. They all fell short, so curses came upon the entire house of Israel. If you study every family tree in the Old Testament, you will notice there is at least one curse following every one of them. Only Jesus kept and obeyed the entire Law and fulfilled it. He did that for us. Hallelujah! Thank You, Jesus!

This is one of the main reasons sicknesses come upon New Testament believers and they are not healed, even though we pray for them. Many do not understand the difference between the Old Testament and the New Testament. Because of pride, human beings love to make themselves feel worthy to receive something. It is hard for them to receive something for free. They want to feel as if they earned it, so many have become passionate about the Levitical laws.

That is why we do not see very many Messianic Jewish believers blessed spiritually and financially. They have the religious look with their prayer shawls and shofars, but they still hang on to the Old Testament Law. When a curse is operating in our lives, we automatically disqualify ourselves from receiving any answers to our prayers and the blessing God promised in His Word.

The solution to the law is grace. In the New Covenant, God deals with us through His grace and not on the basis of Old Testament law. *Law helped people to* cover *their sins, grace helps us to* overcome *sin.* Many do not understand the difference between the Old and the New Covenants. Most believers take one verse from Leviticus and another one from the gospel of John and form their doctrines. Jesus did not come to mix two covenants, but to put an end to the old one and start an entirely new one (Romans 10:4). Nobody taught them classes called New Testament Theology or Apostolic Doctrines. As a result, they got stuck and confused.

They do not get to enjoy any benefit of the New Covenant. Instead, they have become religious and fleshy. What needed to be accomplished in the Spirit, they try to do it in the flesh. They live a life alienated from the grace and promises of God. The Bible calls it falling from grace (Galatians 5:4). All their life they wait to fly away from the very earth God put them on to inherit and influence. Such a waste!

If you want to know more about the grace of God, please get my book entitled, *7 Dimensions of God's Grace*. It will be one of the best investments you will make for your spiritual growth.

I came to the U.S. to study. I met my wife there and married. God blessed us with three children. Our expenses soared high every month. The ministry had also grown and finances got tighter. We had $25,000 in ministry-related debt and almost $30,000 in credit card debt. I began to ask questions again for which I did not have any answers.

Here we were trying to do the will of God and obeying Him the best way we could. Why then had we ended up with this much debt? I knew by reading the Old Testament that debt is a curse, and not a blessing. But I did not know how to break that curse. We were paying tithes every month—both from the ministry and from our salary, but our financial situation did not improve beyond meeting our basic needs. That was clearly not indicative of God's blessing.

God began to open up my understanding and showed me from His Word what He thinks about finances and how it works in His kingdom. When we began to practice those principles, we paid off both our personal

INTRODUCTION

and ministry debt in one year—we were debt free! We became the worst enemy of debt. We stopped using credit cards unless we knew we were able to pay them off at the end of the month, because these days, it's almost impossible to live without a credit or debit card.

Do you know what God did with those peanuts and the twenty cents I gave to Him in faith? He enabled us to plant about a hundred churches in six states of India. God took me to more than forty countries. I was on TBN's Praise the Lord program more than once. We conducted seventeen pastors' conferences and trained more than 7,500 pastors and leaders. 80,000 homes have been reached with the gospel. 1,500 children were reached with the gospel. Hundreds of crusades and outdoor meetings have been held. We have established four orphanages in India.

God enabled me to preach on International Television eight times; the program went all over the world. By His grace we have published twenty books that have blessed hundreds and thousands of people on six different continents. As I am writing this book, I am sitting in an airplane, flying to Germany for a conference. I feel the anointing all over me and I am praying for God to do an extraordinary work in your life as you read this book. I can go on and on, telling what God did with those twenty cents.

There is no limit to what God can do with what you have right now. Whether little or much, when we release what we have into the hands of an unlimited God, what we gave becomes unlimited as well. When we partner with God, we get to do the impossible because there is nothing impossible with Him.

What you thought was unattainable will become normal in this new season. What you thought extraordinary will become ordinary for you. What you thought was supernatural will become natural. When I look at the house we are living in, the car we are driving and the people we are connected to worldwide, I say in my heart, *how did I get here?* Two years ago I thought this was impossible. What was impossible to me, God made possible. If He will do it for me; He will do it for you. He is not partial. I am not special. But you need to learn the principles of kingdom economy and practice them.

To be honest, I never sought a nice house or beautiful car. Those were not my dreams and I never chased them. Materials things mean nothing to me. They have no attachment to my heart. They were added to us as a bonus as we were seeking the kingdom of God first and fulfilling the purpose God created us to do.

How did all these things happen? How did we go from peanuts to living in kingdom economy? This book will open up your understanding about how the kingdom economy works. I have seen hundreds of precious believers who pay tithes and offerings and still are struggling to survive. They want to do more for God and give, but don't know what to do to break into the next level.

This book is written for those precious saints around the world, who are tired of religion but hanging in there. This revelation will break you free, once and for all from every chain that holds you back. You are created to be blessed and to be a blessing. You are supposed to be the head and not the tail, above and not beneath. May the Lord use this book to open your eyes to see everything you are created to do *and enjoy*.

I am excited to share these principles, which will revolutionize your thinking and giving. When you practice them, you will be debt free and always have more than what you need. Your financial situation will never be the same again. I believe this book contains the answers you have been waiting for. You might be a faithful tithe-giver, but do not have much left over. Whatever level you are at right now, God will take you to the next level in giving and receiving. All glory be to His name.

This is not a "how to become rich" book. If you are looking to be rich, this book is not for you. This book is written with the intention of equipping the saints to administer God's kingdom in the area of economy in their nations. If you are looking to become rich, to have a bigger house or a nicer car, please do not waste your time. There are so many other books that could help you do that. This is for those saints who are hungry to discover and fulfill their purpose, and to see the kingdom of God and His will be established *on earth as it is in heaven.*

This is not a book that promotes a "prosperity gospel" nor a "poverty gospel." This book is for those people who are serious about fulfilling their God-given destiny. It's for those who have been faithfully following God and giving to the Lord and His work from their hearts, but have not seen a financial breakthrough in their lives.

In the Old Testament, we read about saints who were blessed beyond measure; they did not have room to contain it all. Moses had to tell the people to stop bringing their offerings to build the Tabernacle, because they had brought too much. This book is for those people who have faith to receive the financial abundance that the Bible talks about and want to be a blessing to the kingdom during this end-time.

CHAPTER - 1

KINGDOM ECONOMY 1.0

The word "economy" comes from the Greek *oikonomos* which means "one who manages a household" or "manager of various resources."[1] The word *oikonomos* is translated as *steward* eight times, *chamberlain* one time and *governor* one time in the King James Version of the New Testament.

God has made us stewards of His kingdom resources. He entrusted us with the earth and one day we need to give Him an account for our performance in that area. We have been squandering those resources by neglecting it and poor management. Reckoning will happen and the "land-Lord" will require from us an account of what we did.

Many of the parables Jesus shared have to do with stewardship or economy, which is basically management of resources. We tend to not take those parables seriously. Instead, we think they are just stories He told. Either that, or we do not understand what they mean.

---

[1] James Strong, "3623. Oikonomos," Biblehub.com, accessed January 02, 2019, https://biblehub.com/greek/3623.htm.

How does God's kingdom and its economy work? God is the Creator and Owner of all riches and wealth on this earth. When most people think of economy, they think of money. They think if they have more money, their problems will be over. God doesn't give money to anyone. What I mean is, He doesn't just drop money from heaven on people. Why? Because the currency of His kingdom is not money made of paper. If God does not give money, then what does He do to bless His people? What is the currency of His kingdom? How does the economy of His kingdom operate? Let's find out the answers to these questions.

I would like to ask you a favor. From now on when you think of heaven, I want you to think of it as a *kingdom*. Heaven is not a large, blue expanse where clouds float and nothing material exists. That is far from the truth. *Heaven is a kingdom.* The Bible calls it the kingdom of heaven. The kingdom of heaven has everything we see in an earthly nation. They have food, clothing, precious metals, stones, and horses in heaven. Someone has to produce or manufacture and manage them.

When God gives, He gives what He owns in His kingdom. He gives riches and enduring wealth that has the potential to create money. Some of the enduring riches and wealth of God's realm are knowledge, wisdom, ideas, and understanding. *Money is a system of this world. Money was invented by man and has nothing to do with God's kingdom.*

The reason many people do not receive answers to their prayers for money is because of this. God does not have any money. The money that you carry in your wallet has no value in His kingdom. What gives value to that paper is the seal of the government that it represents. That country decided its value. The paper itself has very little value. For example, a one dollar bill and a hundred dollar bill cost the same to make. Only the treasury of the United States decides which one is worth a dollar and which is worth a hundred dollars. God, on the other hand, does not print money and does not deal in money. He never said He owns all the money; instead

He said He owns the cattle on a thousand hills and all the gold and silver. They are a part of kingdom wealth.

The economy of God's kingdom works on the riches and wealth principle. God wants you to be rich and wealthy for His kingdom purpose. The person who has a lot of cash is not necessarily rich because that cash can disappear sooner or later, or the government can demonetize the currency, as has happened in many countries.

For example, a couple of years ago, the government of India cancelled many of the currencies. Many people threw sacks of money into the rivers or burned them because the money did not have any value once the government nullified the currency. They did this so they would not be accused of hoarding it illegally. Even so, as long as we live on this earth, we will need money. Money is a tool of the kingdom of darkness. The spirit of mammon works behind the monetary system of this world. Greed and covetousness are the brother and sister of the spirit of mammon. If you ask people who have plenty of money how much is enough for them, they will say, "just a little more."

One of the ways the devil keeps God's children poor and ineffective is by blinding them with money. Once we become enslaved and controlled by the spirit of mammon, we will not understand how the kingdom economy works. Instead, we will live in a state of constantly worrying about money, and spending most of our lives trying to make more of it. Once we are stuck in that rut, it's hard to get out. The devil knows that very well. His intention is to make you serve money all your life and then kill you before you get to fulfill your purpose. Money is a master and it requires your complete subjection to its lusts.

I did not understand this principle for a long time. I was asking God for a raise, more money, and greater income. Nothing much happened in my life until I received this revelation. I stopped asking God for more money and started asking for riches and wealth. *When you put God's riches and wealth principles to work; and do business using them, they will create money for you.*

You may be asking what the difference is between riches, wealth, and money? Let me explain it to you from the biblical perspective. The thing we call money came into existence in recent history. When I say recent, I mean a few hundred years ago. Before then, all transactions were done with silver, gold or other precious substances.

We read in Genesis 13:2 that Abraham was very rich in silver, gold, cattle, maidservants and menservants. He was rich in kingdom economy and wealth. What made Abraham a rich person? Not a lot of money. The secret to his riches was gold, silver, cattle and servants. When God wants to bless you, He wants to bless you with His riches and wealth. We need to understand the difference between riches and wealth too. Most people are working themselves to death trying to make some money because they do not understand what creates money or what money is.

Riches are liquid assets, or something you can turn into cash or money. When God appeared to Solomon, Solomon asked God for wisdom and an understanding heart. God in turn told him that because he did not ask for riches or wealth or the death of his enemies, He would give him riches, wealth, and honor.

> Then God said to Solomon: "Because this was in your heart, and you have not asked riches or wealth or honor or the life of your enemies, nor have you asked long life—but have asked wisdom and knowledge for yourself, that you may judge My people over whom I have made you king—wisdom and knowledge are granted to you; and I will give you *riches* and *wealth* and *honor*, such as none of the kings have had who were before you, nor shall any after you have the like" (2 Chronicles 1:11-12).

The Bible says this about wisdom:

> "Length of days is in her right hand, in her left hand riches and honor" (Proverbs 3:16).

When you go to God, you need to know exactly what to ask for. When you are in the presence of the most wealthy, wise and powerful King, you need to know what you are going to say (Ecclesiastes 5:1-6). Many times, the reason we do not receive the answers to what we are asking, is because we are not asking for the right thing. That is the number one reason for unanswered prayers; we ask amiss (James 4:3).

Right now, your struggle might be to pay off a medical bill, or an educational loan, or some kind of debt or need, so you may be asking God for money to pay off that bill or meet that need. Paying off that bill *is not the end of your financial need*. What will you do after you pay that off? You still need money to live. We keep on asking God for more money. I am not saying He will not provide you with the money you need. It's just that you need something more than just money. *You need something that will create money or generate a stream of income for you*. I am not talking about getting a second or third job either. I am talking about learning to live in kingdom economy.

Believe it or not, *you can create money*. I do not mean you should print money in your basement; if you do you'll probably end up in prison. But if you create a product or service, or provide valuable information that other people need, and price it according to the value of the product, service, or the information, then you have created that amount of money. When you exchange that with someone who needs it, they will pay you money that is worth the value. That is one of the secrets to making money.

God never said money belongs to Him, but He did say that riches and wealth belong to Him.

> "Blessed are You, Lord God of Israel, our Father, forever and ever. Yours, O Lord, is the greatness, the power and the glory, the victory and the majesty; *for all that is in heaven and in earth is Yours;* Yours is the kingdom, O Lord, and You are exalted as head over all. *Both riches and honor come from You,* and You reign over all. In Your hand is power and might; in

Your hand it is to make great and to give strength to all" (1 Chronicles 29:10b-12).

All gold and silver belong to our God.

> "'The silver is Mine, and the gold is Mine,' says the Lord of hosts" (Haggai 2:8).

> "saying with a loud voice: 'Worthy is the Lamb who was slain to receive power and riches and wisdom, and strength and honor and glory and blessing!'" (Revelation 5:12).

In the Bible whenever God blessed someone or transferred wealth, He gave them riches. The Hebrew word for wealth is *chayil* which means "strength, might, efficiency, wealth, army, ability, efficiency, force."[2] I thought wealth was money, but when God talks about wealth He is not talking about money necessarily. The same Hebrew word is used for army, ability, and efficiency. To God, wealth also means strength, power and can refer to an army. When He says He is the One who gives you power to get wealth, He is talking about strength, army, efficiency, not just money. Below are some verses that also use *chayil*.

> "So the Egyptians pursued them, all the horses and chariots of Pharaoh, his horsemen and his *army (wealth)*, and overtook them camping by the sea beside Pi Hahiroth, before Baal Zephon" (Exodus 14:9).

There is another verse in the Bible that preachers use in regards to receiving money. They say the wealth of the sinner is stored up for the righteous (Proverbs 13:22b). We think that all the money the wicked have is going to come to us supernaturally. That is not what it means. *Chayil* is used there for wealth.

---

[2] James Strong, "2428. Chayil," Biblehub.com, accessed January 02, 2019, https://biblehub.com/hebrew/2428.htm.

The strength or the efficiency of a nation or a people are its land and its resources. There is another meaning for wealth and that is land.

In Ruth 2, we read,

> "There was a relative of Naomi's husband, a *man of great wealth*, of the family of Elimelech. His name was Boaz" (Ruth 2:1).

In the olden days, the person who owned the most land was considered rich and most of the time he was also known as a king. Boaz was a mighty man of wealth. In other words, he was a mighty man of strength (or army), because he owned a lot of land. During harvest time, Ruth went to his field to glean. He was respected at the gate and was a man of influence. Wealth brings you money, and money will increase your strength and influence.

The devil has cheated many believers worldwide, deceiving them into thinking they do not need to own anything here on earth. Instead many believe we are just passing through and we will have everything in heaven. Dear friend, if that is you, you need to shake that limping theology that keeps you deprived of the legal inheritance your Father has given you. The only time and place you can be a blessing to someone else is while you are on earth. As I mentioned earlier, heaven is a kingdom and it belongs to God. He has no plan for sharing it with any humans. He did not mention that in His Word. He created the earth and gave it to us as our inheritance.

In His first official message to the world, Jesus said,

> "Blessed are the meek, for they shall inherit the earth" (Matthew 5:5).

One of the reasons God did not transfer much wealth to believers until now, even though they have been crying for more money, is because there are only a few trained people who have an understanding of how to handle and manage wealth. Many are blinded by the religious spirit, the spirit of mammon, ignorance and greed. If they receive wealth, it would destroy them more than it would bless them.

They would run out and start buying things their flesh wants and not have any system in place to handle it effectively. God has been holding back His kingdom wealth for our own good, but He wants to release His wealth and He is looking for His children worldwide who will be equipped to receive it from Him. I believe one of the reasons God gave me this book is to prepare the body of Christ to have the right heart and understanding of how to handle God's kingdom economy.

How do we bring honor, glory and riches to our King, Jesus Christ, as it says in the book of Revelation 5:12? We know that we can't carry anything from earth with us when we die. What are we going to present to Him for the price He paid and for the salvation He has given us? What are we going to give Him in return for defeating the devil and giving us the keys of His kingdom? Will we be able to answer Jesus like the person who received the five talents? "He who had received five talents came and brought five other talents, saying, 'Lord, you delivered to me five talents; look, I have gained five more talents besides them'" (Matthew 25:20b).

When King David was ready to die, he called his son, Solomon, and gave him 650 billion dollars' worth of gold and silver for the building of the temple. David was not just singing praise to God during his life. David sang, "Lord, I give You all the glory and praise," and then he practiced what he was singing. All of the psalms he wrote came out of his experience. David had something to give to the Lord.

Are we just going to tell Jesus that we're sorry, but we just barely made it? That would be the most humiliating thing for Him to hear in front of His angels and enemies. Wouldn't it look like He hadn't done a good job? Everything was created for Him and through Him, but everything is not in His control right now. The enemy has taken over much of what He created. He put us here to take it back for Him. Instead, we have been crying to get us out of here. What a dilemma!

It is time for the body of Christ to receive God's true riches and wealth. Jesus is waiting until all His enemies are brought to His footstool (Hebrews

10:12-13). That is the Old Testament verse that is most repeated in the New Testament. The enemies of God are not going to be brought to His feet simply through our singing, preaching, or conducting of crusades. This will happen when we receive our inheritance that God has prepared for us before the foundation of the world and begin to administer His kingdom on earth. When the church subdues His enemies and invites Jesus the King to come and receive His reign over the earth, that's when He will come back. Until then, He is going to remain seated at the right hand of the Father (Hebrews 1:3; 8:1; 10:12-13).

> "For you know the grace of our Lord Jesus Christ, that though He was rich, yet for your sakes He became poor, that you through His poverty might become rich" (2 Corinthians 8:9).

God wants you to be rich for His kingdom purpose. When you are poor you cannot accomplish your purpose, nor can you be a blessing to others in order to meet their needs. (Either you need spiritual or natural wealth to bless others. The apostle Paul could have been a materially wealthy person; instead of making himself rich, he focused on making others rich.

> "As unknown, and yet well known; as dying, and behold we live; as chastened, and yet not killed; as sorrowful, yet always rejoicing; *as poor, yet making many rich; as having nothing, and yet possessing all things*" (2 Corinthians 6:9-10).

> "You are already full! You are already rich! You have reigned as kings without us—and indeed I could wish you did reign, that we also might reign with you!" (1 Corinthians 4:8).

Everything was at Paul's disposal: Life, death, this world and the world to come; he had all things.

> "Therefore let no one boast in men. For all things are yours: whether Paul or Apollos or Cephas, or the world or life or

death, or things present or things to come—all are yours. And you are Christ's, and Christ is God's" (1 Corinthians 3:21-23).

The moment you prove you are able to handle more, God releases more authority and influence to you. It is a growth process, and He wants us to grow in it.

When we think of rich people we tend to think of people with a lot of money. Rich people do not necessarily have a lot of cash, but they do have assets that can be turned into cash. God wants you to have assets too. When you get the money of this world, find a way to turn it into riches and eventually to wealth and vice versa.

When God wants to meet your needs, He says He will do it according to the riches in His glory (Philippians 4:19). What type of riches does He have in His glory? There is no "money" in heaven. The Word says that Jesus was rich; but for our sake, He became poor and was born in a manger (2 Corinthians 8:9). After the resurrection, He ascended to glory. Jesus is not a poor person anymore. He not only has all the riches in heaven, Jesus now has all the wealth and riches on this earth; they all belong to Him too. He gives them to whomever He chooses.

Many people think Jesus is a poor guy and that is why He was born in a manger. Then they teach that because He was born poor, we should be poor like Him. That is far from the truth. He could have been born anywhere He wanted and at any time He pleased, but for our sake and because of our poverty and to redeem us from it, He chose to be poor for a short period of time. In the same way that He became sin for us so that we could be the righteousness of God, He became poor so that we could be rich (2 Corinthians 5:21).

CHAPTER - 2

THE FOUNDATIONS OF KINGDOM ECONOMY

When we hear the word *economy*, we commonly think of cash, stocks, savings, business or any other things related to money. These things are part of the world's economy. Kingdom economy runs on a different system and is based on the wealth that God has created. It is not based on money, credit systems, or debt and the things I mentioned above. It is dependent upon things that *create* money. As long as the kingdom of God remains, its economy also will remain. *This world's economy depends on the economy of the kingdom of God.*

The enemy's tactic is to blind us from God's economy, and influence us to depend on the monetary system of his kingdom. The devil doesn't or cannot own anything legally. He has to deceive humans and steal from them, and use what originally belonged to us to do his business on earth.

How was it that the early church, which had more than five thousand members, had not one unmet need? They had a revelation about the kingdom economy. One of the first things they established as a congregation was not a mass choir, but a banking system founded on kingdom economy principles. The early church had a banking system to meet the needs of its members. Second, many of them sold a portion of their assets, and brought the money to the apostles and laid it at their feet. The apostles distributed that money so that everybody's needs were met. This is a picture of kingdom living.

> "Now the multitude of those who believed were of one heart and one soul; neither did anyone say that any of the things he possessed was his own, but they had all things in common. And with great power the apostles gave witness to the resurrection of the Lord Jesus. And great grace was upon them all. Nor was there anyone among them who lacked; for all who were possessors of lands or houses sold them, and brought the proceeds of the things that were sold, and laid them at the apostles' feet; and they distributed to each as anyone had need" (Acts 4:32-35).

For a long time I believed what I had been taught by the religious spirit, and that was that they had sold *everything they had*, but this could not have been so. If they had done that, they could not have gone from house to house every day. Those properties would have been gone.

> "Now all who believed were together, and had all things in common, and sold their possessions and goods, and divided them among all, as anyone had need. So continuing daily with one accord in the temple, and breaking bread from house to house, they ate their food with gladness and simplicity of heart" (Acts 2:44-46).

> "And daily in the temple, and in every house, they did not cease teaching and preaching Jesus as the Christ" (Acts 5:42).

Many in the church today believe that if they tithe regularly, one day they will be financially free and wealthy. According to the Bible, that is not true. *The Bible never teaches that if you pay tithes you will be financially wealthy; in the Bible, financially wealthy people paid tithes.* The best example is the father of our faith, Abraham, who began the principle of tithing. He was a very rich man way before he ever gave any tithe. There is also no evidence that shows Abraham paid a tithe regularly. We only read about the one-time encounter he had with Melchizedek, the king of Salem, to whom he gave a tithe.

God said,

> "And you shall remember the Lord your God, for it is He who gives you power to get wealth, that He may establish His covenant which He swore to your fathers, as it is this day" (Deuteronomy 8:18).

There is no "one size fits all" financial principle in the Bible. God worked differently with different people in different times and cultures. And He still does. This is important to keep in mind. Many times we are looking for a formula or a shortcut. There are no shortcuts in His kingdom. His principles and ways are same for everyone everywhere.

God understands better than we do that it requires wealth to establish His covenant, so He has made His power available to His children to create wealth. We need to learn how to tap into that power. What kind of power is He talking about? When we think of power, we think of force or energy. In Old Testament days, the king with the largest army and the most sophisticated weapons was considered powerful. They could conquer nations and plunder their wealth. We can't do that right now.

As a New Testament believer, we cannot build an army and attack neighborhoods to kill and plunder people. We live in the information age. A person with the latest know-how on anything can make money. Knowledge is power. The Bible says God's people are destroyed for lack of knowledge, and wisdom is better than weapons of war (Ecclesiastes 9:18). God wants to impart cutting-edge innovations and revolutionary inventions to us, but most believers do not know how to put them to work. We are not trained in those areas yet.

There are actually angels of inventions in heaven. God releases them to earth when it is time for a new product to manifest. That angel wanders around looking for a believer to receive it, but finds them all busy inside their four walls, waiting and crying out for revival and rapture. So he goes and gives it to an unsaved person who is looking for an idea that could change the world. That person puts that idea to work and creates billions of dollars with it because all the Christians will run to the stores on Christmas and for birthdays to buy those products (made by heathens) for themselves and for their family members. Christians miss many opportunities because they are not tuned in to what God is doing now.

THE FOUNDATIONS OF KINGDOM ECONOMY

God mentioned the foundations of kingdom economy in Genesis. They consist of five things: wisdom, land, agriculture, precious metals and stones, and water. In any nation, the people who own the majority of these controls the rest of the population. As long as these remain, God's kingdom economy on earth will never experience any recession or economic collapse.

The first two chapters of Genesis reveal the foundations of kingdom economy. Actually, the foundation of everything in this life is revealed in those two chapters. We are going to find out how God established His kingdom economy here.

1. WISDOM

Why is wisdom the number one foundation of kingdom economy? The Bible begins by saying, "In the beginning God created the heavens and the earth." What did God do to create the heavens and the earth? What kind of material did He use? We make something out of something. We need matter to create matter or change it into another form. To create the entire mass of the earth and its matter, what did God use? He used a substance called faith and the technology called wisdom, knowledge and understanding. The Bible says that by wisdom God established the earth (Proverbs 3:19).

There is something on this earth that is more costly than silver and gold.

> Happy is the man who finds wisdom, and the man who gains understanding; for her proceeds are better than the profits of silver, and her gain than fine gold. She is more precious than rubies, and all the things you may desire cannot compare with her (Proverbs 3:13-15).

"Wisdom is better than weapons of war" (Ecclesiastes 9:18a). There is something more powerful than weapons of war.

"Wisdom is better than strength" (Ecclesiastes 9:16a). There is something that is harder to find than any hidden treasure. There is something that everyone seeks and only a few find. There is something that is better than strength.

It is wisdom. That is the foundation of kingdom economy.

> "The Lord by wisdom founded the earth; by understanding He established the heavens" (Proverbs 3:19).

Before God created the earth and all its wealth, He created wisdom. Then He used wisdom to create everything else.

> "Length of days is in her right hand, in her left hand riches and honor" (Proverbs 3:16).

The Bible says wisdom has two hands. Everything we look and work for with our life, we will find if we have wisdom.

> "Wisdom is the principal thing; therefore get wisdom. And in all your getting, get understanding" (Proverbs 4:7).

God tells us to find wisdom and find understanding before we seek any material blessings.

Wisdom is the most expensive and precious thing there is. God said in Hosea that His people perish for the lack of knowledge (Hosea 4:6). The foundation of everything we do must be wisdom, whether it is marriage, business, or any other relationship. Everything we do must be established on wisdom. The Bible says a house is built by wisdom and by knowledge its rooms are filled with precious treasures (Proverbs 24:3-4).

Everything God does is grounded in sound wisdom. Before He releases His power to a person, or a situation, He will make sure His wisdom precedes it. That is why the Bible says Jesus increased in wisdom and stature before the power of God came upon Him (Luke 2:52).

On the first day God created light, but He created the sun, moon, and stars only on the fourth day. What was the light He created on the first day? It was wisdom. He separated light from darkness, knowledge from ignorance.

Before we set out to build a business or make money, we need to gain wisdom. That should be our first priority. The root cause of every problem we face in life is ignorance. Wisdom helps us create intellectual property, so that we are not ignorant or making ignorant decisions.

Intellectual Property

Everything began with an idea. Just like people have real estate and lands, some people own intellectual properties and rights. Everything on earth runs on software and hardware. What I mean by that is that every system runs on two levels. One is the unseen and the other one is the seen. It has always been that way—long before the computer age. You can see a machine working but you can't see the mechanical laws by which it operates. You can see the sun rise, but you cannot see what causes that sun to rise. These unseen laws govern the universe, and were established by God.

In the twenty-first century, people who own intellectual properties are some of the wealthiest people on earth. Developing and buying computer software and other programs cost a lot of money. Books are another form of intellectual property. It's considered a crime if you trespass on someone else's property or steal it. In the same way, stealing or copying intellectual property is a crime.

As I mentioned earlier, all the treasures of wisdom and knowledge are hid in Christ and He lives in us. We are supposed to be the wisest and the most knowledgeable people on earth. Unfortunately, the majority of the church around the world are very slow of learning. We learn most things from the people of the world.

It would not be outrageous to say that God left the church many years ago because He couldn't use very many people in the church to do anything that benefited humanity. Too many were so religious and heavenly minded that they lost touch with the real world. So, He had to go to the world to find someone who was willing to think outside the box; to imagine and create products that had never been made before. And He did.

The Bible says this about people who seek and acquire knowledge (Proverbs 15:14; 18:15). As I say in my other books, the number one sign that a person has any fear or reverence for God is their hunger for wisdom. Why? Because the fear of the Lord is the beginning of wisdom. If there is no hunger for wisdom and knowledge, they haven't met the God of the Bible. They might have encountered a religious spirit and thought it was the real God. It is very possible for someone to be deceived by a religious spirit and serve it for all their life, thinking they are serving God. I am talking about Christians here. Unfortunately, the religious spirit or the spirit of this world deceives the majority of the church world.

2. LAND

In the natural, *kingdom economy starts with land*. The words *land*, *earth* and *field* combined, appears 2,875 times in the NKJV. The word *heaven* appears only 692 times. Now, you tell me whether the Bible gives more importance to earth or heaven.

Everything that controls the economy of a nation comes from the land. In any country, it is the people who own land that have influence and wealth. The more land you own, the more influence you have. Just because you own land does not mean you have money. You need to utilize that land to produce something that will create the money you need.

In Genesis 1:1, 9 we read about God making the dry land. He called the dry land *earth*. That is the second foundation of kingdom economy. A kingdom's economy is based on how much land it occupies. In a nutshell, the size of a kingdom is determined by how much land it possesses. In Esther 1:1, we read that the Persian kingdom of King Ahasuerus extended from Ethiopia to India. It was one of the most vast and powerful kingdoms that ever existed on the face of the earth.

Land is the chief foundation of a kingdom and its economy. When God began His kingdom here, the entire earth was the territory of His kingdom. He gave that to His children to manage. As mentioned before, the Bible begins with, "In the beginning God created the heavens and the earth" (Genesis 1:1). It also says that heaven is His throne and earth is His footstool. If heaven is only His throne and the planet Earth is only big enough to be His footstool, imagine the size of His kingdom! It's beyond human comprehension. I read that scientists have discovered that the universe is big enough to hold millions of solar systems like ours.

Why is land the chief foundation of the economy of a kingdom or a nation? Because everything we use for our survival comes from the land. Every product, including our food, water, and clothing—everything imaginable is a product of the land. That is why God began in Genesis with the land.

> "Moreover the profit of the land is for all; even the king is served from the field" (Ecclesiastes 5:9).

Before He introduced His power, gifts, or any other thing, God wants us to know about the relationship He has with the land. It is interesting to note that God calls the land His land[3] just like He calls people His people.[4] We need to call the land our land and love it as much as God loves it.

From the beginning, God gave land: first to Adam and Eve, which they lost, and later the Promised Land, which was also lost through disobedience. The enemy's plan from the beginning is to deceive us with the fruit and steal the garden from us.

The book of Ezekiel contains verses promising land as well,

> "I will make a covenant of peace with them, and cause wild beasts to cease from the land; and they will dwell safely in the wilderness and sleep in the woods. I will make them and the places all around My hill a blessing; and I will cause showers to come down in their season; there shall be showers of blessing. Then the trees of the field shall yield their fruit, and the earth shall yield her increase. They shall be safe in their land; and they shall know that I *am* the Lord, when I have broken the bands of their yoke and delivered them from the hand of those who enslaved them. And they shall no longer be a prey for the nations, nor shall beasts of the land devour them; but they shall dwell safely, and no one shall make *them* afraid. I will raise up for them a garden of renown, and they shall no longer be consumed with hunger in the land, nor bear the shame of the Gentiles anymore. Thus they shall know that I, the Lord their God, *am* with them, and they, the house of Israel, *are* My people," says the Lord God.' "You are My flock, the flock of My pasture; you are men, and I am your GOD," says the Lord GOD" (EZEKIEL 34:25-31).

In nations where the people are poor, they do not love the land God gave them. They do not take care of the land, and they do not appreciate

---

3 See Joel 2:18 and Zechariah 9:16.

4 See Psalm 100:3.

or cultivate it. They think land has no value. Because they do not value it, they sell it to others cheaply and think the cash they receive from the sale will make them rich. However, just the opposite occurs: They will end up poorer later on than they were before. Land is the most expensive and precious commodity you can possess. If you do not value the land, it is because you have no understanding of real wealth and what it can produce for you.

If you look at the land in poor countries, it is usually unkempt and disorderly and dirty. They have no system to take care of garbage and the land is covered with filth. They are always looking for something for free or to travel to a foreign country. This is the fruit of laziness and ignorance. If you look at the richer countries, the land is treated with respect and kept neat and orderly. I have come to the conclusion that the main difference between poor and rich countries is how they care for their land. In poor countries, patriotism (or love for their nation) is also very minimal. Most are trying to get out of their country to find a better living somewhere else, preferably in another country. On the other hand, in rich countries patriotism is a heartfelt attitude.

> "Much food is in the fallow ground of the poor"
> (Proverbs 13:23a).

> "He who tills his land will have plenty of bread, but he who follows frivolity will have poverty enough!" (Proverbs 28:19).

> I went by the field of the lazy man, and by the vineyard of the man devoid of understanding; and there it was, all overgrown with thorns; its surface was covered with nettles; its stone wall was broken down. When I saw it, I considered it well; I looked on it and received instruction: A little sleep, a little slumber, a little folding of the hands to rest; so shall your poverty come like a prowler, and your need like an armed man (Proverbs 24:30-34).

In most parts of the world, a person who owns the most land has more influence than others. Your purpose is connected to a land. If you study the Bible, you will see this pattern: *When God favors a people, He gives them land; and when they disobey Him, they lose their land and go into captivity.* I was surprised to read that God even went to the extent of telling the people of Israel that if they disobeyed Him, they would lose the land He gave them. And they did.

Does God love the land more than He loves people? There are only two permanent things on this earth: one is our spirit and the second is land. God cares for the land so much that He protects and fights for it. He loves people so much that He died for us all so that we will take care of His land. He loves both. Every true believer in Christ should ask God for forgiveness for not taking care of the land He gave us and not loving it as much as He loves it. Most of the wars that took place were for land or disputes over land. Even in the present day, there are many countries that are in dispute on their borders.

I was really surprised by a verse I found about the land. The last part of the verse says God will destroy those who destroy the earth. "The nations were angry, and Your wrath has come, and the time of the dead, that they should be judged, and that You should reward Your servants the prophets and the saints, and those who fear Your name, small and great, and should destroy those who destroy the earth" (Revelation 11:18).

It is very unfortunate that many Christians do not understand the value of land. They are waiting to fly away, and live in heaven. If we do not appreciate the gift God gave to us and do not take care of it, there is no point in going to heaven. He will not be happy with us.

3. AGRICULTURE

On the third day God spoke to the earth to bring forth grass, the herb that yields seed and trees that yields fruit. It was so. Then on the sixth day He created living creatures, animals and cattle (Genesis 1:11-13; 24-25).

The third foundation of kingdom economy is agriculture. The work God gave to the first human being was to be an agriculturist. In Genesis we read that God created Adam, made a garden for him, and He put the man in it. There are two major expenses in life: the first is land, which includes your house (whether you own or rent), and the second is the food you eat.

The economy of any country depends primarily on land and agriculture. The best farmers should be Christians. We should produce the healthiest food. Food is the number one killer in today's world. In the West, people die because of food and in the East they die for the lack of it. Much of the food in the West is produced from genetically manipulated plants and seeds, which does more harm than good to our health. We should rediscover and go back to the original seeds and cultivate healthy food instead.

As long as our life remains, we will need food. People who produce food will have constant income. The restaurant industry is one of the most lucrative businesses because of the return on investment.

Most of the people God used in the Bible were agriculturists, or farmers. If you compare that to our time, a much smaller percentage of believers are involved in such enterprises. We have neglected it and given it to the devil and his children, thinking it is not spiritual enough. It's time to take it back.

4. PRECIOUS METALS AND STONES

The fourth foundation of kingdom economy is precious metals and stones.[5] Every precious stone and metal that is on this planet belongs to God and His children. However, the enemy has stolen most of it from us and is hiding it. He is using these precious metals to build his kingdom. God explained this to Adam:

---

5 See Genesis 2:12-13.

> "Now a river went out of Eden to water the garden, and from there it parted and became four riverheads. The name of the first is Pishon; it is the one which skirts the whole land of Havilah, where there is gold. And the gold of that land is good. Bdellium and the onyx stone are there" (Genesis 2:10-12).

In this verse, God introduced gold and precious stones to us. He said the gold in that land was good. Part of kingdom economy runs on gold. In the Bible, there also mention of gold in heaven. The United States government owns more gold than any other country right now at 8,133 metric tons.[6]

No wonder the nation's capital funds are based on the gold reserve they have. When God is saying something is good, you better believe it and say amen to it. "Yes Lord, the gold is good." If we had come into agreement with God about the things He says are good in His Word a few hundred years ago, the church would be in a different position by now.

Why would God tell us in Genesis that the gold and precious stones in one part of the world are good? Because He is teaching us about kingdom economy. He repeatedly said in His Word that all of the gold and silver belong to Him.

> "Because you have taken My silver and My gold, and have carried into your temples My prized possessions" (Joel 3:5).

> "'The silver is Mine, and the gold is Mine,' says the Lord of hosts" (Haggai 2:8).

When the New Jerusalem comes down from heaven, which we read about in Revelation, its foundation, walls, and gates are made from twelve

---

6 GoldPriceIndia, "Which Country Has the Highest Gold Reserve in the World?" GoldPriceIndia.com, April 24, 2017, accessed January 03, 2019, https://www.goldpriceindia.com/which-country-has-the-highest-gold-reserve-in-the-world.php.

precious stones, pearls, and pure gold.7 There are no unnecessary details in the Bible. God does not waste words. If He says something, there is a reason for it. Why would God give us the details of what is in the land of Gihon, including its gold and precious stones, if they were not somehow important? He would not. *The foundation of any nation's economy depends on how much land they own, what is in that land, and what they do with it.* From that comes the amount and quality of food they produce and the resources they extract from it.

Most people believe and most preachers preach that Lucifer was in charge of worship in heaven. But if you really study the Bible, you will see that he was not just a worshiper. He owned vast amounts of wealth in God's kingdom too. He was in charge of the economy, business, trade, wealth, and manufacturing in God's kingdom. He knew God better than all of us combined because he saw Him with his own eyes and experienced Him firsthand. Most of us haven't seen Him. We believe that He exists, but lack substantial experience to prove anything.

For the devil that is not the case. He knows how God functions and how His kingdom operates. He copied it well and enabled his children to manifest a counterfeit form of it on earth, all the while deceiving God's children because most of us have no idea how God's kingdom operates.

Recently I heard the story about a country in Africa that sold their copper mining rights to an outside company for 25 million USD because they did not have the proper technology. This company came in and made $26 million USD within the first three months of their operation, with a long future of greater profits ahead of them.8 That is just one example of how precious stones and metals can change the economy of a nation.

---

7 See Revelation 21:18-21.

8 Samarendra Das and Miriam Rose, "Copper Colonialism," Foil Vedanta, January 21, 2014, accessed January 03, 2019, http://www.foilvedanta.org/articles/copper-colonialism-foil-vedanta-zambia-report-launched/.

We need to appreciate what God put in the land and take ownership and use it to establish His kingdom, and will, in the nations. It's time for God's children to rise up and manifest as true sons and daughters of the most high God.

5. WATER

In Genesis 2, God introduced a river to us. Why a river? A river is a water source and bring things to life wherever it flows. Water is one of the most precious commodities we have. We cannot live without it. Clean drinking water is becoming scarce in many parts of the world. It is also a billion dollar industry. In 2016 water surpassed carbonated soft drinks as the number one drinking beverage in the United States. When God began the restoration of planet Earth in Genesis 1, He gathered all the water into one place and called it the sea. There are many types of wealth in the ocean too: Oil, fish, minerals, and pearls are just some of them.

I read in the news that the water in the ocean contains more gold than what is hidden in the land. There are $771 trillion dollars' worth of gold in the ocean.[9] We do not have the proper technology to extract it yet, but the nation that comes up with that technology would become one of the wealthiest nations in the world.

In some parts of the United States, when you buy a piece of land, you do not also gain ownership of the water rights to that land. That means you cannot dig water out of the land you *own*. Someone living in a different town or state might own the water rights of the land you purchased. This was a big surprise to me because in India when you buy a piece of land, you own the water rights too. You can dig a well and use the water for your personal use.

---

[9] Trevor Nace, "$771 Trillion Worth Of Gold Lies Hidden In The Ocean: Good Luck Getting It," Forbes, September 15, 2017, accessed January 03, 2019, https://www.forbes.com/sites/trevor-nace/2017/09/15/771-trillion-worth-gold-hidden-ocean/#245e550c23d3.

As long as we live on this earth, we will need water. In Genesis, God taught Adam about the rivers that started in the garden. They were their water sources. God knows water is vital to our life. One of the fastest growing businesses in many parts of the world these days is turning sea water into drinking water.

JESUS USED THE FOUNDATIONS OF KINGDOM ECONOMY

There is a specific reason why when Jesus shared the parables about the kingdom, He always used either land, agriculture, and precious stones or metals as objects to reveal the mysteries of the kingdom of God. Some people think He used them because they were familiar examples in their culture and they helped communicate a particular truth best to the people.

Remember, they were living under the Roman Empire. However, Jesus never used anything related to Rome or its culture to reveal a mystery or truth about His kingdom. Why? He only used the foundations of kingdom economy to explain how His kingdom operates, and as I said, they are all mentioned in the first three chapters of the Bible.

One day God spoke to me, and said, "If you do not understand the first three chapters of the Bible, then you will not understand the rest of the Bible." If we do not understand the first three chapters of Genesis, we will not understand why God created us and put us here. God has hidden solutions to every major problem we face in those first three chapters. The rest of the Bible is the expansion of what happened and the process God is using to restore us to the first two chapters.

Every law that governs natural and spiritual life is mentioned in Genesis 1-3. Every major doctrine of the Bible are mentioned in them as well. Theologians call these the "law of first mention" and look to these verses to set the tone for understanding vital doctrines.

One of the questions I have asked the Lord is this: "Why are saved, sanctified, Spirit-filled believers less productive than people who are not saved and do not believe in the real God?"

Here is the answer He gave me. "You do not need to be saved to be successful on this earth. You do not need to be Spirit filled to invent or create something. You do not need to speak in tongues to run the largest corporation in your country. You do not need to believe in God to be a president of a country." With all those blessings, we are supposed to be more influential than the people in the world, but in most cases, it is not so. It is very sad. We are supposed to be blessing the earth and its people.

Anyone, regardless of color, position in society (caste), or religion can apply the laws that God has set in motion and they will reap the consequence of them. Anyone who is successful in any field has discovered the laws that govern that field and applied them, receiving the benefits they bring. It is that simple.

If there are two farmers living next to each other, and one is a believer in Christ and the other one is a Hindu, the person who knows the laws of the kingdom and applies the best farming skills will get the best harvest. The Christian might pray and go to church and still not receive a bountiful harvest. The Hindu who worships many idols, but studies about farming and equips himself with better skills, may get a better harvest than the Christian.

We see this in everyday life around us. In India there are many prosperous business people who are Hindus. In the Middle East there are many successful Muslims. They have learned and applied the laws that govern their particular business and received the result that brings. They reap what they sow.

Whether you obey it or break it, *every spiritual or natural law has a consequence*. Success is not automatic. Just because you are Christian that does not mean you will succeed or have a good life. You also have to follow God's principles. *Nothing* is automatic. God told Joshua:

> "This Book of the Law shall not depart from your mouth, but you shall meditate in it day and night, that you may observe to do according to all that is written in it. For then you will make your way prosperous, and then you will have good success" (Joshua 1:8).

The Bible is a book of laws. As I mentioned earlier, every law of success and prosperity is mentioned in the first three chapters of Genesis. God told Joshua that if he would meditate on those laws and observe (or do) all that is written in them, he would be prosperous and successful. Success is predictable. *If you observe and apply the laws of success you will succeed; and if not, you are destined you fail.* It's that simple. It's not a matter of luck.

You may ask: What about favor? Will not favor make one person successful? Yes it does. But the truth is that favor is a biblical law too. Favor does not just come to everyone; if it did, then no one would be broke and poor, especially Christians. There are principles mentioned in the Bible that when applied attract favor—either with God or from man.

Luke 2:52 says,

> "Jesus increased in wisdom and stature, and in favor with God and men."

What do you think gave Jesus favor with God and men? It was the wisdom He obtained that gave Him favor.

> "For whoever finds me *(wisdom)* finds life, and obtains favor from the Lord" (Proverbs 8:35).

So if you need favor, the solution is very simple: Get wisdom! Why did God give Joseph such favor? Because he was wise. How do I know that? Because he ran away from a woman who tried to seduce him. In

Proverbs it says that a person who commits adultery lacks understanding and destroys himself (Proverbs 6:32). Wise people run away from such women, and the results of such decisions. Eventually, Pharaoh appointed Joseph to teach wisdom to his elders.

God has blessed us with all we need. There is not a blessing in heaven that God has not blessed us with too. He did not withhold anything from us, not even His own Son (Romans 8:32). Those blessings exist either in the invisible (spirit) realm or in the visible realm, and the hands of the wicked. How do we bring them from the invisible to the visible? From the hands of the wicked to the house of God.

HOW TO CREATE MONEY

Did you know that you can create money? This is actually how we take the wealth of the wicked and bring it into the kingdom of God. Money is a medium of exchange—something you exchange for something else of value. If you make something that has a value of ten dollars, you have just created ten dollars. When you exchange that product, idea, information, skill, entertainment, service, or whatever it is, with someone who needs it, they will pay you ten dollars. It could be anything. Your financial provision is connected to one or more of the following principles, which will generate income to your life. Your purpose will encompass at least one of these areas.

HAVE A PRODUCT

At any given time, we might be using ten kinds of products, made by different companies, on our bodies alone. This number may be greater or smaller depending on your needs. We paid money to buy those products, and on top of that, we use hundreds of products in our homes. Someone made those products and made money when we bought them!

You might be a person in whom God has deposited an idea for a product. It does not have to be something as large as an airplane; it could be as small as a paper clip or a rubber band. Not everyone is created to produce a product, so if you do not have an idea like that, there is no need to worry about it. You may be called to help someone who manufactures something instead.

There are many roles you can play in the process of launching a new product. The first is design. Every product needs a designer to plan it and build a prototype. Then someone has to test it before it is manufactured and sold.

The next role is the manufacturer. This can be as basic as making it and selling it start to finish, or much more complex. For instance, you could start a company that manufactures parts for others or one that makes someone else's idea (their design). Someone told me that a car is made of almost twenty-five thousand parts, and various companies in different countries make many of those parts. They are all brought to one place and the car is assembled. All you have to do to make money is to manufacture one of those parts.

Another is packaging. There are companies that specialize in making packaging materials alone. There is also marketing. A product will go nowhere if it is not marketed, so some people expend their energies in the promotion of products and are paid to do that. Some others are distribution, transportation, and advertising. You could provide the raw materials, parts or any form of services or tools, to any of the above areas. All of these services generate money, and the people who do these things become blessed financially.

MEET A NEED

The second way money will come to you is through meeting a need. There are needs all around us. In our nation, church, and community, there are needs waiting to be met. When you meet a particular need, you will be blessed financially. Food meets the need of hunger. Watches solve a time-telling problem. Gasoline makes a car move and people need it supplied to them. Lonely people need companionship. Single parents often need help keeping up. Those without families need friends. The possibilities are endless.

SERVE A CAUSE

There are causes that are worth committing your life to serving too. There are many social and charitable organizations around the world, and they all serve a cause. Our ministry had a vision center in India in which we trained orphans and destitute children to discover and fulfill their purpose. It's been one of the best programs we ever created as a ministry, to see children who never had opportunity to go to school become entrepreneurs, learn skills, and become who God created them to be. Everyone who has come to visit has said they have never seen a program like ours anywhere else. This is just one example. There are many others.

God will guide and help you discover such a cause if this is the direction He wishes for you to go. Even if you cannot establish a cause, you can support those He touches your heart to serve.

SOLVE A PROBLEM

You are created to solve a problem. Jesus solved the sin problem. Bill Gates solved a computer problem. Ford solved the automobile problem. Clothes solve the nakedness problem. Whatever problem grieves your heart and makes you cry, you might be created to solve. Every business out there solves a problem, and people pay money when that problem is solved for them.

ADD VALUE TO OTHERS

When you add value to others through your wisdom, gifts, service, teaching, companionship, or however God uses you, you will in turn be blessed, financially and otherwise.

THE WEALTH OF THE WICKED

> "A good man leaves an inheritance to his children's children, but the wealth of the sinner is stored up for the righteous" (Proverbs 13:22).

I have seen many people claim this verse without understanding what it really means or how it works. What was the wealth of the wicked in the time and day that the verse was written? It was mainly land (everything comes with and from the land), servants, cattle, gold and silver. God told the Israelites that He would give them the Promised Land (which was the wealth of the wicked). What is the wealth of the wicked in our day and time?

When you see the wealth of the wicked, you cannot simply take it for yourself. If you do, they would kill you. Nor are the wicked going to bring their wealth and leave it at your doorstep. There is very little chance of it happening that way. *We need the wisdom of God to know how to bring the wealth of the wicked into the kingdom.*

We must possess it. Just because God said He has given you something does not mean you possess it. The Lord told the Israelites that He had given them the Promised Land, but it wasn't theirs until they possessed it. *They had to fight to inherit the promises of God.*

How do we *fight* in this day and age to possess the wealth of the wicked? There are five ways you possess the wealth of the wicked.

BUSINESSES/PRODUCTS

When you come up with a valid product that is good for humanity, you are creating a legitimate path to tap into the wealth of the wicked. When you have a product, people will spend money to buy that product. The better and more useful the product, the more people will buy it. Each time someone buys your product, you are inheriting some of the wealth of the wicked.

SERVICES

When you offer a service that people need for which you are paid, that is another way we obtain wealth. If you own a telephone company and you have many subscribers, they pay you for using your service. If you cut and style hair and own a barber shop, you are paid for that. Everyone needs a haircut at some point in their life. If you are a dentist and provide that service to the people in your community, you will be blessed through that service. When you provide a service that people need, you will inherit the wealth of the wicked and build relationships at the same time.

FAVOR

The third way the wealth of the wicked is transferred to you is through God giving you favor. It's happened many times in history, but may not happen to everyone. If you are supposed to start a business, you are not going to receive wealth through favor, but through the business God is leading you to develop. God gave the people of Israel favor with the Egyptians and they plundered them of all their valuables. Another example is Nehemiah. He received the resources he needed from the king to go back to Jerusalem and rebuild its walls. There is usually a bigger purpose in God's mind in all this as you can see in those two examples.

MEET A NEED

Another way to create money is to meet a need. I have a friend who is rich and wanted to do live shows on social media. This person had no experience with social media. Hearing about that need, I offered my time and the technology he needed to do it (and meet that need). I did not ask for any payment nor was I expecting anything in return, but just because I recognized an unmet need and stepped in to fulfill it, I was eventually blessed in more ways than I ever thought possible. What needs do the people around you have that you could step in and meet? Don't let people take advantage of you. You need to use wisdom to know which need you should step in and meet and which one you should not. As you put these needs before God, He will guide you into what you should or should not do.

KNOWLEDGE, WISDOM, AND UNDERSTANDING

To do any of the previously mentioned endeavors, we need knowledge, wisdom, and understanding. Wisdom is the most precious treasure we can possess. The Bible says all the treasures of wisdom and knowledge are hid in Christ and He dwells in us (Colossians 2:3). We should be the ones with the answers to the most pertinent and demanding problems this world has. When you solve a problem, you will be rewarded by others.

CHAPTER - 3

KINGDOM PERSPECTIVE ON MONEY

Are you going through a financial crisis? Have you ever asked God for a financial miracle? Have you ever wished you had more money? It is the desire of most human beings to have more money. That is why people go to work every day. Regardless of what you think about money, money is a good idea and you cannot live without it.

I have not yet met a person who does not want to have more money. Whether it is to meet your living expenses, pay off some debts, help your children, pay for medical treatment, or reach the next status quo, everyone is striving to have more money. The Bible talks about blessing, prosperity and similar words 566 times in the New King James Version.

There's more financial wealth on this earth today than at any other time in the history of the world. There are more millionaires today than at any other time in history. There are also more poor people today than at any other time. As time progresses, these two extremes are emerging: the extremely rich and the extremely poor.

There are over 7.5 billion people on the earth.[10] Out of that number, "26.2 percent of the world's population, were living on less than $3.20 per day in 2015. Close to 46 percent of the world's population was living on less than $5.50 a day."[11] America has only 5% of the world's population, but has 70% of the world's money, and 45% of the world's "super rich population."[12]

In biblical days there was no "money" as we have today. What they used for business transactions was precious metals like silver, gold and other such materials. We have been programmed from our childhood to use paper money; and when we do not have it, we get nervous.

Money is a good thing if we know how to manage it properly. Money is a kind of power, similar to electricity. If we channel electricity properly and manage it wisely, it can be a very productive source of energy. On the other hand, if you do not manage electricity well, it can be very dangerous and cause great damage. Money works the same way.

Some people are afraid of having more money. They think if they get more money, it will cause them to sin and disobey God. That is a deception. Money is a good tool if you learn how to manage it with wisdom. As long as the devil can deceive and keep you poor, you cannot be fully effective for the kingdom of God.

There is nothing that divides people today into different classes more than money. People are treated and respected based on how much money they have. The rich, middle-class and poor exist in every nation.

---

10   "Current World Population," Worldometers, accessed January 03, 2019, http://www.worldometers.info/world-population/.

11   "Nearly Half the World Lives on Less than $5.50 a Day," World Bank, accessed January 03, 2019, https://www.worldbank.org/en/news/press-release/2018/10/17/nearly-half-the-world-lives-on-less-than-550-a-day

12   Benjamin Cosman, "The U.S. Has 5% Of the World's Population, and 45% Of the World's Super Rich Population," Mic, October 24, 2015, accessed January 03, 2019, https://mic.com/articles/74547/the-u-s-has-5-of-the-world-s-population-and-45-of-the-world-s-super-rich-population#.2VgRbOHB1.

Kingdom economy is not about money or making more of it. It is about what creates money. Before we can handle it, we need to be set free from the spirit that controls the monetary system of this world. That is the first step that needs to happen for us to qualify to handle kingdom economy.

Many of those that talk about the kingdom today are still controlled, or influenced by, covetousness, greed, and the spirit of mammon. All they care about is making more money. When you are in the kingdom, making a little more money should not be our priority. *Establishing God's will is our priority.* We will need money to do that, but we need to put money at the place where it belongs.

We should not let money control our decisions, or us. The Holy Spirit should lead us. How do we know when we are free from the spirit of mammon or covetousness? We are free when money has no influence on our decisions. It is when we see money as a tool and not as a source or a master.

Unless we are free from the hold of money, God will not release His economy to us. There are only a very few people whom He can trust with kingdom economy. Most are controlled by it unawares. They think they are living for God, but only to the limit their money allows them. They are stuck in the system. Why? Because they are not seeking to fulfill their purpose first. When we do that, God releases all we need to do it.

How do we become free from money? God will give us several opportunities to be free from it in our lifetime. These come primarily through allowing us to go through financial hardships and Him asking us to give away what we have. Most won't obey because of fear and will remain a slave, spending the majority of their lives working for money.

God wants all of us to be financially blessed and prosperous. When God created Adam, Adam was neither rich nor poor. He had the potential and the resources around him to become rich. God creates people and they decide whether they want to become rich or poor. The choice is yours, not God's.

Some people become rich because of what they know and how they use what they know. Some people remain poor because of what they do not know, and the way they think and believe about themselves and money.

Many Christians believe and say, "If God wants me to be rich, He will just give me millions of dollars by chance and I will be rich." That's a wrong mindset. Let me tell you, even if God wanted them to be rich, those people will never become rich. The reason they say such things is because they do not know God, neither do they understand His ways and principles about wealth and prosperity. The truth of the matter is that God (our Father) wants all of His children living healthy and prosperous, just as any parent would want their children to be.

"Beloved, I pray that you may prosper in all things and be in health, just as your soul prospers" (3 John 1:2).

God does not give away free money! There is no incident in the Bible where God dropped money from heaven and blessed someone. *People became wealthy because they obeyed God and put into practice the opportunities and ideas He gave them according to the principles in His Word.* The opposite is also true: People remain poor when they disobey God and do not put into practice the principles from God's Word about money. He will give you resources, materials, ideas, opportunities, dreams and wisdom or connect you with someone who has money.

Solomon said,

"Money answers everything" (Ecclesiastes 10:19).

Finding a job or a better job is not the solution to financial freedom or for creating wealth and riches. They are only temporary fixes. Many of us are programmed to believe that having a job is the solution to acquiring money. Kingdom economy doesn't work that way. In the kingdom, discovering your purpose, embracing your calling, identifying your gifts by gaining specialized knowledge and developing and mastering a skill, are the keys to unlocking the kingdom economy in your life.

You were created to be the solution to someone else's problem. You are an answer to someone's prayer. You have the harvest for someone's need. When you live with that kind of motive and attitude, life will never be boring nor will you lack anything. Financial prosperity is one of the blessings that God has promised His children. No father likes to see his children living in poverty and in need. Our heavenly Father not only cares about us, He wants to see us blessed and prospering in everything we do (Psalm 1:3).

God promised Joshua to make his "way prosperous" and give him "good success" if Joshua kept God's Word. God also promises us good success if we keep His Word in our heart, meditate on it, and speak it with our mouth. To me that is the simplest way to success. Many people spend years in colleges and universities to succeed in life, but still fail.

Financial prosperity is not the invention of some preachers in the West. God has placed the choice between a blessing and a curse before every person. It is the personal choice of each individual to take one or the other.

> "Behold, I set before you today a blessing and a curse: the blessing, if you obey the commandments of the Lord your God which I command you today; and the curse, if you do not obey the commandments of the Lord your God, but turn aside from the way I command you" (Deuteronomy 11:26-28a).

It is up to us which one to choose. God will not force anything on us. Blessing and curse are just a reciprocity of our response to His commandments. In the New Testament, following the way of His commandments means to be led by the Holy Spirit. When we are led by the Holy Spirit, we will automatically fulfill all the commandments.

Jesus said He came that we might have life and life more abundantly (John 10:10). The Greek word for "abundantly" is *perissos* which means "all-around, excess, more than, beyond what is anticipated, exceeding expectation; more abundant, going past the expected limit, and more than enough."[13]

There were rich believers both in the Old Testament and in the New Testament. The Bible mentions money and possessions over 2,300 times. More than eighty percent of the parables Jesus shared related to the subject of money and investment.

Many believers that I know are very committed to the Lord and give tithes and offerings to their churches and other ministries, but they do not enjoy the financial abundance God has promised. They stay at the same financial level for decades. It hurts my heart to see most unsaved people prosper and have abundance because they put into practice biblical principles; while believers, who carry around their Bible all their life, do not know how to put into practice the principles that are taught in it about money.

They begin and end financially at the same point in life. They have the same debt that the people in the world have. The Bible says we will not borrow but lend to many nations. Instead, I see most Christians borrow and glorify the process, declaring it is wise. Maybe it is the wisdom of the world. If I do not have the money to do something or buy something, though the situation looks pressing, then it is not God's will for my life to do it or to have it.

Whenever I borrowed money and did something significant with it, I always got in trouble at the end. It did not end productively as I thought it would be. Some Christians says it is OK to borrow money if you are going to make more money with it. That means you can twist the Word and get around it. It renders the Word of God changeable according to circumstances, just as a pro-abortionist would choose to kill a baby for

---

[13] James Strong, "4053. Perissos," Biblehub.com, accessed January 13, 2019, https://biblehub.com/greek/4053.htm.

their convenience. Or perhaps you could kill someone if you knew you were going to save someone later? I do not think so. The Word of God is not changeable.

Many have a heart to give but do not have anything left to give after meeting their living expenses, while many wealthy people have much left over, but do not have the heart to give.

God created Adam and gave him the entire earth and its wealth to be a steward of it. The only thing God told him not to eat was from the Tree of the Knowledge of Good and Evil. God gave him gold, silver and all other precious metals. In fact, in Genesis 2 God proclaimed the gold in the land of Havilah as good (Genesis 2:11-12).

When we think about money, we think of something that is made of paper with the seal of a government on it. God does not think the same way. To Him, the paper money we carry is worth nothing; and in actual fact, it has no value other than the value attached to it by the reserve bank of its country, which can be cancelled at any time by the government. However, there are some things that your government cannot cancel or diminish in value because the value of those things is not determined by them. Those are the things we need to look into when we think about "money" rather than focusing our attention on paper money.

There is a powerful spirit working behind the monitory system of this world. I believe there are three major areas of this world system that Lucifer himself oversees and they are: the government, religion and economy of each nation. Out of the three, the economy plays the major role because all other systems function based on money. If there is no money, neither government nor religion or any other area would be able to function at all.

The Bible mentions only two masters and they are God and mammon. Mammon is the spirit that works behind the economy of every country here. Believe it or not, the majority of the people on this earth serve mammon. Most believers do not serve the purposes of God, neither do they have any time to do it. The majority of their time is spent serving the monetary system of their country by trying to make more money to buy food, shelter and clothing. God gave these things to Adam for free and promised to give them to us freely too—if we seek His kingdom first and His righteousness.

Most people that I know are fearful about money. They go to church on Sunday and say Jesus is their Lord; but in reality, their trust is in the money or the job they have. It is not their fault nor am I accusing anyone. We have all been programmed from childhood. As a result, many of the ways we think and things we practice as a normal part of our life were never meant by God to be normal at all.

Let us look at the life of the father of our faith, Abraham. The Bible says Abraham was rich in gold, silver and cattle. He had 318 servants that were born and brought up in his own house (Genesis 14:14). Since they were born in his house, that means they had parents. These 318 were grown and trained men. They might have had wives and children. I calculated about how much it might cost to take care of 500 plus families a year. If it takes just a minimum of $10,000.00 to support one family in a year, then it comes to $5,000,000.00 (5 million). Plus, we need to add Abraham and his own family and all their expenses. Imagine the wealth our father Abraham had!

When Abraham's servant went to look for a wife for his son Isaac, the Bible says the servant took ten camels loaded with gold, silver and precious substances to give away as gifts to the bride and her family. Job, David, Boaz, and Solomon were other wealthy people in the Old Testament.

It never says God was upset with them for having wealth. Instead He was honored by His servants representing Him well on the earth, not just in the spiritual realm, but in the financial arena too.

TWO KINDS OF MONEY

In Luke 16, Jesus spoke about true riches and unrighteous mammon. Unrighteous mammon is the monetary system of this world and the true riches are the economy of the kingdom of God. That means there are two kinds of money. The entire chapter of Luke 16 deals with money and how to manage it properly. It talks about the place of money in our life.

Jesus never promoted financial wealth or prosperity as bait to follow Him. He taught about money and money management because money plays an important role in our lives. Jesus never dealt with people based on their financial status, nor promoted prosperity as a sign of spirituality. He put money in the proper place where it belongs. We should do the same.

> "And I say to you, make friends for yourselves by unrighteous mammon, that when you fail, they may receive you into an everlasting home. He who is faithful in what is least is faithful also in much; and he who is unjust in what is least is unjust also in much. Therefore, if you have not been faithful in the unrighteous mammon, who will commit to your trust the true riches? And if you have not been faithful in what is another man's, who will give you what is your own?
> No servant can serve two masters; for either he will hate the one and love the other, or else he will be loyal to the one and despise the other. You cannot serve God and mammon" (Luke 16:9-13).

The righteous money is what we receive as part of our inheritance from the Lord and earn using proper rules and principles, and the unrighteous money is what people make through lucrative means.

In every society, people with money are considered more powerful, and they always get a special place in the society as well as respect from people. Jesus knew this and He told the Pharisees, who loved money and respect, this:

> Now the Pharisees, who were lovers of money, also heard all these things, and they derided Him. And He said to them, "You are those who justify yourselves before men, but God

knows your hearts. For what is highly esteemed among men is an abomination in the sight of God" (Luke 16:14-15).

To further confront them, Jesus told the parable of the rich man and Lazarus (the poor man) in Luke 16:19-27. The rich man paraded himself with his riches and Lazarus desired to eat the crumbs that fell from the rich man's table. After death, the rich man was taken into the place of torment (Hades) and Lazarus to the bosom of Abraham.

We should never think of having more or less money as a sign of our spirituality nor promote it. If God has given us riches, we should use them for His glory to establish His kingdom and not to show others how smart, wealthy or spiritual we are.

REWARD FOR FOLLOWING CHRIST

One of the concerns that Jesus' disciples had was about their reward for following Him and leaving everything behind. Jesus made sure they knew what they would receive as their reward.

> So Jesus answered and said, "Assuredly, I say to you, there is no one who has left house or brothers or sisters or father or mother or wife or children or lands, for My sake and the gospel's, who shall not receive a hundredfold now in this time — houses and brothers and sisters and mothers and children and lands, with persecutions—and in the age to come, eternal life" (Mark 10:29-30).

Many misunderstand the teachings of the New Testament. They teach that we have to forsake everything and become like nomads to follow Jesus. They also teach that we are not supposed to have any wealth or money, and that all these things are kept for us when we reach heaven. That is far from the truth. Why would we need money or wealth in heaven? It is true that many times we need to leave behind what was holding us back from following Christ, and that could be something or someone; but it is not true that we are to wander the earth, live in poverty, and suffer to please God.

Some of the disciples of Jesus were rich. Luke was a doctor and Matthew was a tax collector. Joseph who buried Jesus was a rich council member. Nicodemus was a Pharisee and a member of the Sanhedrin.

> "Now when evening had come, *there came a rich man from Arimathea, named Joseph,* who himself had also become a disciple of Jesus" (Matthew 27:57).

Jesus did not ask him to sell everything he had in order to follow Him.

Poverty came as a result of the fall, not from spiritual enlightenment or commitment as some believe. Sickness, curse, death and all other evil that we see came after the fall. Jesus died to redeem us from sin, the curse and death. *Jesus became sin to redeem us from our sins. Jesus became cursed to redeem us from the curse of law. Jesus became poor to redeem us from poverty.*

Poverty does not glorify God. Poverty does not make you more spiritual or holy. These kinds of thoughts are straight from the devil, and designed to keep us stupid and under his bondage. Poverty and need are a curse. There are religious sects that require you to make a vow of poverty if you want to be part of them. That is also against the Word of God.

Throughout the Bible, God's intention concerning prosperity towards His people is the same. God created Adam and Eve and put them in the garden where they lacked nothing in their lives. When sin came, we lost God's prosperity and a poverty mindset came into us. But God did not leave us in that state. He took the children of Israel into the Promised Land. The whole experience of coming out of Egypt and going to the Promised Land is symbolic of what we experience in Christ through redemption.

> "For the Lord your God is bringing you into a good land, a land of brooks of water, of fountains and springs, that flow out of valleys and hills; a land of wheat and barley, of vines and fig trees and pomegranates, a land of olive oil and honey; a land in which you will eat bread without scarcity, *in which*

you will lack nothing; a land whose stones are iron and out of whose hills you can dig copper" (Deuteronomy 8:7-9).

The key phrase in the above verse is in verse 9 where it says, "You shall lack nothing." That is God's will for our lives.

> "The young lions lack and suffer hunger; but those who seek the Lord shall not lack any good thing" (Psalms 34:10).

Let us see what God's will is for us in the New Testament. There is no place in the gospels where Jesus and the disciples needed anything while they were doing ministry. They did not lack food, clothing, nor a place to stay.

When the church started, Acts says the believers' needs were all met. The Bible says in,

> *"Nor was there anyone among them who lacked;* for all who were possessors of lands or houses sold them, and brought the proceeds of the things that were sold, and laid them at the apostles' feet; and they distributed to each as anyone had need" (Acts 4:34-35).

That was a peculiar situation in which everyone sold a portion of what they had and shared with the rest. There is no mention of this practice again in Acts or the epistles, neither did the apostles, including Paul, teach this as a doctrine for the New Testament church.

Later Paul writes to the saints that it is God's will for them to be in plenty and lack nothing.

> For I do not mean that others should be eased and you burdened; but by an equality, that now at this time your abundance may supply their lack, that their abundance also may supply your lack—that there may be equality. As it is written, "He who gathered much had nothing left over, and he who gathered little had no lack" (2 Corinthians 8:13-15).

> "That you may walk properly toward those who are outside, and that *you may lack nothing*" (1 Thessalonians 4:12).

> "Send Zenas the lawyer and Apollos on their journey with haste, that *they may lack nothing*. And let our people also learn to maintain good works, to meet urgent needs, that they may not be unfruitful" (Titus 3:13-14).

> "And God will generously provide all you need. Then you will always have everything you need and plenty left over to share with others" (2 Corinthians 9:8, NLT).

> "Command those who are rich in this present age not to be haughty, nor to trust in uncertain riches but in the living God, who gives us richly all things to enjoy" (1 Timothy 6:17).

Just like poverty does not make us spiritual, riches also do not make us spiritual. But having riches gives us more advantages on this earth than being poor does. Money and wealth are a type of power that God uses to accomplish His purposes. When we bless others and help those who are in need, it really glorifies God. When we have money, we can do a lot more for God's kingdom than we can if we don't.

> "And He said to them, 'Take heed and beware of covetousness, for one's life does not consist in the abundance of the things he possesses" (Luke 12:15).

When we have riches, we have to be careful that we do not put our trust in them or boast in our riches. We must never put the riches in the place of God. Money is not the root of evil, but *the love* of money is the root of all evil.

PAUL'S STORY

Many saints of God misunderstand Paul's writings. They think he was poor and took glory in his poverty. That is not true at all. Paul went through financial difficulty as well as financial abundance. He learned to be happy in both situations. He was a traveling minister who roamed extensively throughout the world.

Just as it is costly to travel today, it was also expensive for Paul and his team to travel and minister all over the known world. All the money to do that had to come from the ministry or the business he was doing. Let us read his testimony. He was traveling on ships most of the time, which was the most expensive form of travel in those days. I believe if there had been airplanes in those days, Paul might have flown in them too.

Paul was born into a wealthy and prominent family, and was well-known among the Jewish community (Acts 22:3). He had influential friends in the government when he was in the ministry (Acts 19:31). In Acts 24:26, the Roman leaders tried to get money from him as a bribe to release him. If you are poor, rulers won't expect you to pay them, so he was not poor.

> "Not that I was ever in need, for I have learned how to be content with whatever I have. I know how to live on almost nothing or with everything. I have learned the secret of living in every situation, whether it is with a full stomach or empty, with plenty or little. For I can do everything through Christ, who gives me strength. Even so, you have done well to share with me in my present difficulty.
>
> As you know, you Philippians were the only ones who gave me financial help when I first brought you the Good News and then traveled on from Macedonia. No other church did this. Even when I was in Thessalonica you sent help more than once. I don't say this because I want a gift from you. Rather, I want you to receive a reward for your kindness.
>
> At the moment I have all I need—and more! I am generously supplied with the gifts you sent me with Epaphroditus. They

are a sweet-smelling sacrifice that is acceptable and pleasing to God. And this same God who takes care of me will supply all your needs from his glorious riches, which have been given to us in Christ Jesus. Now all glory to God our Father forever and ever! Amen" (Philippians 4:11-20, NLT).

Paul had a personal conviction about his financial life. He decided not to have any personal wealth to set an example for other fellow ministers and believers. He wanted them to know that he was not doing what he was doing for financial gain. He worked with his own hands to support his life and ministry (Acts 20:34). He did not burden the churches to give. Though he always received what the churches gave to him willingly, Paul could have easily asked and received sufficient support from the churches he started.

"My defense to those who examine me is this: Do we have no right to eat and drink? Do we have no right to take along a believing wife, as do also the other apostles, the brothers of the Lord, and Cephas? Or is it only Barnabas and I who have no right to refrain from working? Who ever goes to war at his own expense? Who plants a vineyard and does not eat of its fruit? Or who tends a flock and does not drink of the milk of the flock?

Do I say these things as a mere man? Or does not the law say the same also? For it is written in the law of Moses, "You shall not muzzle an ox while it treads out the grain." Is it oxen God is concerned about? Or does He say it altogether for our sakes? For our sakes, no doubt, this is written, that he who plows should plow in hope, and he who threshes in hope should be partaker of his hope. If we have sown spiritual things for you, is it a great thing if we reap your material things? If others are partakers of this right over you, are we not even more?

Nevertheless we have not used this right, but endure all things lest we hinder the gospel of Christ. Do you not know that those who minister the holy things eat of the things of the temple, and those who serve at the altar partake of the offerings of the altar? Even so the Lord has commanded that those who preach the gospel should live from the gospel.

But I have used none of these things, nor have I written these things that it should be done so to me; for it would be better for me to die than that anyone should make my boasting void. For if I preach the gospel, I have nothing to boast of, for necessity is laid upon me; yes, woe is me if I do not preach the gospel! For if I do this willingly, I have a reward; but if against my will, I have been entrusted with a stewardship. What is my reward then? That when I preach the gospel, I may present the gospel of Christ without charge, that I may not abuse my authority in the gospel" (1 Corinthians 9:3-18).

"Nor did we eat anyone's bread free of charge, but worked with labor and toil night and day, that we might not be a burden to any of you, not because we do not have authority, but to make ourselves an example of how you should follow us" (2 Thessalonians 3:8-9).

So if you have poverty mindset about money, I would encourage you to get rid of it and receive a biblical perspective about money. It is not helping you or anyone else. As long as you live on this earth you need money, just like you need water and air. It is not an evil thing.

Paul decided to keep the money where it belonged. He knew the danger of trusting in money or man for his well-being. He lived as if he had nothing, but in the spirit he possessed everything (2 Corinthians 6:10). It is better to possess everything in the spirit than to have lot of money and possess nothing in the spirit. When you possess everything in the spirit, you will never lack anything in your life.

GOD'S WILL FOR OUR FINANCES

Does God care about our financial needs? Of course He does. The first miracle Jesus did in His ministry was to meet the material need of a family. He was invited to a wedding party and it was a common practice to offer wine as part of the meal. Unfortunately, the wine was insufficient for everyone. He turned the water into wine and met the need of that family (John 2:1-10). The Bible says this miracle was the manifestation of His glory (John 2:11).

Jesus said,

> "The thief does not come except to steal, and to kill, and to destroy. I have come that they may have life, and that they may have it more abundantly" (John 10:10).

As mentioned earlier, the Greek word used for "abundantly" is *perissos* which means "over and above, more than necessary, superseded, exceeding abundantly, an extraordinary." That is the kind of blessing God wants to grant us. The Bible also says we shall not borrow, but lend, to many nations (Deuteronomy 28:12).

The credit system in America is glorified to such an extent that people do not even give it a second thought when they borrow money. It has become a part of the culture and lifestyle. They do not understand that there is a spirit behind it. It is not God's perfect will for them to borrow money.

How can we fulfill the assignment God has given us if we stay on the same financial level as the rest of the world? God's Word says we will not borrow, *but lend,* to many nations. How come we do not have more than enough to give and bless God's work and His people? Why do pastors or ministers beg believers week after week to support them, telling us to give in order to meet a financial need in the church?

Wouldn't it be nice if as soon as a need was mentioned, someone was waiting to meet that need, whether the need was for a building project, mission, or a TV program? I believe God is going to make the church operate that way in the coming days.

God never intended for His church to experience financial difficulty. God never intended for finances to be a problem for His children—ever! He is a God of abundance. Whatever He has, there is no limit to it. His wisdom, His wealth, His power, His mercy, His love has no limit whatsoever.

In the Old Testament Moses had to tell the people to stop giving because they gave so much, and what they received was more than they needed to build the tabernacle (Exodus 36:4-7).

There are three things the devil hates the most:

1) Believers walking in the righteousness of God
2) Believers living in financial abundance
3) Believers walking in God's power

He will do everything in his power to keep you from experiencing those three things.

Is it God's will for people to live in sin? No, because Jesus became sin for us and died for our sins (2 Corinthians 5:21).

Is it God's will for people to be under a curse? No, because Jesus became a curse for us and took our curses on the cross (Galatians 3:13).

Is it God's will for people to be sick? No, because Jesus became sick for us. He took our sickness and disease on the cross (Isaiah 53:4-5). Sickness came because of sin and the debt of sin was paid off; therefore, sickness cannot survive.

Is it God's will for people to be poor? No, because Jesus became poor for us, so that you and I can be rich. 2 Corinthians 8:9 says poverty is a curse and there is a spirit that works behind that curse called the spirit of poverty.

The first miracle Jesus did in a synagogue was healing a man with a withered hand. This man could not bless anyone because his hand was withered. A part of this curse is still working in many lives in the church today. They cannot stretch their hand to bless any one—either because they are living on such a tight budget or they do not have the heart to give. In either case, it is the same sickness.

Jesus wants to heal our withered hand and release the spirit of generosity, so that we can be agents of blessing in the world. When disaster strikes an area, it would be nice if the people in that area looked to the church for help rather than some social organization. Thank God for churches that are making a difference in their community, but most churches that I know of are known for their hunger to receive rather than their dedication to giving. People avoid those types of churches.

Abundant does not mean just enough, living on the bare minimum, and just getting by every month. If you have to use your credit cards every month to meet your needs, that is not living in abundance.

How many of you know that salvation is only *the initial step* that we take to enter the kingdom? Unfortunately, the religious spirit made many believe that salvation is *the final step* and the next stop is heaven. We have to learn how to live in the kingdom. Many believers get saved, get comfortable, and never grow in the Lord. For them, going to heaven is the next big event and there's nothing in-between.

Once a person is saved, he needs to be trained to be productive and grow in the kingdom. Tithing is like a sign-up fee to enter God's economy. Just because you tithe, you may not receive a financial miracle, unless you give like Jacob did—in faith when he had nothing in his life.

Today the church envies the world by seeing the prosperity of the unsaved. There is something wrong with that picture. The Bible says that God shall supply all our need according to His riches in glory by Christ Jesus (Philippians 4:19). I began to ask God, "Lord, why do most believers who pay their tithes faithfully, not receive financial miracles in their life? Why do they struggle like other people in the world with debt and need?"

If you are a faithful tithe-payer to your church or organization, you might have asked this question yourself. I have seen people struggle and sometimes go broke financially, though they were giving their tithe and offerings to other ministries. Seeing this over and over again made me ask God that question. He opened my understanding and showed me that *giving tithes alone will not bring a financial miracle.*

First of all, some do not tithe consistently and we need to be a consistent giver in order to reap consistently. If we give only occasionally, we will reap occasionally. The second thing is that people think that once they pay their tithe, they need to wait around for money to show up on their front door or get dropped on their lap by an angel.

In the Bible, we do not see anyone receive a financial miracle because they paid their tithe. Abraham was a rich man before he started paying tithes. The Bible does not teach any of those things. Most Christians use Malachi 3:10-11 as their key verses to support tithing.

Many believers pay their tithe, but when God gives them an idea or opportunity they will not step out to do it. They still wait and pray to God for a financial miracle, but they are not willing to put their hand to work. They are missing out.

It is like the man who was drowning in a river. He had great faith that God would send help to rescue him. First a helicopter came and lowered a rope, but he declined saying that he was waiting on God to save his life. He did not believe that God would use a natural method to save his life. Then a friend came by in a boat and asked him to get into the boat, but again he declined, and said, "I am waiting on God to save my life." He would not swim either, thinking God was big enough to save him from any trouble.

Finally, a sudden surge of flood water came, wiped him away and he died and went to heaven. He was very upset and asked Jesus why He didn't come to rescue him when he was drowning. Jesus very lovingly spoke to him and said, "First I sent a helicopter to save you, but you did not respond. Then I sent your friend in a boat, but you declined his help too. You also knew how to swim; you could have helped yourself." The poor guy did not know what to say.

Our faith in God should not become a handicap. It should make us productive and more fruitful than other people. Because of mistaken ideas, *many believers expect God to do what they should be doing.* That is why we do not achieve more with our lives.

In the same way, many believers are waiting around for God to give them a financial miracle. They believe one day they will walk out the door and a bundle of money will be waiting for them on their doorstep, or they wait for a million dollar check to come in the mail. While many opportunities and open doors are passing them by, they will not take hold of them because of their ignorance and fear. Either that or they believe if they just work harder or take another job, then they would be paid more.

CHAPTER - 4

PREPARING TO PROSPER

If you want to be prosperous and live in the kingdom economy, you need to be willing to go through the process of preparation. God will present an opportunity to every human on earth, regardless of where they are born, to improve and learn His ways. Many are not willing to "bend" or change their ways. They are stubborn or ignorant and remain where they are in life.

In the following pages we are going to learn from a few others God has used. They went through the process to fulfill their destiny. They did not go to a university, as we think of them today, but when they finished God's university, they were more prepared than most of us who has a college degree.

JOSEPH

The first person we will learn from is Joseph. There are five "Ps" that stand out in Joseph's life. The first one was the **P**it, then **P**otiphar, next was **P**rison, then **P**alace and finally **P**rime Minister. Each of those "Ps played an important role in fulfilling His destiny.

Joseph became the prime minister of Egypt. You might call it a miracle, but I would call it preparation meeting opportunity. He was already prepared when he received that promotion. He had a trail behind him that he had been walking on for a long time and it had not been an easy path. It had been a difficult path. It was a lonely walk. First of all, he was put in charge of his brothers at home. He was like a supervisor to them and reported back to his father about how they were doing. Because of this, his brothers hated him, as he reported accurately that they were not faithful in what they were doing.

Additionally, Joseph had a dream about his future, and what he was going to become in the long run. Like Joseph, God has planted a dream in everyone's heart. Most ignore it and others sleep on it and the majority sit on it for the rest of their lives. Few prepare and capitalize on it. This book is for those who are willing to prepare and not wait around for a miracle to show up.

Joseph was sold as a slave to an Egyptian government official. When he was appointed as a slave that was his college education. He was faithful to follow the instructions that Potiphar, his boss, had given him. He didn't have an "attitude" when he was told to do something. I see many young people and I feel sorry for them because they don't like anyone telling them what to do.

They don't listen to their parents, teachers and so they don't listen to people at their workplace when they are older either. They are constantly changing jobs, or complaining about the one they have. "What is the problem?" you ask them. "My boss just fired me for no reason," they reply. When you get fired three times, you'd better realize the problem is not with the boss, but with you. Joseph knew how to submit to authority.

Soon Joseph was promoted to a manager's position over Potiphar's entire household. He was in charge of all of his servants, his wealth, and his properties. Potiphar was like a millionaire. Joseph was a young boy and he was not afraid to follow instructions because he knew that if he was ever going to lead, he must first know how to follow. What you sow is going to catch up with you. I know many people who are literally starving because they don't want to work for someone else.

I see young people everywhere who want to be their own boss. They do not want to work for anyone else. They forget or never have been taught that before they can be a boss, they first need to learn to take orders from someone else and do exactly as they are told.

Let me ask you this. If you started a business, you would need other people to work for you, right? What if everyone you hired had the same attitude you had? You'd better get under some authority and learn how to follow instructions. If you are ready to follow instructions exactly as someone else over you gives them—maybe your boss, partner, father, or husband—then you are ready for a promotion.

Many follow instructions, but only according to their own way. That won't work. The number one problem in the body of Christ today is rebellion. No one wants to hear anyone else telling them what to do. They are all waiting to become a CEO, or the next big minister, but until they are able to submit to the authority that God has placed over them, they will continue to do just that—wait and wander.

Joseph successfully completed college and was ready for graduate school. He was accused of a crime that he didn't commit and sent to Pharaoh's jail. It was not just any prison, but the prison where people who committed a crime against the king or the government were sent. This was the place for a future prime minister? Why? In this jail you met people that were going to be your future problems. It was an opportunity to learn from them. The same will be true for you: the kind of people you go through a trial with are going to be your problem and blessing once you are appointed to your position.

Joseph studied them and learned from their experiences. He found out why they ended up in prison, and why they did what they did and offered them solutions to their problems. He was taking notes from each of them about their abusive pasts and problems with the government. He may have asked what they thought must be changed in their country or what caused them to rebel against the king.

Joseph was successful, even in prison, and was promoted to being in charge there as well. He finished his postgraduate studies and was ready for his appointment. He had a spirit of excellence in everything he did. He was using his God-given brain. He didn't speak in tongues and shiver nor was he *slain in the flesh*. He had a dream and he was committed to getting prepared, regardless of the circumstances. You might say that you don't have the money to go to college or to get an education. Well, Joseph didn't either.

Once I tried to convince God by telling Him it requires billions of dollars to change or disciple nations. He asked me, how much money did Joseph and Daniel have to change their nations? I said, "None." That is true even today. What we really lack is the right vision and wisdom, not resources. Money will show up eventually because people are attracted to wisdom and a properly executed vision.

What matters in life is not where you are right now. *Your response to your immediate circumstances will create the momentum for your future.* Either you will be stalled or promoted. Whether you're at your home, church, or on a temporary job, you have the potential to go anywhere you want. Where you are right now is the starting point to where you want to go. There is no future if you don't "live" your present well.

How you use your time now determines the harvest you are going to reap in the future. Your present creates your future. Many worry and try to live in the future that is not here yet and miss the present! They are dreaming about the "someday" they want by wasting the only thing they control over: that is their "today" and what they do with it.

Joseph was not lazy and didn't have an attitude. He was willing to follow in order to become a leader in the future. If you don't learn to follow, you can't lead well. Nobody can be an effective leader if they don't follow someone. He was promoted to a place where he was managing the wealth of the entire nation of Egypt. He was in charge of the whole land, agriculture, economy and the people. That's kingdom living.

Do we really want to change or restore a nation? Then we need to know how to influence governments, economy, agriculture or any of the major sectors by which a nation is made. We will never impact a nation by just conducting crusades and healing rallies. That takes us to our next example.

MOSES

Moses had a dream to become a deliverer of his people from Egypt. He was ignorant of how to accomplish that dream and needed to be prepared. He received his basic education from Egyptian schools, but that was not enough. The Bible says, he was taught in all the wisdom of Egypt (Acts 7:22), but the wisdom of Egypt was not enough to deliver God's people or to restore a nation. He needed the wisdom of God, so he had to go through the process of preparation.

Egypt was the superpower of that day. Their school system can't be compared to ours today. Today, kids are left to learn their own way and we call it "freedom of choice." How can a fool help others make the right choices? Education must be good in order to get rid of foolishness and pride.

After completing the Egyptian school, Moses thought he was "something" and knew "everything" and was ready to fulfill his destiny. But, God said that he needed to go to graduate and postgraduate school. So, he was taken to God's school in the wilderness where he learned how to follow instructions.

He was appointed as a shepherd of sheep that he didn't own. He was feeding his father-in-law's sheep. Imagine that. What a humbling experience for an Egyptian prince: feeding someone else's sheep day after day, night after night, year after year. Jethro told Moses when to take the sheep out, and when to bring them back. He had to give an account and feed them well. Moses was faithful and took care of the sheep for *forty years.*

Moses didn't say in his heart, "They are not my sheep, so I will just sleep and let them go where they want. Jethro is not watching, so I can steal some of the money he got from shearing the sheep." No. Moses was faithful. The Bible says that if you are not faithful with someone else's wealth, God will not give you your own. Those who are faithful with little will be faithful with much too (Luke 16:10,12).

Moses led the sheep faithfully and led them up to the mountain of God, Horeb. How did this mountain become the mountain of God? There was no mention of it before in the Bible. Let me tell you how Mount Horeb became the mountain of God. It is because of Moses. Let Scripture interpret Scripture. Psalm 15 asks, "Who can dwell at the mountain of God?" Psalm 24 tells us the qualities of a person who can ascend the mountain of God.

Moses reached that place in his life; and because of Moses, Mount Horeb became the mountain of God. Every major incident in the Bible involves a mountain or a garden. Whenever God decides to do something new on earth, it always starts on a mountain. Whenever God releases something new to the earth, He does it from a mountain. You and I are connected to one of God's mountains. There are different types of mountains that represent different spiritual principles and spheres.

You can choose your own mountain to be the mountain of God, but you need the qualities that God requires. Moses finished his postgraduate studies by feeding his father-in-law's sheep. He was going to lead God's people one day to the same mountain, and God trained Him for that position by feeding and caring for sheep.

Are you faithful in managing somebody's wealth, money, or possessions? If you are not, God will not give you your own wealth. God is looking for people who are good at following instructions; because He knows that if they won't follow someone else's instructions, they won't follow when He gives them instructions. Interestingly these people will tell you they will follow God if He tells them something, but they won't follow a human. They do not understand the way God uses His authority and works through His chosen leaders.

I have seen spiritual and super-spiritual people who won't let you tell them anything. They are full of pride, egocentric, egotistic, stubborn and rebellious and won't stop talking about themselves. Unless God has mercy, I don't know where they will end up. They are their own gods. They love themselves more than they love God, and bite the hand that feeds them.

Moses, on the other hand, followed his father-in-law's instructions for forty years and passed with an A+. Now God was ready to give him instructions, and the Bible says that Moses was faithful in all things (Numbers 12:7). When I graduated from Bible school, I was sent to work with a team whose leader was a new Christian.

By the grace of God, I followed every instruction he gave. When he asked me to sweep the floor, I swept the floor. When he asked me to wash dishes, I washed dishes without question. Result? I was sent for leadership training within the first three months when it might have taken two years to reach that level. Because I was willing to follow instructions, they couldn't wait to appoint me as a new team leader.

Today, people ask to join our ministry, but they do not like to follow instructions. All they are looking for is a "salary" to do what they like to do. If you don't help someone else fulfill their dream, there won't be anyone to help you fulfill your dream. If you don't help someone reach success, there won't be anyone to help you do the same. How wonderful if you realize you need someone's help to be successful.

Whatever the company you are working for, or the organization which you are a part of, give your heart to them in order to be successful. Work overtime and be willing to do the job that no one else wants to do. Then watch out. Nobody will be able to stop you because promotion comes from God (Psalm 75:6-7).

DANIEL

Daniel is another person who was elevated to one of the highest positions in a foreign country. The Bible says that he was taken to Babylon because he and his friends were wise, skillful and quick to learn new things. Daniel had a heart to study and gain knowledge and understanding of many things. While other kids spent their time playing video games or reading fictional books (or something similar in their culture), he was doing his research in history, math, and science.

While other kids were watching sports or music videos, he was developing a skill, which was going to help him in the future. While other kids spent their time on chitchat, or social media, he was developing his social skills for teamwork. While other kids were eating at the best restaurants, Daniel was fasting.

More than that, he prayed three times a day and had a vibrant relationship with the God of His fathers. He was prepared when opportunity knocked at his door. He did not have to look for a job. When you are prepared, opportunity will come seeking you.

JESUS

The greatest Leader of all. How did He develop His leadership skills? I believe He learned them from His earthly father, Joseph. He was submissive and was willing to follow His parents' instructions until He was of age to do the task that God had for Him.

Jesus had to learn obedience just like you and me (Hebrews 5:8). It was not easy for Him. It didn't come naturally. He learned it through the things He suffered. He didn't move out of His home when He was sixteen to explore life and do stupid things because He felt like it. He waited until the appointed time came.

At thirty years of age, the Father said, "He is ready now." Later in life, what He learned at home helped Him to follow His Father's instructions. He didn't make a mistake because He had learned obedience through the things He suffered. Then when he was an adult, he was mature and perfect.

Jesus learned the trade of a carpenter through His earthly father. People around Him knew Him as a carpenter or the son of a carpenter. That was only His job until the time came to fulfill His destiny. They failed to recognize who He was in the spirit. He was shaping rugged wood into beautiful pieces of furniture that were useful to people.

Later, Jesus was shaping broken lives into purposeful lives. Before, He was repairing broken furniture and fixing it with new pieces of wood. Later He was changing hearts and lives and removing the hardened heart and replacing them with ones that were compassionate. Before, He was fixing wooden pieces that no one thought were any good.

Afterward, Jesus carved pieces of wood into decorative items. Later, He was restoring and renewing lives that were neglected and forgotten. This is our Jesus, whom we follow. Obedient till death. He was not worried about ruining His heavenly status by working as a carpenter while He was here. What better job could have prepared Him for His destiny?

You might say that time has changed and people have changed. Yes, that is true. *But God's principles have not changed.* I would rather prepare myself now so that I would be ready, rather than have the opportunity come and not be prepared. If you are believing to win a heavyweight championship title, you'd better get into the ring and start practicing and building up some muscle. It would require years of practice before you could win a title like that. Speaking in tongues and paying tithes alone may not help you win the title. You need to learn how to punch and when to punch, in order to knock down your opponent.

Many Christians unfortunately, do not believe in this. They expect God to do what they should be doing. They wait until their hair turns gray and waste their time away. All their life they have been waiting for a miracle. This same principle applies to any area of excellence. *You need to spend your time and effort preparing yourself.*

In my opinion and based on my experience, Christians are one of the laziest groups of people. They get jealous and envious when worldly people get blessed or make millions. They will say the devil is blessing them, but if you study the lives of successful people in the areas of sports, business, or ministry even, you will see that they traveled the same roads and applied the same principles as Christians. God is not a respecter of persons. He blesses and rewards people who are diligent, and put the potential He has given them to work.

CHAPTER - 5

SIGNS OF TRUE PROSPERITY

Throughout the Bible, God differentiates between the people who love Him and the people who do not respect and honor Him. The Bible is actually a story about two trees and two seeds: the Tree of Life and the Tree of the Knowledge of Good and Evil, and the seed of the righteous and the seed of the wicked one. The first group fears the Lord and the second group does not fear the Lord. The first group are those blessed by God and second group are those cursed by God. The first group is called righteous and the second is called wicked.

In this chapter, I would like to share what the signs of true prosperity are. There are many.

God adds no sorrow.

> "The blessing of the Lord makes one rich, and He adds no sorrow with it" (Proverbs 10:22).

Their house is blessed.

> "The curse of the Lord is on the house of the wicked, but He blesses the home of the just" (Proverbs 3:33).

The next verse says the result of humility and the fear of the Lord are riches, honor, and life. The first result of humility, and the fear of the Lord, is riches.

> "By humility and the fear of the Lord are riches and honor and life" (Proverbs 22:4).

There is no chapter like Psalm 112 that talks about the signs and qualities of a person who is blessed by God. Let's take it apart verse by verse. Psalm 112:

> "Praise the Lord! Blessed is the man who fears the Lord, who delights greatly in His commandments" (Psalm 112:1).

The word used for "blessed" in the Hebrew is *esher*, which means "happiness or blessedness."[14] The most important thing is to fear the Lord and stay close to His Word. For a believer, our blessing from God is proportionately connected to our obedience and respect for the Word of God. The following verses talk about the signs of those who fear the Lord and delight greatly in His commandments.

> "His descendants will be mighty on earth; the generation of the upright will be blessed" (Psalm 112:2).

The blessing of the Lord is generational. If a person obeys God and walks in His commandments, not only is he blessed but his family and posterity after him will also be blessed. In the Old Testament, God called Abraham and blessed him and promised him that his descendants would be blessed as well. God said He would be faithful to His covenant to *a thousand generations.*

---

14 James Strong, "835. Esher," Biblehub.com, accessed January 04, 2019, https://biblehub.com/hebrew/835.htm.

> "He remembers His covenant forever, the word which He commanded, for a thousand generations" (Psalm 105:8).

God is just.

> And the Lord passed before him and proclaimed, "The Lord, the Lord God, merciful and gracious, longsuffering, and abounding in goodness and truth, keeping mercy for thousands, forgiving iniquity and transgression and sin, by no means clearing the guilty, visiting the iniquity of the fathers upon the children and the children's children to the third and the fourth generation" (Exodus 34:6-7).

David said,

> "I have been young, and now am old; yet I have not seen the righteous forsaken, nor his descendants begging bread" (Psalm 37:25).

It does not matter where you are from or what country you are living in today, God's Word shows clearly that He is not a respecter of race or nationality. If you believe and obey His voice, you will be blessed both spiritually and naturally.

> "Wealth and riches will be in his house, and his righteousness endures forever" (Psalm 112:3).

After He blesses family, the next area God blesses is finance. "Wealth and riches shall be in his house" means God will fill his house with all kinds of treasures. It is interesting to note that the words "wealth and riches" are used here. I believe this refers to liquid assets and other possessions that can be turned into cash.

> "Through wisdom a house is built, and by understanding it is established; by knowledge the rooms are filled with all precious and pleasant riches" (Proverbs 24:3-4).

God wants to bless us; and He wants to bless us in the right order. We have to put God first, our family next, and then our wealth and riches.

> "Unto the upright there arises light in the darkness; he is gracious, and full of compassion, and righteous" (Psalm.112:4)

Those who are blessed of the Lord shall not walk in darkness, but in light. It also means when others are talking about recession and economic challenges, God will open up new opportunities for the upright. When everything seems dark and slow, promotion and increase will come to the righteous, no matter what.

When a godly man is blessed with money, he is gracious, full of compassion, and righteous. That is opposite to what the world says a wealthy man should be. In the world, people with money are arrogant, self-reliant, grasping, and prideful. You and I need to watch our attitude once God blesses us with riches.

> "A good man deals graciously and lends; he will guide his affairs with discretion" (Psalm 112:5).

This refers to financial investment. Once you have some money, you need to know how to make more money and not spend it all on consumables. A good man deals graciously and lends to other people. There is nothing wrong with lending to people if both parties benefit. If the person who's borrowing is making more money with the money he borrowed, then he should pay it back with interest. If the person who borrows is doing that for his survival or his family, then we should not charge interest. That is called *usury* in the Bible and is a condemned practice. That is why it says in the next line that he will guide his affairs with discretion. When you are prosperous, you will not borrow but lend to many nations.

> "Surely he will never be shaken; the righteous will be in everlasting remembrance" (Psalm 112:6).

The person who fears the Lord and keeps His commandments has riches and wealth. He invests from his wealth to increase his riches. These kinds of people will never be shaken. Even their memory will be blessed.

> "He will not be afraid of evil tidings; his heart is steadfast, trusting in the Lord" (Psalm 112:7).

The economy will go up and down, the stock market will crumble and all kinds of financial trouble may come in the world, but the righteous will not be afraid of evil tidings. His trust is in the Lord, and not in His riches.

> "His heart is established; he will not be afraid, until he sees his desire upon his enemies" (Psalm 112:8).

The key is to have an established heart. As long as we are on this earth, bad things and bad news will continue to occur. But we should not be afraid. Our heart needs to be established in the Lord.

> "He has dispersed abroad, he has given to the poor; his righteousness endures forever; his horn will be exalted with honor" (Psalm 112:9).

When we are blessed, we are in a position to bless others. We need to give to the poor liberally. It pleases the Lord and He will bless us more.

> "The wicked will see it and be grieved; he will gnash his teeth and melt away; the desire of the wicked shall perish" (Psalm 112:10).

The wicked should see our blessings and grieve. Unfortunately, today the reverse is true, and many so-called righteous people see the blessings of the wicked and grieve and gnash their teeth. May the Lord have mercy on us!

Redemption through Christ is not just for our spirit to go to heaven when we die. To "redeem" means to buy back what was stolen or lost. We did not lose heaven when Adam sinned; instead we lost the blessedness, favor and glory of God. God wants to restore His children to their original purpose. Many are waiting to go to heaven. Jesus brought heaven to us, but only a few dare to experience it on earth.

WEALTH IS POWER

As we saw before the meaning of the word "wealth" is force or power in the Hebrew language. It is interesting to note that wealthy people are often powerful or influential. In Deuteronomy, God told the people that it was He who gave them "power to get wealth" (Deuteronomy 8:18). It is the power of the Lord that causes one to get wealth. We need to ask God for that power. In the same way we ask for the power of the Holy Spirit to cast out demons and heal the sick, we need the power of God to get wealth. The reason He gives that power is to establish His covenant on this earth.

God will give power to get wealth to those people who are interested in establishing His covenant on the earth. The Lord delights in the prosperity of His servants (Psalm 35:27). The Bible never says anywhere that God delights in the poverty of His servants or we need to take a vow of poverty to serve Him. God is happy when you are prosperous and healthy.

God is getting ready to release a financial anointing upon His church. The world is talking about financial recession, economic collapse, layoffs and incredible price hikes. Is there a hope for believers?

As children of God and citizens of the kingdom of God, we should not live based on the economy on the earth. Though we participate in it, the rules that govern our financial lives are different from the rules that govern the financial life of this world. We live and operate according to the kingdom economy and this book will help you learn how to walk in it.

Anytime in history when financial collapse or recession took place, there were people that became wealthy during that time. They were positioned in such a way that they took opportunities and ran with them. This book will prepare you to become one of those people. You will prosper in every season, the normal seasons and when famine comes.

There are more millionaires on the earth today than any other time in the history of the world. There is more wealth (liquid cash) on this earth today than any other time in history. Most of the wealth is controlled by a handful of people and corporations.

Many believers that I know are suffering with the rest of the world and do not have much left over. Research says most people make more than a million dollars in their lifetime, but at the end of it they have only 25 to 50 thousand dollars in liquid cash. Many people earn income but their wealth level is not increasing.

It seems money and wealth travels a certain route and most people miss it. Or it travels around a certain circle of people. Either you attract money and wealth or they move away from you. It depends on your personal money management habits and your attitude towards them.

ABUNDANT LIFE

John 10:10b is the most used verse regarding prosperity. Jesus came that we might have life and life more abundantly, but only some Christians understand what abundant life is all about. Most people equate an abundant life with having a lot of material things. That is far from the truth. Jesus said He came to give us life and life more abundantly. *Abundant life refers to the quality of life, not the abundance of stuff.* Jesus came to give us abundant life, not abundant stuff. When you have abundant life in you, whether you have few or many material possessions, you will be content.

The question then is this, "What is life?" The Bible says,

"In Him was life, and the life was the light of men" (John 1:4).

If we want to know what life is, we need to look at Jesus. He had the best quality of life, and it was not based on His circumstances or material abundance. It came from the relationship He had with His Father. As I shared earlier, we are all waiting to live outside in, rather than inside out. God always starts inside and later, the outward will change. We all want to live and live well.

The Bible says, "In Him was life." What kind of life was in Jesus? Did He drive a Mercedes or BMW? Did He ride the most elegant Egyptian stallion? No! He walked with His disciples through the mountainous terrain of Galilee. But He had abundant life.

Many rich people that I know do not live an abundant life. They are sad and dissatisfied though they have everything they want and an abundant cash flow. We want the life that Jesus had, which was abundant life. The Bible says to rejoice always. When was the last time you really felt joy in your heart? You might laugh circumstantially at various things, but real joy is that which bubbles out of your spirit and inner man. When was the last time you really felt that?

Let me tell you, joy only comes from the presence of God. The Bible says,

> "You have put gladness in my heart, more than in the season that their grain and wine increased" (Psalm 4:7).

Prosperity according to this world's standard is having a lot of money. Prosperity according to God's standard is having a full life. People in the Bible, like Joseph and Paul, had abundant lives, even when they were in prison. They were rejoicing and became a blessing to others. *They had life without limits.*

CHAPTER - 6

YOUR PURPOSE AND CALLING: ULTIMATE KEYS TO KINGDOM ECONOMY

Before we understand the kingdom economy, it is imperative that we understand why God made us. Every blessing we receive is connected to our purpose. We need to know why God made the human race before we can understand our individual purpose.

There are four fundamental questions every human asks. The sooner they find the answers to those questions, the better their lives will be. They are: Who am I? Where did I come from? Why am I here? Where do I go from here? Every individual needs to answer those four questions before they die. Unfortunately, not everyone find the answers.

When I say purpose of mankind, I mean the entire human race which includes both men and women. From Genesis 1-3, we understand that God created mankind for one single purpose. Let us see what the Creator had in mind when He made us.

Since I have been around Christian circles for a while, I have noticed that even believers have all kinds of ideas about why God created them. Some say it was for His pleasure; others say we are created to fellowship with Him; still others say we are created to worship Him or for Him to have a family. Maybe the last one is the most popular. Though they are all part of our function, the truth is that none of them are mentioned in Genesis as our purpose.

Why do we have difficulty in accepting what God the Creator spelled out very clearly and distinctly about our purpose when He decided to create us. Why do we need a second opinion or believe someone else's opinion above God Himself?

Genesis 1:26-28 spells it all out.

> Then God said, "Let Us make man in Our image, according to Our likeness; let them have dominion over the fish of the sea, over the birds of the air, and over the cattle, over all the earth and over every creeping thing that creeps on the earth." So God created man in His own image; in the image of God He created him; male and female He created them. Then God blessed them, and God said to them, "Be fruitful and multiply; fill the earth and subdue it; have dominion over the fish of the sea, over the birds of the air, and over every living thing that moves on the earth" (Genesis 1:26-28).

This tells us how and why God created us. We were created in the image and likeness of God to have dominion over the earth. To make it very simple, every human being has the same purpose, which is to rule and reign on earth. In like manner, every apple tree has the same purpose, which is to produce apples, and every cow has the same purpose, that is to give milk. Each of us are created to have dominion over a particular area of life and God has equipped each human being with the capacity and ability to do that. We call that a vision or calling; and everyone has the same one; but it shows itself differently in each life. It is accompanied by a unique vision and its subsequent result in each of us.

Genesis 1:26 is the foundation of our purpose. If we miss that part, we will be cheated out of our best. The devil has done a good job of talking most Christians out of their purpose, or blinding them from it. Meanwhile, the devil also empowers his children to take over almost all the geopolitical systems in the world.

God deposited our purpose in us in the form of a seed. When we discover that seed and follow the principles or steps he laid out in verse 28, we will prosper without a doubt. As I mentioned above, if you ask most people about why God created them, and they will mention things like worshiping or glorifying God or even to bring God pleasure. They have been misinformed.

There is no one born on this earth without a purpose. The problem is that many have not discovered it yet. We also call that seed, potential or a talent. Each seed needs a particular environment to grow and be fruitful. Why do people fail to discover their purpose? The main reason is because they do not know why God created the human race. Only when we understand our corporate purpose, will we also understand our individual purpose.

Mankind was created with just one single purpose and seven different functions. Those functions are intended to help fulfill that one purpose. Many great men and philosophers have told us we have a purpose, but few tell us what it is.

Even so, I was committed to help others discover their purpose. Then one day, the Holy Spirit made it simple and helped me crack the code of purpose. He said that every single human being has the same purpose. I thought every single person had a different purpose. That is not what the Bible teaches.

We all have the same purpose and are called to do different things to fulfill that purpose. To help us fulfill that purpose, God gave us different gifts. In the same way, every car has the same purpose, which is transportation. Yet there are different sizes and models of cars and they all function differently. Even so, the basic principles are same for every car, whether it is a limousine or a four-door sedan.

If we focus on the functions and don't fulfill our purpose, our life will be wasted. We have been ignoring our purpose for too long by focusing overmuch on the function. What is the difference between purpose and function? Purpose is the original intent for which something is created and function is how we operates. Now let's explore the purpose and function of mankind.

THE PURPOSE OF MANKIND

MAN WAS CREATED TO HAVE DOMINION OVER THE EARTH

> Then God said, "Let Us make man in Our image, according to Our likeness; let them have *dominion* over the fish of the sea, over the birds of the air, and over the cattle, over all the earth and over every creeping thing that creeps on the earth." So God created man in His own image; in the image of God He created him; male and female He created them. Then God *blessed* them, and God said to them, "Be *fruitful and multiply; fill the earth* and *subdue* **it**; have *dominion* over the fish of the sea, over the birds of the air, and over every living thing that moves on the earth" (Genesis 1:26-28).

Here God, the Creator, mentions His purpose for creating man. *Only the manufacturer knows the purpose of a product.* It is very important that we understand this. We all have preconceived assumptions, from the religious spirit, in our heart and mind. So when we read the above verses we assume we understand, but in truth, only a very few people do. Most reject it, thinking it doesn't apply to them now.

We have been taught that God created man to worship Him. This is not mentioned anywhere in Genesis. This is one of the biggest deceptions of the enemy. He has deceived us in order to keep us ineffective. He knows that if he can keep us deceived, we will not bother him with the dominion of the earth. We will just stay inside our homes and church buildings and sing songs day and night.

The second biggest deception that the enemy has employed is to make people believe that God created us to live in heaven. This also is not mentioned in Genesis or Revelation. The devil knows that if he can keep us deceived into believing that the earth does not belong to us, but to him instead, then the devil can freely misuse the whole earth and its resources for his evil intents, and man will not bother him. God created man to live on this earth and gave mankind the earth to manage. We are going to reign with Christ—not in heaven, but on the new earth. Scripture makes it clear that our eternal purpose is connected with the planet Earth, not heaven (Genesis 1:26; Revelation 22:5).

Dominion means to rule, govern, manage, subdue, maximize, excel, fruitful, and master something; and each of us are created to rule or master at least one area of life. That is our individual purpose. Once we recognize that purpose, our next step is finding what God called us to do to fulfill that purpose. God gave gifts to each one of us to fulfill our calling, so we need to focus on developing those gifts.

FUNCTIONS OF MANKIND

MAN WAS CREATED TO HAVE A RELATIONSHIP WITH GOD AND ONE ANOTHER

We are created as sons of God. Our sense of worth and identity come from our relationship with our heavenly Father. Unfortunately, we try to find our identity from what we do, or based on the color of our skin or our nationality. We received our body from our parents, but they did not create our spirit. God created our spirit, so our identity comes from Him. Unless our relationship with God is in the right place, nothing else will flourish in our life. We will always feel an emptiness or feel like something is amiss in our heart.

We were also created to have intimate relationships with each other. Family life is the best example for that. We are always longing for a close and intimate relationship with someone. That is deep in our nature. When any of our relationships are not in order, nothing else will work out for good. The number one commandment in both the Old and New Testaments is to love God with all our heart, soul, and mind; and to love others as we love ourselves (Luke 10:27). Everything in the kingdom of God flows through relationship.

MAN WAS CREATED TO WORK OR ACHIEVE

God recreated the garden of Eden and put man in it to till and keep, or guard, it.

> "And Jehovah Elohim took Man, and put him into the garden of Eden, to till it and to guard it" (Genesis 2:15, Darby).

It is interesting to examine what God asked Adam to do in the garden. He was not only to till the garden, but to guard it. Guard it from what? God knew the devil would try to enter into the garden and He warned and prepared Adam for that. As it says in Ezekiel, the devil had been in the garden of Eden once before. The word used for "keep or guard" is *shamar*[15]; a primitive Hebrew root, that means "to hedge about (as with thorns), guard, and generally, to protect and attend to. It is from this root that we get our English word *watchman*.

It was Adam's responsibility to protect the garden from evil forces entering into it. Adam did not pay close attention, so Satan disguised himself and entered the serpent and came into the garden undercover.

---

15 James Strong, "8104. Shamar," Biblehub.com, accessed January 04, 2019, https://biblehub.com/hebrew/8104.htm.

Satan knew he could not directly enter the garden because Adam would see that. Instead the devil had to find a different way to get in. He found it through the serpent because the serpent was more cunning than any other creature God had made.

God had warned man by telling him to guard the garden, take dominion over the earth, and subdue it. Additionally God had given man absolute authority over all the creatures on the earth. He gave him dominion, power, glory, and finally, He gave man His Word. Man's only responsibility was to keep and obey that one Word. (The only command God gave him to keep was not to eat the fruit of the tree which God said not to eat). As long as man obeyed the Word of God, no power on earth or hell could defeat the man.

What Adam and Eve might not have known was the history of the earth. They stepped into a realm in which Lucifer had once ruled, and one in which he was not happy, especially now that man was occupying and ruling his former territory, most notably the garden of Eden. He became jealous once again and wanted to take over the earth by any means. To know more about the pre-Adamic world, please read the book *Releasing Kings and Queens to Their Original Intent*.

MAN WAS CREATED TO EXPAND AND GROW

The garden was not as big a country as we might think. It was a small area. God wanted man to expand it and make the whole earth like it. That was Adam's purpose, to expand the garden, and to grow, and take dominion, over the entire earth. There was a river which originated in the garden that divided into four heads and ran across the whole earth.

In the Bible, a river is always a picture of the anointing of God or life. Jesus said that from our belly the rivers of living water will flow (John 7:38). In Psalms we read that there is a river that makes glad the city of God (Psalm 46:4). Rivers shows growth and expansion, keeping in mind that before the fall the whole earth was like one continent, with the dry land in one place and the sea in one place.

> Now a river went out of Eden to water the garden, and from there it parted and became four riverheads. The name of the first is Pishon; it is the one which skirts the whole land of Havilah, where there is gold. And the gold of that land is good. Bdellium and the onyx stone are there. The name of the second river is Gihon; it is the one which goes around the whole land of Cush. The name of the third river is Hiddekel it is the one which goes toward the east of Assyria. The fourth river is the Euphrates (Genesis 2:10-14).

The name of the first river was Pishon, which in Hebrew means "increase or spring forward."[16] Can you believe God named the first river "increase"? He wanted them to know what He was expecting of them, and He wanted them to increase. God did not start a lake in the garden to water it; a lake is a stagnant body of water, and does not flow or increase. However, a river flows over every obstacle that is in its path and you cannot stop it. It is in the DNA of a river to expand and spread forth. God put that river in you. He did not put a lake or a tank in you; the river within you has to flow, and it needs outlets.

The river Pishon encompassed the whole land of Havilah, which means, "circle,"[17] meaning it flows to one region and then it spreads and goes to the next. Then the Bible says there was gold in Havilah, which is very precious. Bdellium and onyx stones were there too. There is no mention of any gold in Eden. If they had remained in Eden, they would not have found these precious metals and stones. They had to move and expand to find the new treasures that God had hidden. As long as you remain in

---

16 "What Does Pishon Mean in the Bible?" CompellingTruth.org, accessed January 04, 2019, https://www.compellingtruth.org/meaning-of-Pishon.html.

17 Smith, "Havilah," Biblehub.com, accessed January 04, 2019, https://biblehub.com/topical/h/havilah.htm.

one place, you will not discover the treasures God has deposited *for you and in you*. It is God's idea for you to expand and grow.

The second river was called Gihon, which means in Hebrew "bursting forth."[18] You cannot stop this river; it bursts forth from you. This is the same as when Jesus said, "out of his belly shall flow rivers of living water" (John 7: 38b, KJV). The more you give out, the more God will put into you; and you will reach a place of bursting forth. If you keep it for yourself, you will lose it, or God will take it and give to someone who will use it (Matthew 25:29).

The third river was called Hiddekel, which in Hebrew means "rapid."[19] Whatever God does He does rapidly, because it is not by might nor by power but by the Spirit of the Lord (Zechariah 4:6). What we try to make happen in twenty years of effort, God can do in one minute. This river goes toward the land of Assyria, which means a "step."[20] Sometimes all it takes is a step, just none step, to step into the destiny God has for you. God is waiting for you to take a step by believing in Him.

The fourth river was called Euphrates, which in Hebrew means "fruitfulness or sweet water."[21] That is what God wants from all of us, fruitfulness. Jesus said to go and bear fruit. There are different kinds of fruit that we can bear as Christians. There is the fruit of our body, the fruit of righteousness, the fruit of the spirit; additionally, every invention is a fruit of our imagination.

---

18 James Strong, "1521. Gichon," Biblehub.com, accessed January 04, 2019, https://biblehub.com/hebrew/1521.htm.

19 Smith, "Hiddekel," Biblehub.com, accessed January 04, 2019, https://biblehub.com/topical/h/hiddekel.htm.

20 Francis Brown, Samuel Rolles Driver, and Charles Augustus Briggs, "Ashshuwr - Old Testament Hebrew Lexicon - New American Standard," Bible Study Tools, accessed January 04, 2019, https://www.biblestudytools.com/lexicons/hebrew/nas/ashshuwr.html.

21 Easton, "Euphrates Definition and Meaning - Bible Dictionary," Bible Study Tools, accessed January 04, 2019, https://www.biblestudytools.com/dictionary/euphrates/.

The breath of God that was in man had all these qualities. After the fall, man lost that creative ability and succumbed to his own circumstances. He lost the anointing to expand and spread out. People remained in one place and increased in number, but failed to expand the kingdom of God as they had been commanded to do.

MAN WAS CREATED TO MANIFEST THE GLORY OF GOD

Man was the only visible form of God on earth. God wanted to live through man, and those who see him should see God too. He gave us His glory. It is possible to have preconceived ideas about the word "glory." Usually we use and hear this word in relation to worship or a feeling. That is not the only type of glory mentioned in the Bible. We are created to manifest seven dimensions of God's glory.

1. MAN'S GLORY: GLORY RELATED TO THE SONS OF GOD.

Man was filled and covered with the glory of God in the garden. That is our inherent glory. It did not come through worship or by doing anything, but by just being the children of God. Through that relationship, we inherited His glory. When we sinned, we lost the glory of God. The Bible says, "All have sinned and fall short of the glory of God" (Romans 3:23). Because we lost that glory through sin, we lost the capacity to know God; and we also lost the capacity to represent Him.

Jesus came to restore that glory. Those who believe in Him become the children of God and receive His glory. He said in to His Father, "The glory which You gave Me I have given them" (John 17:22).

2. SOLOMON'S GLORY: GLORY RELATED TO OUR PROSPERITY.

Luke says,

> "Consider the lilies, how they grow: they neither toil nor spin; and yet I say to you, even Solomon in all his glory was not arrayed like one of these" (Luke 12:27).

What was Solomon's glory? It was the glory of God manifested through his wisdom and prosperity. He was the wisest and richest man who ever lived on this earth. Your prosperity is directly in proportion to your wisdom. The wisdom and riches of our God is unsearchable. We are created to manifest that here on earth.

3. MIRACLES: GLORY RELATED TO THE SUPERNATURAL.

In the Gospels, we read that Jesus manifested His glory through the miracles He did. The first miracle He did was to turn the water into wine. The Bible says,

> "This beginning of signs Jesus did in Cana of Galilee, and manifested His glory; and His disciples believed in Him" (John 2:11).

When Jesus was informed that Lazarus was sick, He told His disciples that his sickness was not for death, but for the glory of God. When He came to raise Lazarus from the tomb, He told Martha this: "If you believe, you shall see the glory of God." The same is true for us. When we move in the supernatural power of God, we manifest God's glory.

4. CREATION: GLORY RELATED TO OUR WORK

All creation reveals the glory of God. Psalms says,

> "The heavens declare the glory of God; and the firmament shows His handiwork" (Psalm 19:1).

We are supposed to manifest the glory of God through the works we do too. Whatever we do should represent our God. Jesus revealed the glory of His Father through the works He did while here on earth.

> "There are also celestial bodies and terrestrial bodies; but the glory of the celestial is one, and the glory of the terrestrial is another. There is one glory of the sun, another glory of the moon, and another glory of the stars; for one star differs from another star in glory" (1 Corinthians 15:40-41).

When we manifest God's glory through our work, we will fill the earth with His glory.

5. PRAISE: GLORY RELATED TO PRAISE

We are familiar with this kind of glory. This is the glory we experience when the presence of God manifests.

6. ETERNAL GLORY: RESURRECTION GLORY

We shall become like Jesus.

> "So also is the resurrection of the dead. The body is sown in corruption, it is raised in incorruption. It is sown in dishonor, it is raised in glory. It is sown in weakness, it is raised in power" (1 Corinthians 15:42-43).

Paul says this present affliction is light and nothing compared to the "exceeding and eternal weight of glory" that will be revealed in us (2 Corinthians 4:17).

> "Beloved, now we are children of God; and it has not yet been revealed what we shall be, but we know that when He is revealed, we shall be like Him, for we shall see Him as He is" (1 John 3:2).

7. MARRIAGE: REVEALING THE NATURE AND GLORY OF GOD

> "For a man indeed ought not to cover his head, since he is the image and glory of God; but woman is the glory of man" (1 Corinthians 11:7).

When a man and woman come together in marriage, they reveal the nature and quality of God. Man or woman alone cannot reveal His glory. God is revealed in the Bible as a father as well as a mother.

MAN WAS CREATED TO FIGHT AND CONQUER

Mankind was created in such a way that they need something for which to fight. They need a woman, country, kingdom or a cause to motivate them. They need a new horizon to conquer, a new challenge to overcome, a new boundary or limit to break. It's in their nature to fight. They need a king and kingdom to fight for.

Almost every nation that exists today was once ruled by a king. Why were kingdoms powerful in the olden days? Thousands of people gave their lives to their king and the kingdom in which they lived. They either supported him or died for him. It is in the nature of man to need something to fight and live for, because it thrills and motivates him.

In our day and time people still fight for their country. When I say fight, I am not talking about fighting our family members or our neighbors. We need to fight against the kingdom of darkness and the gates of hell to establish the will and the kingdom of our King Jesus Christ.

MAN WAS CREATED TO FUNCTION LIKE GOD

The reason we are created in God's image and likeness is to function like Him on earth. What God is in heaven, we are on earth. What He does in heaven, we are supposed to imitate or copy on earth (Ephesians 5:1). The only way we will live successfully is if we learn to function like Him.

We read in 1 John that "as He is, so are we in this world" (1 John 4:17b). That verse is extremely powerful. "As He is right now" means the present state and function of God or Jesus. We are supposed to emulate Him now in this world, not the world to come. We have a long way to go.

When Adam fell, we lost the ability to function like God. We became prey to outside forces and circumstances. If you would like to know more about how to function like God, please read the book *Kingdom Family*.

MAN WAS CREATED TO MANIFEST AND REPRESENT GOD ON EARTH

Those who see us should know God and see God through us. Jesus said, "He who has seen Me has seen the Father" (John 14:9). Those who see us should see our Father. I am not talking about His physical form, but evidence of His existence through the works we do. Jesus said that by seeing our good works, people would glorify our Father in heaven. Jesus was, and is, the exact representation of God the Father. We are supposed to represent God to the rest of creation and the demonic world too. One of the purposes of the church is to teach the wisdom of God to principalities and powers in the heavenly places (Ephesians 3:10).

To fulfill our purpose, God has called each one of us to do something specific. Once you realize your purpose, the next step is to discover your calling. Your financial blessing is connected to your calling. There are different types of calling. Some are called to be in ministry, others may be called to be in politics, but each one is different in what they are called to do.

I have written a powerful book called *Purpose, Calling, and Gifts*. Please order a copy and study it so you will never again be financially broke.

CHAPTER - 7

SEED: THE SECRET TO YOUR CALLING AND EXERCISING DOMINION

"Another parable He put forth to them, saying: "The kingdom of heaven is like a man who sowed good seed in his field; but while men slept, his enemy came and sowed tares among the wheat and went his way" (Matthew 13:24-25).

One of the mysteries of the kingdom of God is seed. The whole earth functions on the principle of seed. Without seed, it is impossible to sustain life. When God gives you something, He gives it to you in seed form. The reason many people think God did not give them anything is because they did not recognize the seed God gave them. Seeds are mostly tiny in nature; and we tend to look for larger gifts or better yet, the finished product, most of the time.

The problem with most of us is that we have both seeds and weeds in us. Many of us are more aware of the weeds (weaknesses and the works of the flesh) than we are of the seeds (potential, gifts and talents) God planted in us. Let me tell you the good news: *God is more aware of the seed He planted in you than the weeds you are worried about.* He did not plant any weeds in you; it is the devil, exploiting your sinful nature, who planted those weeds. Jesus said everything His Father did not plant will be uprooted. In fact, God created you, your body, and your life in order to deposit that seed. That is the whole purpose.

> "But He answered and said, "Every plant which My heavenly Father has not planted will be uprooted" (Matthew 15:13).

Throughout history God used people in spite of their weaknesses or failures, or their weeds, because of the seed He planted in them. This is very important. I want you to grab this truth with both hands, hold onto it, and never lose it. Everything you need in life is in that seed. A seed never has to go to school to learn on how to become a tree or to learn how to grow. Those qualities were built into that seed by its Creator.

When you look at someone, you might see only the weeds, but do not throw them out. Everyone has received a seed from God (1 John 3:9). Our job is to help them find that seed. The reason the weeds have overgrown the seed is because they failed to recognize the seed and give it the needed attention. I can guarantee you that God will never take back the seed He planted in you.

At other times we see a fully-grown tree, a finished product, someone who is fully functioning in his or her calling. We think, how come I don't have what they have? Or, I wish I could be as talented as they are! The truth is, they developed their seed, they invested time and money, and now they are receiving a return for their investment.

I was reading in the news the other day about an Olympic contestant that had been preparing eight years for a performance that only lasted a hundred seconds. I was stunned to read that. Imagine, someone being in training, on a strict diet, and doing a special exercise routine for eight long years, just focusing on developing one skill. How many of us can say we have done anything close to that? And we complain to God that He hasn't given us any gifts or seeds!

There are miracles in your hands and fingers. Those ten fingers can do amazing things. The only thing is that they are not trained yet. They can play music, sports, cook, care for others, create, heal, write, bless, and there is almost no limit to what your two hands can do. It is sad that a majority of people remain poor, simply by thinking they have not received any blessings or won a lottery. Meanwhile their hands remain idle and are never put to use in acquiring a skill or ability.

To be honest with you, each part of your body has seed in it. The thousands of works and actions your hands can perform are all seeds. The question is: Which action are you going to focus on, nurture and develop into a gift or a talent? For example, your hand can play a musical instrument, but it will take thousands of hours of practice to become a musician. Your feet, your brain, eyes, you name it, each of those body parts are created for a specific function. You choose how they are trained.

Your miracle is not in someone else or going to come from somewhere else. *Your miracle is in your seed.* The seed to the miracle you are believing God for, is with you right now. That is why, whenever God did a material miracle in the Bible, He always used something the people already had. What He used was the seed that created the miracle they needed.

When Moses cried out to God because of the Red Sea in front of him, God told Him to stretch his rod over the sea. That rod was the seed to the miracle. He already had the key to the miracle in his hand. When the people of Israel cried out to God for deliverance, God sent Moses, who was one of the Jewish people. When a widow came to Elisha, complaining about her debt, the man of God asked her what she had in her house. She said a jar of oil. That was the seed to her miracle.

The first miracle Jesus did was to turn water into wine. He told the people to fill the jars with water and the water became wine. The same principle applies to the multiplying of the five loaves and two fish. These are all seeds, and each had unlimited potential to reproduce its own kind when they were given to God.

Your calling is hidden in you as a seed. God deposited that in you when He created you. You need to recognize it and develop it as early as you can. Everyone has a calling, whether it is small or great. God has put something in you or in your hand, which has the ability to multiply and reproduce. When you put them to work or maximize them, you will prosper.

Your food is in your seed. When God gave man the seed, He said it was for food. The reason many people are hungry and in poverty is because they do not recognize the seed God gave them. Every nation and every person has received seeds. There is not a country on this earth that does not have seeds. They do not value the seed God gave to them, so they starve and wait for someone to come along with free food.

> "And God said, "See, I have given you every herb that yields seed which is on the face of all the earth, and every tree whose fruit yields seed; to you it shall be for food" (Genesis 1:29)

The good news is that God gave the seed to every single human on the earth. When I say seed, I am not referring only to natural seeds from plants. A seed is anything that has unlimited potential to multiply its own kind. A seed could be a talent, passion, a gift, a desire, resource or an opportunity. God never created a person without depositing a seed.

Your words are seeds that determine your future. You will reap the harvest of the seeds that you sow today. The harvest you have today is the result of the seeds you have sown in the past.

Your purpose is in your seed! God has hidden the purpose of your life in seed form in you. It needs to be recognized, planted (you stay in one location), nurtured and cultivated. Most of the time, when we eat or cut a fruit or vegetable, we throw away the seeds. Because we do not value seeds, we think they're unnecessary; but to God those seeds are vital for the propagation of the species.

Your future is in your seed! The Bible mentions different kinds of seeds. Your children are your seed. Your children are your future. The Bible calls us the seed of Abraham. If you nurture, train and cultivate your children in the ways of the Lord, you will have a great future and have a blessed generation after you.

Your financial miracle is in your seed. The Bible calls money a seed. When you are believing God for a financial miracle, God may not give you the full amount you are believing for; in fact, most of the time He won't. Many people get mad at God because He did not provide for their need. He promised to supply the seed, not a harvest. When we sow the seed, He is faithful to produce a harvest.

> "But this I say: He who sows sparingly will also reap sparingly, and he who sows bountifully will also reap bountifully. So let each one give as he purposes in his heart, not grudgingly or of necessity; for God loves a cheerful giver. And God is able to make all grace abound toward you, that you, always having all sufficiency in all things, may have an abundance for every good work. As it is written: "He has dispersed abroad. He has given to the poor; His righteousness endures forever." Now may *He who supplies seed to the sower*, and bread for food, supply and multiply the seed you have sown and increase the fruits of your righteousness" (2 Corinthians 9:6-10).

In order to understand our purpose, we need to know the principle of a seed and how it works. God has hidden the wisdom that we need to know so we can discover and fulfill our purpose in a seed. There are nine principles hidden in a seed:

A seed is something that has unlimited potential to reproduce its own kind. As we know the old saying, anyone can count the seeds in an apple, but no one can count the apples in a seed. The seed God planted in you has the capacity to multiply without limit. Within the limit of your purpose, you can grow to any level you want. You are the one who decides your limit.

A seed needs a particular environment to grow and produce fruit. Every seed does not grow everywhere. I live in Denver, Colorado. If I bring home a mango tree from India and plant it on my backyard, there is little hope that it would grow and produce any mangoes. It might grow a little bit, but it will never reach its full potential because mango is a tropical fruit, and Denver does not have tropical weather. Your purpose has a specific location, and only when you reach there can you unfold the potential God has put in you.

A seed needs to go through a process of change in order to become what it's created it to be. If a seed remains as it is, it will not produce any fruit. It has to go through a painful process of change in order to become a tree. The seed must "die" in order to become a tree. Dying does not mean a natural death but a change of form or state.

Many are not willing to go through any change in their lives. They want to achieve something without paying any price. They want a gold medal but do not want to train and run the race! There is a saying in my language that goes like this, "People want to take what is on top of the shelf, but they do not want lose what is in their armpit." I hope you get the idea. In order to reach for something higher, you should be willing let go of what you are holding onto. It could be a tradition, belief system, location, excuses, habits, laziness, or anything that God and your purpose require from you.

I had to give up almost everything to do what I am doing today. I gave up my culture, language, food, relatives, weather and much more to be doing what I am now doing. If I had fought God and resisted the change, I wouldn't be here today. It wasn't easy, but when I look back it was worth it.

A seed needs to be planted for it to grow and become a tree. You cannot grow a seed on your shelf. As long as it remains there, it remains as a seed.

When you plant it in the ground and wait a few days, you will see a sapling coming out of the ground. The reason is that it needs the help of different factors to become everything God created it to be. It needs the help of the ground, the water, heat, and minerals for the process to begin.

You also cannot become everything God created you to be without the help of others. God will send people to your lives: some will cause pain and others will offer resources. Everyone who comes to your life is there to change you or help you in some way. When a seed is planted in the ground, the same ground that is causing discomfort, is actually helping with the process of change.

God will use the very circumstances that you feel are the most painful to you, for your benefit. He will use that circumstance to change you into the person you were meant to be and help you enter into your new season. Once you plant a seed, it needs to remain there for a while to grow. You cannot dig it out every day or every other day and expect it to grow. It will die. You need to remain planted in one place until you accomplish what God sent you there to accomplish.

A seed needs time to become everything it was created to be; it does not grow overnight. As the Bible says, there is a time to plant and a time to harvest. You cannot plant seeds whenever you want. There is a particular time and season for sowing. If you miss it and sow your seed during winter, you will not receive a harvest. Many people do not recognize the time of their sowing, the time of hard work, to prepare for their future. They just wait and wait for God to do a miracle for them, when all along God gave them the seed, and they are not doing anything with it.

For example, you cannot become a good musician overnight. That only happens in dreams. It takes years of practice to master an instrument; that is the season of sowing. When you've mastered that instrument, God will open venues for you to perform. That is your harvest.

A seed has in itself every potential that's required to grow and become a tree. Though the seed needs the help of other external factors, it has everything it needs to grow and become a tree. *You have everything you need right now to become everything God created you to be.* You just need to be planted in the right ground.

A seed has the power to overcome obstacles and adverse circumstances. A seed may look tiny and powerless, but it has the inherent ability to push through any obstacle that's in its way. Just like a blade of grass cracks through a sidewalk, your purpose has the potential to overcome any obstacle you will ever face. Nothing can destroy your purpose—except you. So, stop worrying about other people and enemies; they can do nothing to stop you. If you focus on the seed, God will take care of the rest.

A seed will not ask another seed what it should do. Can you imagine a pumpkin seed asking a tomato seed what it's supposed to be doing? Each seed is completely equipped with everything that's required to become what it is meant to be. All it needs is the right environment.

A seed does not need another seed to become what it was created to be. That might sound strange. We do need the help of other people to fulfill our purpose, but there is a difference. Let me make this clearer. A seed will not go looking around for someone else's help because the help it needs comes to the seed. Do not think that you need the help of someone to become what God created you to be? If He sends someone to you, praise God, but you do not need to depend on people. Depend and trust only in God.

Whatever you need to take the next step, to fulfill your purpose, to move toward your destiny—it is already with you. Most people wait and hold back until they have everything together. It will never happen. They keep making excuses or believe the lie that says they don't have what it takes. Stop waiting for someone to come and discover your greatness or help you. It won't happen. Start where you are and everything you need will follow.

When you sow a financial seed, it's a harvest for someone. In turn, when they sow a seed, it becomes a harvest for others. Right now, you have someone else's harvest. The cycle goes on and on. You are created to be an answer to someone else's problem. The Bible says you are not your own, you are bought with a price (1 Corinthians 6:20).

Remember the parable of the talents that Jesus shared? A talent is like a seed. If you keep it as it is, it remains the same, but if you plant it or invest it, it will produce a harvest. God has given to each individual, seed/s according to their ability.

After you recognize the "seed" in you, you need to find the right environment or education to grow that seed. All seeds do not grow everywhere. Each seed requires its own special weather and environment. That is why God takes people away from their birthplace to a different city or country to train and develop them. The way God develops us is not the same as the world does. His system of education works a little differently than our regular schools and colleges.

We see that God created man for six distinct purposes. In Genesis 1:26, we read that God said, "Let us make man in our image and likeness." Then He said, "Let them have dominion over the fish of the sea." In creation, God said, "Let us create," but in having dominion over the earth, He did not include Himself; instead He said, "Let them have dominion." That means man had total freedom in what he should do on the earth. God was not going to intrude into man's business or freedom of choice.

God created us to have dominion over the earth. There are two applications of this truth. The first one is natural and the second one is spiritual. The natural application is this: In verse 28, God is explaining how to have that dominion over the earth. First of all, He blessed them. Then He explained the process of obtaining dominion. He said to be fruitful, multiply, replenish, subdue and then have dominion. This process is the key to understanding our purpose. Being fruitful means not only to have children but to be productive. God wants us to be productive.

That means God put at least one seed in each of our lives. That seed needs to grow and produce fruit. That means there is a product in each of us that is waiting to be released. That is the key to your prosperity in the kingdom. When you discover your product or service, you become an essential part of life. Thousands or maybe millions die without ever discovering their product. The reason for poverty here is that people are not productive, because they do not know their purpose.

God put a desire in your heart to do something. That desire is a clue to the product that is hidden in you. It could be ministry, business, an invention, a song or a book, music, serving, a talent, or so much more. There are a variety of ways in which God wants us to manifest that product to the world.

Once you discover your product (fruit), you need to multiply it (manufacture it). After you manufacture it, you need to fill the earth (market it) or replenish the earth with that product so that others can benefit from it. The next step is to subdue (take control), and implement a managing system for your business. As a result, you will have dominion over a particular area of life.

When we think of computers two names comes to our mind, Bill Gates and Steve Jobs. Why? They have implemented the above principle and have taken dominion over the computer business. What if Bill Gates and Steve Jobs sat in their living rooms and sang, "Amazing Grace, How Sweet the Sound" all day? Or sang, "This Earth is Not My Home, I Am Just Passing By"? They may not be tongue-talking, holy-rolling believers, but they have lived true to the purpose for which God created them. Every successful business uses biblical principles as their foundation. What about you and me?

You are created to take dominion over a particular sphere of life. The seed of God in you is waiting to be released. Do not go to the grave with that seed still in you. You need to discover and reproduce that seed to bless humanity. Do not leave the earth before you make your mark on the pages of history. The whole earth is waiting for the manifestation of the sons of God.

In Genesis 1:28, God blessed them and explained to them the steps to having dominion. There are five steps. They are:

1. FRUITFUL

The first thing God told man was to be fruitful. To have a fruit, first you need a seed. Fruit does not grow on its own; it needs a tree, and the tree needs ground, and the seed has to be planted in that ground. In turn, the tree produces the fruit to disperse the seed further later on. Also, the tree bears fruit not for itself to enjoy, but for someone else.

You are created to be a blessing to someone. God sometimes does not explain the whole process when He says something. He will tell you the result, but we have to go through the process. There are multiple meanings of the word "fruitful"; the Hebrew word used for fruitful is *parah*[22] which means "to bear fruit, be fruitful, branch off, to make fruitful, to show fruitfulness."

The general idea of being fruitful is having children, which is the fruit of our body. Even for that there is a process involved. A baby does not just appear out of a man; he needs to deposit his seed into a woman's womb and then it takes nine months to birth a baby.

Man is a three-part being, made of spirit, soul and body. Each of these parts has the ability to produce fruit. When God said to be fruitful, He was not just talking about the fruit of our body, which is our children. He was also talking about producing fruit through the other two facets of our being: soul and spirit.

Unfortunately, most people only produce the fruit of their body. The other two areas of fruit remain barren, so they do not prosper in life. If you keep producing only children and do not produce any other fruit, you will not have anything to feed your children. That is the reason for

---

[22] James Strong, "6509. Parah," Biblehub.com, accessed January 04, 2019, https://biblehub.com/hebrew/6509.htm.

poverty in many parts of the world. They produce children, but their soul and spirit remain barren.

The key to prosperity lies in the fruit of the other two parts of our life, which are soul and spirit. At the same time, our soul and spirit cannot function without our body. The fruit of the mind and spirit have to manifest through our body. A fruit is also called a product. Children are our natural product, the product of our body. You need to bring forth some product from your mind and spirit as well. Just like God has put seed in your body, He also put seed in your mind and spirit. We need to discover and develop that seed too, if we are going to prosper and fulfill our purpose. The Bible talks about different kinds of fruit, and I am not talking about the kind we eat.

Fruit is something that benefits others. A tree does not eat its fruit. The fruit is there to attract others to the tree. When you bear fruit, it is for someone else. They want to eat that fruit; and if it is good fruit, they will pay you for it. If your fruit (or product) feeds or meets any of the needs of others, they will pay you for meeting that need. Every product you buy from stores is the *fruit* of someone. It meets your need and you spend your money to have it. That is the secret to prosperity. No fruit, no money.

Just having fruit will not bring you money. There are other steps involved before you can make any money from your fruit. I will explain that below.

For now, just take a moment and say, "Father, thank You for making me fruitful in my spirit, soul and body." The Bible talks about the fruit of our body, spirit and soul. Please read the following.

FRUIT OF OUR BODY

The children we give birth to are the fruit of our body. We also labor or work with our body and that produces fruit. This is called the fruit of the land. If we do not work, there will not be any fruit.

> "He will also bless the *fruit* of your womb and the *fruit* of your land" (Deuteronomy 7:13).
>
> "When you have gathered in the *fruit* of your labors from the field" (Exodus 23:16).
>
> "Give her of the *fruit* of her hands, and let her own works praise her in the gates" (Proverbs 31:31).
>
> "Blessed shall be the *fruit* of your body" (Deuteronomy 28:4).

FRUIT OF OUR LIPS AND OUR WORDS

The words we speak are seeds. They will bring a harvest into our lives sooner or later. Our prosperity and health depends on the words of our mouth. The Bible says that "death and life are in the power of the tongue" (Proverbs 18:21).

> "A man will be satisfied with good by the *fruit* of his mouth" (Proverbs 12:14).
>
> "A man's stomach shall be satisfied from the *fruit* of his mouth; from the produce of his lips he shall be filled" (Proverbs 18:20).
>
> "I create the *fruit* of the lips" (Isaiah 57:19).

FRUIT OF OUR MIND AND SOUL

Your prosperity depends on the fruit of your mind and spirit and not necessarily the fruit of your body. By fruit of the body, I'm referring here to children. Our soul is made up of our emotions, intellect, will, and memory. The fruit of our mind is our imagination. Every product and invention was the fruit of someone's imagination, or mind. Some minds do not produce anything good, because their imagination is constantly evil. We need to train our mind to think good thoughts because every thought has the potential to produce either good or evil fruit. Every good and evil deed we've ever done began in our imagination or as a thought in our mind.

God put the picture of our future in our mind. I call it a vision. The mind is not evil and all imaginations are not evil. Our mind is a blessing from God, if we use it for the right cause. Our mind is God's manufacturing plant on earth. He wants to use it to release new products and inventions. When God wants to release something new to this planet, He releases that idea to someone's mind or spirit.

The fruit of the mind is comprised of ideas, books, songs, drawings, specific knowledge, creativity, inventions, speech, and anything else that we can use our imagination to complete. The Bible says we have the mind of Christ (1 Corinthians 2:16). Therefore, we should be the most productive and creative people on earth.

The richest people on earth are those who use their minds. If you look at the life of rich people; they are not necessarily working with their body, but they put their minds to work. Your wealth is in the fruit of your mind. The more you put your mind to work, the more productive and prosperous you become.

> "Commit your works to the Lord, and your *thoughts* will be established" (Proverbs 16:3).

> "The *plans* of the diligent lead surely to plenty" (Proverbs 21:5).

> "The *fruit* of their thoughts" (Jeremiah 6:19).

FRUIT OF THE SPIRIT

Our spirit can produce fruit. We are familiar with the fruit of the spirit: love, joy, peace, and so on. We also need to bear a different kind of spiritual fruit—souls. When you bring a person to Christ, they are the fruit of your spirit, your spiritual children. The more spiritual children you have, the more you will be blessed.

> "But the *fruit* of the Spirit is love, joy, peace, longsuffering, kindness, goodness, faithfulness, gentleness, self-control" (Galatians 5:22-23).

Souls that we bring into the kingdom are also the fruit of our spirit. We call them our spiritual children. The fruit of the spirit can also be an idea, speech, book, song, a massage, and many other things; but they all have to come through our mind and body to benefit other people.

FINANCIAL FRUIT

When we sow a financial seed, it produces a harvest. It is also called a fruit.

> "Not that I seek the gift, but I seek the *fruit* that abounds to your account" (Philippians 4:17).

FRUITFUL IN EVERYTHING

> "You did not choose Me, but I chose you and appointed you that you should go and bear *fruit*, and that your *fruit* should remain, that whatever you ask the Father in My name He may give you" (John 15:16).

> "That you may walk worthy of the Lord, fully pleasing Him, being *fruitful* in every good work and increasing in the knowledge of God" (Colossians 1:10).

When we recognize the seeds God planted in our spirit, soul and body and begin to produce fruit; we need to move into the next step, which is to multiply.

2. MULTIPLY

The next thing God told man was to multiply. After we produce a fruit, we need to multiply that fruit. This means we need to find a way to mass produce it. I am not talking about children here. I am talking about the fruit of your mind and spirit. When a person invents a product, he or she goes to a manufacturing company and asks them to reproduce it. The Hebrew word used for multiply is *rabah*[23] which means, "be or become

---

[23] James Strong, "7235. Rabah," Biblehub.com, accessed January 05, 2019, https://biblehub.com/

great, be or become many, be or become much, be or become numerous (of people, animals or things), to make large, make many, enlarge."

When you have an idea, song, book or anything God puts in your spirit or mind, you need to design it and find a way to multiply it. After you do that, we move to the next stage.

3. FILL THE EARTH

To fill the earth means to distribute or market it. Many of us do not prosper, not because we do not have an idea or a product, but because we do not know how to turn an idea into a product or a service. Others have a product but do not know how to distribute it. The more you distribute, the more you prosper.

The Hebrew word for "fill the earth" is *male*[24] which means to fill, be full, fullness, abundance, and to be accomplished.

The people in the world are smarter in these things than believers in the church. You need to fill the earth with your product. Companies spend billions of dollars to advertise their products. It does not matter how valuable or beneficial a product is, if you do not advertise it, no one will know about it; and as a result, you will not prosper.

Companies like Coke, Pepsi, McDonald's, and Microsoft fill the earth with their products. They are some of the richest companies in the world. Once you fill the earth then you can move into the next stage.

4. SUBDUE IT

Once you distribute your product, then you take control of that one area you are focusing on with your product. Bill Gates subdued the area of

---

hebrew/7235.htm.

24 James Strong, "4390. Male," Biblehub.com, accessed January 05, 2019, https://biblehub.com/hebrew/4390.htm.

computer technology and software for a long time, all over the world. Subdue means to take authority over something. Do what you do like no one did it before. The Hebrew word for subdue is *kabash*[25] which means "to subject, subdue, force, keep under, bring into bondage, or make subservient."

To subdue something, you need power and authority. Your product gives you power and authority to subdue that area of life. When you subdue, you will have dominion over that area, and that is the next step.

5. DOMINION

Dominion is the ultimate purpose of God for man. Most people know in their heart they are created to rule and have dominion. Since the fall, when man lost his dominion over the earth, and did not understand the process of dominion, they began to dominate each other. A person who does not have dominion over an area of life through their purpose and product will always try to dominate or control their fellow human beings through the use of force because they feel insecure and left out of the crowd. Others may use their money and power to dominate. We are not created to rule over people.

The Hebrew word for dominion is *radah*[26] which means "to rule, have dominion, dominate, and tread down."

From Genesis to Revelation it is God's plan for man to have dominion. God is a king and we are His children. What kings do is rule over a territory, which is called his kingdom. Adam was a king. Since the fall, God added another level of ministry to us, which is the ministry of priesthood. It is only for a period of time. At the end (after the redemption of creation),

---

25 James Strong, "3533. Kabash," Biblehub.com, accessed January 05, 2019, https://biblehub.com/hebrew/3533.htm.

26 James Strong, "7287. Radah," Biblehub.com, accessed January 05, 2019, https://biblehub.com/hebrew/7287.htm.

there will be only kings just as it was in the beginning. That is why whenever God mentions the position of man, He always puts the kingship first and not the priesthood. Please read the following verses, then you will know what I am talking about.

Right now, everyone in the body of Christ is a king and priest at the same time. In some circles, they divide the body into two parts, saying people who are in ministry are priests and others are kings. They do that because of the distinction we see in the Old Testament between priests and kings. David was a king, but he also had the anointing of a priest and prophet. Samuel is another example of someone who was a judge, priest, and prophet.

When God brought the people of Israel out of Egypt He said He wanted them to be a kingdom of priests. Exodus 19:6 says, "'And you shall be to Me a *kingdom of priests* and a holy nation.' These are the words which you shall speak to the children of Israel."

We see the same thing in the New Testament. "But you are a chosen generation, *a royal priesthood*, a holy nation, His own special people, that you may proclaim the praises of Him who called you out of darkness into His marvelous light" (1 Peter 2:9).

> "And from Jesus Christ, the faithful witness, the firstborn from the dead, and the ruler over the kings of the earth. To Him who loved us and washed us from our sins in His own blood, and has *made us kings and priests* to His God and Father, to Him be glory and dominion forever and ever. Amen" (Revelation 1:5-6).

> "And have *made us kings and priests* to our God; and we shall reign on the earth" (Revelation 5:10).

> "'There will never be night again. They will not need the light of a lamp or the light of the sun, because the Lord God will

give them light. And they will rule as *kings* forever and ever" (Revelation 22:5, NCV).

None of the above scriptures say that God made some people, kings and others, priests. Instead they say He made us all kings *and* priests. That includes everyone. In Revelation 22, it mentions only kings. Amen.

CHAPTER - 8

GENETIC CODE OF YOUR SEED

The Bible says, "While the earth remains, seedtime and harvest, cold and heat, winter and summer, and day and night shall not cease" (Genesis 8:22).

Sowing and reaping is a principle set by God for the earth. In the natural, there is a season for sowing and a season for reaping (or harvesting). We have read about this, and heard sermons preached about it many times, but rarely do we gain a clear understanding of how it actually works. One of the things God gave to man at the time of creation was herbs and trees that bore seed. Many believers sow money into different things, but they do not receive a harvest. I am going to explain why. Many think that to receive a financial harvest, all they must do is sow money and wait for the harvest. It does not work that way!

SEED

The first thing we need to know about is the seed. What is a seed? A seed is a substance that has unlimited potential to reproduce its own kind. The main point in that definition is "reproducing its own kind." Every seed is preprogrammed to reproduce its own kind.

I have already quoted the proverb that says, "We can count the seeds in an apple, but cannot count the apples in a seed." God created every seed or herb to produce after its own kind. That means, if we plant an apple seed we will get an apple tree which has the potential to produce apples. We cannot expect oranges from an apple tree. Many people do that. I will explain more about that later.

If you are expecting a particular harvest, then you need to sow a particular seed. Every seed is designed to produce a specific type of harvest. God has designed the code that determines the size, color, flower, and fruit of each plant in its seed. It is already written in the seed. This is called the genetic code. You cannot change it. If you do, you are messing with God's order.

What is a genetic code? It is the set of rules by which information is encoded in genetic material. We call it the DNA, which stands for deoxyribonucleic acid. That means each seed has information written on it about its future. It is very specific and detailed. All the seed requires is the right environment to manifest what is already written on it.

Each of us are a manifestation of the seed our father planted in our mother's womb. The size of our body, color of our skin, eyes, shape of our face: everything was written on that seed. Every form of life—plant or animal—has a genetic code. The genetic code is that which reproduces the next life.

The Bible calls money a seed too. When the apostle Paul talks about giving in the Corinthians, he compares it with the natural process of sowing and reaping.

> "Now may He who supplies seed to the sower, and bread for food, supply and multiply the seed you have *sown* and

increase the fruits of your righteousness, while you are enriched in everything for all liberality, which causes thanksgiving through us to God" (2 Corinthians 9:10-11).

BE SPECIFIC

God wrote the genetic code for each seed and living organism. When you sow your financial seed, *you get to write the genetic code for your seed*. You need to be very specific and detailed about what you are expecting from that seed. God expects specific harvests from every seed He has made, and that is why He has written their genetic code. Some people do not believe in expecting a specific harvest when they sow finances. That means they do not understand the basic principles of farming, or the process of sowing and reaping.

There is nothing wrong with expecting a specific harvest; in fact we are supposed to. If God expects a specific type of harvest from each seed, then we should assign each seed we sow to a specific harvest. That is one of the reasons why many faithful givers do not receive their harvest. They give and give and give, but do not assign their seed for a particular harvest.

Money is a general seed and we get to participate in deciding the type of harvest it should produce. In the natural seed, the type of harvest is predetermined by God. *In the spiritual realm, you and I get to decide what type of harvest we are believing the Lord for.*

PREPARATION

I grew up near a rice field and every year I used to watch the process of sowing and harvesting rice. Before the farmer sowed the rice seed, he had to prepare the ground and that was very hard work. It took time and did not get done in one day. The farmer had to stand under the scorching heat of the sun for the whole day for many days, and by the time he was done for the day he was tired and ready to go to bed.

No farmer will get up one morning and decide that he is going to just sow his seed that day. *It takes preparation to sow.* Another reason some believers do not receive a financial breakthrough is because they do not prepare ahead of time when they decide to sow.

Some people decide at the time of the offering what they are going to give. They pull out from their pocket what they can find and put it on the offering basket. That shows no preparation or planning. That kind of giving will never get you from one level to the next in your financial life.

When a farmer harvests his crops, he separates the best seeds and puts them aside for the next year for sowing. He knows it takes the best seeds to produce the best harvest. *Before you give, prepare your seed in advance; and pray and bless your seed.* Write what type of harvest you are expecting from God on the offering envelope or the check or a piece of paper. Then watch what God will do.

A long time ago I made a commitment to give the best and the biggest currency I have in my wallet when I give, if I am giving an offering that is unplanned. I have kept that commitment 99.9% times. I want the best God has for me. So I choose to give Him the best I have.

RIGHT TIME

"A time to plant and a time to harvest" (Ecclesiastes 3:2, NLT).

There is a time and season for sowing and reaping.

Another important truth we learn from the above verse is that there is an actual seedtime, a specific time for sowing seed. In the natural, there is a particular time when we need to sow the seed. If we miss the season it does not matter how good the seed is, we will not receive a good harvest. When sowing rice, the farmer has to sow the seeds before the monsoon season begins; otherwise he will not have anything to harvest when the harvest time comes.

Sowing is also a time of pain. It says,

"Those who sow in tears shall reap in joy" (Psalm 126:5).

Jesus spoke about this process in the context of His own soon-approaching death, saying a seed had to die to itself, so that it could bear fruit (John 12:23-25). Jesus was looking ahead to the joy set before Him. This natural principle holds true for us as well. The seed we sow must die to itself and be entrusted to the Lord to raise it up according to His will. As our vision is submitted to His, He resurrects it.

When you put a seed into the ground, it doesn't grow into a plant unless it dies first. And what you put in the ground is not the plant that will grow, but only a bare seed of wheat or whatever you are planting. Then God gives it the new body he wants it to have. A different plant grows from each kind of seed (1Corinthians 15:36-38).

I believe what determines the length of time between sowing and the harvest season is the size of the seed sown. The smaller the seed, the faster you receive the harvest; and the bigger the seed, the longer it takes for a harvest. I grew up in a coastal area where we had millions of coconut trees. My father used to plant coconut seeds in our backyard and wait for the seeds to germinate.

Coconut seeds are large in size and it takes three months for them just to germinate. It takes five to seven years for the coconut tree to grow and produce the harvest. For three months you won't see any significant change in that coconut; it will remain in the soil as if nothing is going to happen. Beans are very different. They germinate in a few days and bear fruit in a matter of months.

In the natural, there is a particular time for sowing and if someone misses that season they will not receive any harvest. It is also true in the spirit. There are particular times and seasons in our life that God will inspire us to sow into other people's lives and ministries; and if we obey, we will receive a harvest. Whatever you have today—financially, spiritually, or relationally—is the harvest of the seed you have planted in your last season.

> "Do not be deceived, God is not mocked; for whatever a man sows, that he will also reap" (Galatians 6:7).

WAITING

> "Therefore be patient, brethren, until the coming of the Lord. See how the farmer waits for the precious fruit of the earth, waiting patiently for it until it receives the early and latter rain. You also be patient. Establish your hearts, for the coming of the Lord is at hand" (James 5:7-8).

> "And He said, "The kingdom of God is as if a man should scatter seed on the ground, and should sleep by night and rise by day, and the seed should sprout and grow, he himself does not know how. For the earth yields crops by itself: first the blade, then the head, after that the full grain in the head. But when the grain ripens, immediately he puts in the sickle, because the harvest has come" (Mark 4:26-29).

Both of these scriptures are about the process of sowing and reaping. You do not receive a harvest just after you sow. All truths are parallel. I have watched this year after year. After the farmer sows the seed, he has to protect that seed from mice and other insects that like to eat it. In like manner, once your financial seed is sown, you need to stay in faith and not doubt or complain. The enemy is clever about stealing your seed and aborting your harvest.

When you sow the seed, it will germinate if it is the right seed in the right environment. You will get a little sprout of the plant or tree you planted. Then that plant needs to be nurtured in order to grow and produce a harvest.

When you sow a seed, you get an opportunity to receive your harvest. What you do with that opportunity will decide your harvest. Because many are waiting for their harvest to arrive on their doorstep, they tend to ignore the opportunities that God sends their way and the processes open to them to accumulate the harvest.

God may open up an opportunity for you to start a business, or get a new job. ; or He might send you to a person who is capable of blessing you. You may have to ask or present your need to that person with wisdom. He may give you an idea to do something, or invent something. He may put a book or a song in your heart, and you'll need to sit down and write it.

ITS OWN KIND

Another important thing to know about seed is that it reproduces *only in its own kind*. Apple seeds produce apples, mangos produce mangos. As I mentioned earlier, when you sow a seed, you need to know what you are expecting from that seed. Then you need to sow into someone who has the same need. What does that mean? If you are believing God for a house, then find someone who needs a house and sow into that person's life. All seeds reproduce according to their own kind. If you are believing God for a car, find someone who needs a car and sow a financial seed into that person's life.

You cannot sow into someone who needs a car and expect a house in return. Every seed produces its own kind. The Bible says, "God is not mocked; for whatever a man sows, that he will also reap" (Galatians 6:7). If you sow a car you will reap a car. If you sow a house you will reap a house.

That means you cannot expect a different type of harvest from the kind of seed you are sowing. Jesus said, "Whatever you want men to do to you, do also to them" (Matthew 7:12). The same measure we give will be measured back to us.

CHAPTER - 9

YOUR GIVING DETERMINES YOUR FUTURE

---

*T*he kingdom of God operates on the principle of sowing and reaping. One of the main keys that God uses to promote people is through sowing financial seeds. One of the greatest desires God has for your life is that He wants to bless other people through you.

*In the kingdom, before you can receive something, you need to give. Everything you have, and will receive, in your life is a harvest of what you did or gave previously. There is no limit to **what** you can have, or **how much** you can have, in the kingdom. It all depends on how much you are able or willing to give. Your harvest is proportioned to your sowing.*

I believe with all my heart that we will not go anywhere in the kingdom until we obey God in some critical moments of financial giving. Until you loose something on earth by faith, nothing will be loosed in heaven (Matthew 18:18). This is especially true when going from one financial season to another, and from one financial level to another; the key is to sow a sacrificial seed when God prompts your spirit.

We see this principle at work throughout the Bible. It is not the invention of prosperity preachers; it is a pivotal truth of God's Word. Much of what Jesus taught was about money or financial investments. He preached about finances more than He preached about being born-again, prayer, faith, or hell.

Your giving determines how God responds to your need. Your giving determines how God will cause other people to show you favor too. Favor is defined as God causing other people to bless you unexpectedly, and giving you blessings for which you are not qualified. God's favor will take you places nothing else can.

The first murder took place when someone reacted poorly to the favor his brother's giving had brought him. Cain brought his offering to God first, but God did not respect his offering. Then Abel brought an offering—the firstborn of his flock and God respected Abel's offering. This inspired jealousy in Cain's heart; and when they were in the field, Cain killed his brother, Abel (Genesis 4:3-8). *Your giving creates a reaction in the spirit world.* God takes your giving seriously and pays attention to it, whether you notice it or not.

God was pleased with Abel's offering and rejected Cain's. The Bible says Abel brought the best of what he had to God. It cost him something to give that offering. If an offering does not cost you something and does not get registered in your heart when you give it, it will not get registered in heaven either.

The first judgment, after the Israelites reached the Promised Land, occurred as a result of improper giving too. God specifically ordered Joshua to invade Jericho, the first fortified city in the Promised Land. He was to take all the silver and gold, and vessels of bronze and iron, and have them consecrated to the Lord, so they could bring them to the treasury of the Lord (Joshua 6:19). No man was allowed to touch or take anything from it. It was the firstfruits of the Promised Land, and the firstfruits always belong to the Lord. However, one of the men disobeyed God and took some of it and hid it in their camp and sinned against the Lord.

> "Israel has sinned; and they have also transgressed My covenant which I commanded them. For they have even taken some of the accursed things, and have both stolen and deceived; and they have also put it among their own stuff" (Joshua 7:11).

It was a serious crime against the Lord to do this. They could not stand against their enemies because of it, and they were defeated by the people of Ai. Their restitution for the crime was to punish Achan and his family. Then God restored His favor upon Israel. Your giving determines your victory over your enemies. Your giving determines how God will respond to you and deal with your enemies too.

The first judgment in the New Testament church also happened because of improper giving. Acts 5 tells the story of a married couple in the early church who sold a possession and kept back part of the proceeds for themselves. They brought the rest of the money to the apostles. When they brought the money, they lied to Peter saying that it was the whole amount of money that they got from selling their property. The Bible says Ananias fell down dead and people took him and buried him. Three hours later his wife Sapphira came, and Peter asked her about the money and she lied to him too. She fell down dead as well, and the people buried her next to her husband (Acts 5:1-10).

It amazes me how serious God takes our heart when we give to the Lord. It is a matter of life and death—curse and blessing. At first I could not believe that God would judge someone in the New Testament about giving. I had to ask God to forgive me for not respecting Him with my own giving.

The door for the ministry to the Gentiles was opened because of the giving of a man called Cornelius.

> "There was a certain man in Caesarea called Cornelius, a centurion of what was called the Italian Regiment, a devout man and one who feared God with all his household, who gave alms generously to the people, and prayed to God always." (Acts 10:1-2).

God noted Cornelius's giving and that caused God to send Peter to his house and preach the gospel to him and his household. He was the first fruit of the Gentile believers. The Bible says he was a generous man. Your giving can determine your salvation and the salvation of your household. Thank God for Cornelius and his giving. If it was not for him, we might not have received the gospel so quickly.

Cornelius had a vision of an angel. Note what the angel told him.

> "And when he observed him, he was afraid, and said, 'What is it, lord?' So he said to him, 'Your prayers and your alms have come up for a memorial before God" (Acts 10:4).

This verse demonstrates again that God notices our giving and keeps a record of what we give towards Him and His kingdom.

It does not always have to be money that you sow to receive a breakthrough either. Anything that costs you, including your time, material possessions, money, opportunities, food, water, any resource can be the tool. When you give sacrificially to someone in need, it can unlock a new season in the Spirit.

From the beginning, we see that when a person gives wholeheartedly to someone else or to God, it invokes God's favor to manifest in their lives. It is not because God needs something from us; but He is a God of love and love always gives until it hurts. When a man or woman shows the nature of God to others through his or her life, it pleases Him to move on their behalf.

When you look back, the offerings and gifts that you remember are those God remembers because they were valuable to you. If you want something valuable from God, you need to release something valuable from your hand or from your life to someone else.

In Luke 21 we read about a widow who put two mites into the offering. Jesus noticed and commented on her offering. There were many rich people who gave big offerings, maybe thousands of dollars, but none of them were noticed by Jesus.

> And He looked up and saw the rich putting their gifts into the treasury, and He saw also a certain poor widow putting in two mites. So He said, "Truly I say to you that this poor widow has put in more than all; for all these out of their abundance have put in offerings for God, but she out of her poverty put in all the livelihood that she had (Luke 21:1-4).

After the flood, when Noah came out of the ark, his first act was to offer a sacrifice to God. He built an altar to the Lord and took some of every clean animal and clean fowl and offered burnt offerings on the altar (Genesis 8:20-21). It cost Noah to make that offering and it took time and effort to build an altar. He did not try to build himself a house first when he came out of the ark. Instead he put God first in his life. Scripture says God was pleased with that sacrifice and then promised to never again "curse the ground." Then God came down and blessed Noah and the earth (Genesis 9:1).

We have studied Abraham's life in detail before, but I want to mention one more time how critical it was for Abraham's destiny that he was obedient and willing to sacrifice Isaac. He had only one son. He had waited for Isaac's birth almost his entire adult life. I do not believe Abraham ever forgot that experience. It became a part of the history of the world. It was painful, but as the Bible says, obedience is better than sacrifice.

Every pain you endure for God's sake or for His kingdom will be multiplied back to you as a blessing. As the Bible says, "Give, and it shall be given unto you; good measure, pressed down, and shaken together, and running over, shall men give into your bosom" (Luke 6:38, KJV).

Before Abraham's death, he commanded his servant to go to his kindred to find a wife for his son, Isaac. His servant took camels and the wealth Abraham had and departed to Mesopotamia (Genesis 24:10). Abraham was a wealthy man with silver, gold, and all manner of material blessings. Imagine this servant leading his camels loaded with gold, silver, gifts and expensive clothes that might have been worth millions of dollars.

On the way, he prayed to God and asked for a sign (Genesis 24:12). He stopped by a well to get some water for himself and the camels. The sign he asked God for was that the girl who would give him water and also give water to the camels, would be the girl that God had chosen for Isaac.

You may think this water was an easy thing to give, but there was no motor or technology to draw water from a well those days. I believe she might have come to get water for her animals or for her household. She had to go to the well and bring up the water in a pot. Walking up and down with a pot of full of water is hard work and a sacrifice.

I know this because when I was growing up, we did not have an electric motor and running water in my house. Each house had a well and it was fifty to sixty feet deep. There was a pulley that was attached to the top of the well and you used a long rope that was tied to a bucket to draw water. I used to do that for my mother every day, helping her to get water for our use in the kitchen as well as for our personal needs. It was good exercise and my arms grew stronger through this labor.

As soon as he was done praying, Rebekah came and did exactly what he asked. In fact, she gave more than what was asked. He only asked her for water for himself, but after she gave it to him she offered to draw water for his camels too. He had ten camels and each of those camels would drink at least thirty gallons (113.56 liters). That one act of giving changed Rebekah's entire life. She married Isaac and inherited the entire wealth of Abraham.

What if she had said this? "I don't know this guy? I am not going to spend my time taking care of some stranger and his animals. I have my own work to do. I just got my nails done the other day and I am not going to mess them up! My hands would hurt and I don't want my clothes to get wet and sweaty." She could have come up with an excuse so easily, but she did not, and that showed her character. She would have missed her season and would not have inherited the blessing.

Do you see the pattern? When you do more than what you are asked to do, you will be paid more than you are required to be paid. When you give more than what is required, you will inherit the abundance of God without any limit. As I have heard, "Nothing leaves heaven until something leaves your hand."

There are many examples in the Old Testament about how giving brought breakthroughs and deliverance to people. Before the Israelites came out of Egypt, God asked them to observe the Passover. Every family was supposed to take a lamb which was without any blemish and apply its blood to the doorpost of their houses and eat the meat as a family.

Everyone who did not observe the Passover lost their firstborn child. Passover was an act of giving that protected them and destroyed the yoke of bondage off their lives. Killing that lamb was a sacrifice.

In 1 Samuel 1, we read about Hannah, who did not have a child and was despised by her rival. She went into the house of God and prayed. Hannah made a commitment to God that if He would bless her with a male child, she would give that child back to Him (1 Samuel 1:11). She believed God for a son. Before she ever had him, she gave him to the Lord. The rest is history. God heard her prayer and Samuel was born a year later. After he was weaned, she took Samuel up with her, along with three bulls, one ephah of flour and a bottle of wine and presented them to the house of the Lord (1 Samuel 1:24).

Samuel grew up to be a mighty prophet of the Lord and brought Israel back from spiritual apostasy. God used Samuel to anoint David and institute kingship in Israel. There are two books in the Bible named after Samuel. This all happened because Hannah was willing to give up something precious to her. God answered her prayer, honored her sacrifice, and blessed many other people through her. And He provided even more to her as He gave her more children after Samuel.

Everyone knows about the wealth, glory, and wisdom of Solomon, but few know how he got it all. Solomon was not the wisest and wealthiest man when he became king. It all began when he went to Gibeon to sacrifice to the Lord. He offered an unusual sacrifice that day by giving one thousand burnt offerings (1 King 3:4-5). That was over and beyond what was required to bring to the Lord, and He noticed!

That same night, the Lord appeared to him in a dream and said, "Ask! What shall I give you?" Whatever Solomon asked the Lord, it would be given to him. He asked for wisdom and understanding; God was pleased with his request (1 King 3:9-10).

This was the beginning of the greatness of Solomon, and it all started with giving an unusual offering to the Lord. If you want unusual blessings, you need to give unusual offerings. *If your offering does not cost you something, do not expect to receive something that is costly.*

CHAPTER - 10

GOING TO THE NEXT LEVEL

When we study the Bible we see certain people received a financial breakthrough in their lives. It was not giving tithes that brought that breakthrough. It was a different type of giving. God took me to His Word and began to show me and teach me about these people who experienced a financial miracle. That is what I want to share with you in this chapter.

In the Old Testament, the Gentiles envied the prosperity of God's people. Genesis 26 tells the story of when Isaac sowed during the famine and received a hundredfold harvest.

> "There was a famine in the land, besides the first famine that was in the days of Abraham. And Isaac went to Abimelech king of the Philistines, in Gerar....Then Isaac sowed in that land, and reaped in the same year a hundredfold; and the Lord blessed him. The man began to prosper, and continued prospering until he became very prosperous; for he had possessions of flocks and possessions of herds and a great

number of servants. So the Philistines envied him" (Genesis 26:1, 12-14).

I have found that not everyone who gives receives an unusual blessing. Churches in America are big on tithing, and teach it faithfully, and many people give their tithe just as faithfully. However, not everyone who tithes receives unusual financial blessings.

I have known families who have tithed faithfully for years. Years could mean many decades, and I have seen them struggle and face financial crises. I used to wonder, "Lord, what is wrong? Your Word says that if we bring the tithe to the storehouse, You will open the windows of heaven and pour out a blessing that we are not able to contain."

However, if you carefully study the incidents in which people received unusual financial breakthroughs in the Bible and in the church, those are people who recognized their spiritual timing and gave sacrificially in the midst of their great pain or need. In the Old Testament they were commanded to bring tithes. In the New Testament there is no such commandment. Instead we are commanded to give, not just the usual but to go the extra mile. The New Testament teaching actually transcends the Old Testament commandment.

So the New Testament emphasizes giving more than the Old Testament. *The only offering that will bring a financial breakthrough is the offering that you give sacrificially, according to God's timing and direction.* Most often those times come in the midst of great financial struggle and lack. It is not easy to obey God at that time. God will bring to each of us those moments in our lives and we need to be obedient to His Spirit. If you have missed a chance, He will bring another opportunity. That may be the reason some people go through financial challenges on a regular basis. God is giving them opportunities to sow a seed to receive their breakthrough.

In the New Testament we read about the boy who gave five loaves and two fish to Jesus. Jesus blessed it and fed five thousand hungry men besides women and children. When you release something to God, He multiplies that and will give it back to us, not just to bless us but to be a blessing to others. In my own life and ministry, every time we received a financial breakthrough it was preceded by sacrificial giving.

There is only one way to go from one level to the next level financially. It is to give sacrificially. *If you want to step into the next level of your financial blessing, watch out for what God is saying to you and obey it.* Each level requires a higher level of sacrifice. I started with sowing twenty cents by faith and now I am beyond the thousand-dollar limit in my one-time giving. It hurt when I gave my first thousand dollars offering. As I continued to use that faith muscle, it got stronger and stronger and now it is not painful anymore. I would encourage you to do the same. God is waiting for you to step out and believe for the unusual.

I have given away cars, motorbikes, furniture, clothing, and helped build houses, and more, according to God's guidance. He blessed me each time I needed those things in my own life. It was not easy to obey God when He asked me to give away some of those things. I had to go through great mental struggles to give away something that was very precious to me. You cannot expect to reap from where you have not sown. When you sow, make sure you sow the best you have and not the used and broken.

SPIRIT-LED GIVING

I know believers who follow the letter of the law and tithe their money, time, even space to a church and still have not seen a financial breakthrough. Tithing is an Old Testament principle, first practiced by the father of our faith, Abraham. I have never seen a single person who was blessed abundantly just because they paid their tithes. You will not find an example of this in the Bible or present day. People who are blessed more give more than tithes.

Still others give randomly, to anyone or any place they feel like giving. Hindus, Muslims and some Christians throw coins at temples, mosques, and churches while they are driving by! One of the reasons Christians in India do not receive a financial harvest is that they do not take their giving seriously enough. That kind of giving is not Spirit-led.

Spirit-led giving is another principle that is mentioned in both the Old Testament and in the New Testament that brought great financial miracles to many individuals in the Bible. We are commanded to be led by the Spirit. In how many areas of our life do we need to be led by the Spirit? Either every area or none. That means *we are supposed to be led by the Spirit in the area of giving.*

When we try to do things on our own we get into trouble. Jesus said without Him we can do nothing. Without being led by His Spirit, nothing we do will prosper. I have many experiences in life and ministry of trying to do various things and expecting God to bless it. I was trying my own way and time to accomplish God's purpose. I fell into deeper debt and discouragement as a result.

The Bible says,

> "For as many as are led by the Spirit of God, these are sons (children) of God" (Romans 8:14).

The way outlined by Scriptures to receive financial miracles is sowing by faith when the Holy Spirit tells you to do so. If I can say it another way, it is giving when God says to give, and to whom He says to give and how much He says to give. This is Spirit-led giving or sacrificial giving.

The reason God has me writing this book is to encourage believers who have been tithing and giving generously, but are not moving into the next level in their finances. Abraham was a man of faith and a Spirit-led giver. God did not require him to pay tithes, even though he was a giver. We do not see him tithing before or after that one incident. For Abraham, tithing originated in faith, not the law.

Most believers tithe because of the law or they believe it is a commanded practice in the Bible, so they bring themselves under a curse by remaining under the law. When Abraham met Melchizedek, he was led by God to give a tithe to him. How do I know that he was led by God? There was no requirement prior to that to give tithes. The Bible says,

> "For it is God who works in you both to will and to do for His good pleasure" (Philippians 2:13).

Abraham was not following a written Word of God, for there was no written Word during his lifetime. Abraham lived and fulfilled his purpose by listening to the voice of God at each pivotal point and season in his life. We can do the same.

God's Word remains forever. He can't change His own principles; they are written in stone. If He made changes like that, it wouldn't be just. Paying tithes alone or going to church three times a week is not enough for us to accomplish our purpose or reach our potential in the Lord.

We need to work and be willing to get our hands dirty. How many of you have seen musicians in concert or on TV and wished you could play an instrument like they do? I have. But later I realized that they spent most of their life working with that instrument before they could play like that. If I wish that would happen to me overnight because I pay my tithe, forget it. Many Christians wait a long time doing nothing, attempting nothing and then blame God for not giving them any miracles and not blessing them.

I am not saying you should not give tithes. If God tells you to do it, then do it. What I am saying is this: Don't stop there. You need to be growing in your giving just as you grow in other areas of life. It's up to us which financial level we want to stay at. *After you pay your tithe, God will give you an idea in your heart and you need to get out there and put it to work.* He will help you and give you favor with people. But, whether you are a Christian or a non-Christian, you need to work and spend time on your area of expertise.

FOUR INGREDIENTS THAT DETERMINE YOUR FINANCIAL HARVEST

To receive the harvest you are expecting when you sow a seed, there are specific factors integral to the process of sowing and reaping. No farmer receives the same amount of harvest, even if they sow the same amount of seed on adjacent pieces of lands.

One of Jesus' most famous parables is the parable of the sower and the seed. This one parable contains some great spiritual truths concerning the kingdom.

Then He spoke many things to them in parables, saying:

> "Behold, a sower went out to sow. And as he sowed, some seed fell by the wayside; and the birds came and devoured them. Some fell on stony places, where they did not have much earth; and they immediately sprang up because they had no depth of earth. But when the sun was up they were scorched, and because they had no root they withered away. And some fell among thorns, and the thorns sprang up and choked them. But others fell on good ground and yielded a crop: some a hundredfold, some sixty, some thirty. He who has ears to hear, let him hear! (Matthew 13:3-9).

There are four major focal points in this parable: the sower, the seed, the ground, and the harvest. In truth, this parable is about the Word and how it works in different hearts of people. Jesus is using a natural principle of sowing and reaping to reveal a spiritual mystery. It is not just about the Word and the results of preaching; first of all, it is about sowing and reaping.

Verse 8 says, "But others fell on good ground and yielded a crop: some a hundredfold, some sixty, some thirty." Note that the seed that was planted in the good ground yielded a crop of various sizes: some thirty, sixty, or a hundredfold. Sowing good seed in the good ground alone does not guarantee a hundredfold return.

Many precious saints have been supporting good ministries for years. They sow into that good ground faithfully every month, but they do not see any supernatural increase in their own finances. They receive only the thirtyfold miracle. Thirtyfold is the minimum return.

I began to study this, and asked, "Lord, why did some seed that was sown in the good ground yielded only thirtyfold?" Some people I know stopped supporting some ministries because they did not receive the financial miracle they were expecting. I believe some people do not receive anything, even though they sow into good ground. Even their thirtyfold harvest is stolen by the enemy and they do not even know it. The Lord began to open my eyes and show me why we sow into good ground, but do not receive a hundredfold return in every instance.

He began to teach me the factors involved one by one: factors that determine the size of a particular harvest. *There is a way that you and I can know the level of harvest (not the amount) we are going to receive when we sow the seed.* That way is through understanding the four factors that determine the harvest: faith, timing, ground and the seed itself.

FAITH

When you sow a financial seed to someone in the kingdom, *the most important thing is not the amount, but the amount of faith you needed to sow that seed.* That means if you gave 100 dollars when you had a thousand dollars it did not require much faith, but it requires much faith to sow the whole amount or at least half of it.

The level of faith you exercised when you gave, determines the greatness of your harvest. Many people sow sporadically and do not exercise their faith. In Genesis, Isaac sowed during famine and received a hundredfold return. It takes faith to sow in famine. Most people do not sow in famine. They will try to survive by eating the seed instead.

We saw in previous chapters how people of God gave in their time of need and received a mighty harvest.

You can sow one dollar and receive a thousand or ten thousand dollars as a harvest. This depends on the faith that was exercised in the giving. God had only one Son and He gave that Son and received 3,000 sons and daughters on the fiftieth day. These were His firstfruits.

IT IS IMPOSSIBLE TO PLEASE GOD WITHOUT FAITH

The Bible says it is impossible to please God without faith (Hebrews 11:6) Faith is the substance of things we hope for and the evidence of things not seen. That means that when we go to God in prayer, we need to go with the substance of things we are hoping for and with evidence of things we have not seen yet.

INTENTIONALITY

When you sow your financial seed, you need to know why you are sowing it. On what scriptural basis are you sowing that seed? Next, you need to know what you are hoping for as a result of your sowing. Then, you need to have evidence, right here, about the harvest you are expecting. What are you believing for? This can be in written form, but it must be something you have not yet seen with your natural eyes. It would build our faith if we recorded these intentions in a journal and kept track of the way God moved. Looking back at that would be encouraging to us and to others.

GOD GIVES US THE SEED

God is the One who gives us the seed to the sow (2 Corinthians 9:10). That means you need to listen and sow the amount that God directs you to sow. Since He is the One who provides you with the seed, He is also the One who provides the harvest. All that we must provide is our obedience.

1) God gives the seed.
2) He chooses the ground.

3) He gives the harvest.

4) He gives us the faith.

When God asks us to sow a seed or to do something, it will always require faith to do it. The Bible says, "Whatever is not from faith is sin" (Romans 14:23b).

That means, if we do not sow in faith, it is sin. If it did not require our faith, it is not pleasing to the Lord. We will not get a hundredfold harvest.

Most of the time, God will ask us to sow a certain amount of seed (money or possibly resources) that seems unreasonable into unexpected grounds. We will kick and scream. Our immediate obedience is necessary for a hundredfold harvest. God knows what He is doing. Our obedience is the springboard that releases His power and blessing. When we obey, He responds. Our resources can refer to just about anything: our time, our talents, our gifts, our possessions (cars, boats, land): anything at all. God will use it.

The Bible says,

"Those who sow in tears shall reap in joy" (Psalm 126:5).

God knows that sowing time is a weeping time, because it will hurt when we give out of faith. All our natural means are stretched to the limit but not broken.

TIMING

The second factor that determines the amount of harvest is the time you sow the seed. In the natural there is a sowing time and harvest time. God said, "As long as the earth remains, seed time and harvest…shall not cease" (Genesis 8:22).

There will be times in which you will sow in the spirit for a while and not receive any harvest. You might wonder why. Do not worry about it;

you are in a sowing season. You are storing up your harvest and when your account is full, it will come down as rain. Solomon said in Ecclesiastes 11 that when the clouds were full of rain, it would fall down on the earth (Ecclesiastes 11:3).

God is the One who determines the seedtime and harvest. Even in the natural, man cannot decide the sowing time and harvest. The farmer must wait for the right time to sow the seed. You cannot sow in winter. He must wait until the weather permits him to sow. If a principle is true in the natural, it's also true in the spiritual. God decides when to have you sow, and when to give you a harvest.

There are times when you will receive an immediate harvest and other times, the harvest will arrive in due season. Please read the following scriptures:

Do not be weary in well-doing (Galatians 6: 9)

The reaper will overtake the sower (Amos 9:13)

The farmer waits patiently for former and the latter rain.

> "Therefore be patient, brethren, until the coming of the Lord. See how the farmer waits for the precious fruit of the earth, waiting patiently for it until it receives the early and latter rain" (James 5:7).

You need to sow when God asks you to sow. The Holy Spirit will tell you to sow a certain amount of seed. When He does, your immediate obedience is required to get the maximum harvest. Many people go back and forth; they are wishy-washy or double-minded in their giving. They ponder, "I do not know whether it is God's will or even if it is God who is telling me to give this. I never gave this much before. I could really use this money to pay off a bill." Their flesh will come up with all kinds of excuses and miss God's timing.

Usually when God tells you to sow, it is when you are in a financial crunch. At other times He will ask you to give everything you have. God will tell you to sow in the most unusual times and in the most unusual circumstances. God will tell you to sow the most unusual amount and ask you to give to the least expected person or ministry. Why? Because He has an unusual harvest in mind for you.

One of the most famous Bible verses ever is John 3:16. God had only one begotten Son and when the fullness of time came, He gave that Son to die on the cross. It is noteworthy that it says that when God gave His Son. He waited for the right time, meaning when the right time came in the Spirit. That is why the Bible says,

> "When the fullness of the time came, God sent forth His Son, born of a woman, born under the law" (Galatians 4:4, ASV).

God knew the spiritual timing and when to send His Son. He knew the harvest of His giving before He gave His Son. As a result, God reaped a family that is made up of millions and millions of people. That is the power of a seed sown at the right time and during the right season.

GROUND

When you sow a seed in the natural you always look for the appropriate ground (soil) for that seed to grow. Different kinds of seeds require different types of ground. You cannot sow any kind of seed in any kind of soil. If you do, you will receive any kind of harvest, or possibly no harvest at all.

You should listen to the voice of the Holy Spirit and sow in the ground He tells you to sow in. Just because a ministry is large, it does not mean you have to sow a large amount into it. You must ask Holy Spirit what you should give and obey Him.

The parable of the sower tells us about four different kinds of soil, which represent the hearts of people.

1) The Wayside

The wayside represents those people who sow their seeds randomly and without preparation and expectation. They know they need to give but they do not take it seriously. When a farmer prepares to sow, he spends a lot of time preparing the ground and preserving the seed.

When you give, you need to prepare for it and take it seriously. Your giving is a holy thing to God. As we read before, our giving is important to God. In India when it is time to give, many people offer the least amount of cash they have in their possession in the basket.

If we sow by the wayside, there is no harvest and the enemy will eat our seed as soon as we sow them. You should not give your financial seed to just anyone. You could erroneously give your alms to those who really don't deserve it. Some who are begging are not true beggars; they are just trying to scam people.

2) The Stony Place

Stony places represent those people whose hearts are hardened toward people and God. Do not give to those people who will not appreciate your gift. As Jesus said, "Do not throw your pearls before swine" (Matthew 7:6).

Stony places represent those people who have hardened their hearts toward God. They are not productive. They talk about doing great things, but they produce no lasting fruit. When someone talks about giving they will show excitement, but when the time comes to give they will retreat.

3) The Thorny Places

Thorny places are those people whose hearts are pressured by the cares of this world. They are easily offended and inwardly bitter toward God and people. They would like to grow and produce fruit but outside pressures are so great, they are unable to live the kingdom life they would like to live. That is why Jesus said that when you bring your offering and remember that your brother has something against you, you should leave the offering and go and be reconciled with your brother (Matthew 5:23-24).

They are not happy to give but do so only out of obligation and necessity. The Bible says the Lord loves a cheerful giver. We should not give grudgingly. Freely we have received freely give.

4) The Good Ground

Good ground represents those people who are serving God happily and with a heart of integrity. They represent soil that has been prepared to produce good fruit. We will produce an abundant harvest when we sow in the right time, in obedience to God.

When you give in obedience to the voice of God, you do not get to choose the ground unless He tells you where to sow. When God tells you to sow in a particular place, it will always be good ground. He is the One who determines the harvest.

God chooses the ground and tells you where and how much to sow. When you give a gift or special offering, you have the freedom to choose the ground and ask God how much you should sow. Most of the time, God will tell us the amount and the ground before we sow.

Good ground is those whose hearts are pure and pliable, willing to obey God and ready to receive the Word. According to Jesus there are four types of hearts. He differentiates them on the basis of receptivity to the Word of God.

THE SEED

In the natural, if you sow good seeds your harvest will be good. If you sow seeds that are not good and unhealthy, they will not grow well and will not produce a good harvest. The better the seed, the better the harvest. *The quality of the seed determines the quality of the harvest.*

In my experience, whenever I needed houses, cars, clothing, anything at all, God brought them to me. Whenever I moved (and we have moved thirteen times in the last fifteen years) to a new city or country, I have never had to look into the Apartment Finder for a place to live. Why? Because I have sown into that area: into many people's lives and God is faithful to bring the harvest each time I have a need.

In the natural, if you sow papaya seeds you will reap papayas and not mangoes. Many people think differently in the spirit. They sow mango seeds and expect apples. What I mean by that is that they sow money without any preparation or forethought on their end, and then expect what they need in their life to show up at their door.

Just because you sowed money does not mean you will reap a car. If you want a car, give away your old car or sow a seed to someone who needs a car and write the genetic code for your seed to receive a car. If you need a house, sow into someone who needs a house or help someone build a house. Again, *I want to say that you cannot expect to reap where you have not sown.* All truths are parallel, whether in the natural or in the spirit.

As I said earlier, in the natural you cannot expect an apple from a papaya seed. In the spirit, you can sow money intentionally and expectedly towards something you are believing God to do for you. It can be sown toward material things like houses, cars, jobs, money, or better yet, for spiritual blessings. Money is a common seed that has the ability to reproduce what you desire and believe God for when you sow it in faith.

CHAPTER - 11

WHY OUR TITHING DOESN'T WORK?

God has taken me to more than thirty-five countries and met believers from over fifty countries. 99.9% of all believers I know are in survival mode or financially strained. This bothers me a lot. Why don't believers prosper? Many of them are under the stress of huge debt. I said to myself, there must be something wrong with the financial system we have been following. This must change.

We hear from the pulpit that we should bring our tithes into the storehouse so God will open the windows of heaven and pour out such blessings that there won't be enough room to contain it. I have heard that only eight percent of believers actually give their tithes. If tithing worked as it is taught, why don't we have more people giving tithes? If something is working for the betterment of some people, then others would also try to follow what is working.

Don't you think if someone found a cure for cancer, everybody who has cancer would want to try it? Of course they would! People would travel from the ends of the earth to get that treatment for their cancer. If the tithing system that we follow cured our financial struggles, people would stand in line outside our church buildings to bring their tithes in.

I have not yet seen a believer who was blessed so much that they had no more room to contain their blessing. If anyone knows someone like that, please let me know. I would like to come and collect some of the blessing that they ran out of room to contain.

Instead, I have known believers who tithed, but still went through horrible financial crises. It broke my heart; some of them were our dear friends. I know it broke the heart of God as well. We have been taught that if we pay tithes, God will supernaturally bless us with financial abundance. That it is not so in most peoples' lives. Abraham was a rich person before he ever started tithing. Later, God incorporated that principle into the Law to bless the Levites.

Levites were the priestly tribe of Israel. This meant they did not receive any material inheritance when they came to the Promised Land; they had no land to support them. Instead, the Lord said, "The Lord is his inheritance" (Deuteronomy 10:9). The other eleven tribes were commanded to bring tithes of all their produce and any income they received from their labor. They brought it to the priests; and the priests divided it among themselves to support their families. The priests received the best of the best: Eleven times more than all the other tribes.

There was no direct promise of blessing for tithing when God gave the Law. In fact, there was no blessing mentioned for tithing until God spoke through the prophet Malachi about a thousand years later. Does that mean anyone who tithed before did not receive any blessings? Malachi was a contemporary of Nehemiah. God promised to open the windows of heaven and pour out a blessing that no room would contain. These blessings were not material, but spiritual and intellectual.

Tithing will keep you in survival mode unless you activate or put into action the dreams, ideas, insights and wisdom that God pours into your spirit after you tithe.

I slept on a cement floor for eighteen years on a single mat made from reeds. I did not have a mattress, a bicycle, or a football. We barely had enough to make it through each month. We never experienced the financial abundance God promised in His Word. My father could not take me out to eat or buy me some nice clothes.

Just as we did, I know many, maybe hundreds of families who pay their tithes to their churches faithfully but do not see financial miracles in their life. Like our family did, most of them go from one financial crisis to another. Others will stay on the same financial level for four or five decades. They live in the same house, and drive the same car for many years. They have dreams but do not know why they cannot advance from one level to the next financially.

Some of you might have doubts in your heart, wondering if this tithing principle really works or not. Many of you reading this story can relate to what I am discussing. You might be paying tithes regularly and giving offerings to other ministries, but you have not seen the kind of financial abundance the Bible is talking about. You might be wondering what could be wrong. Well, I'll tell you. *It is not working because we have been doing it incorrectly all these years.*

TWO KINDS OF TREES

Why doesn't our tithing work? What went wrong with it? How can something good not work for us? If God's Word is true, *and it is*, then why is it not working for us? According to the grace given to me, I will attempt to explain what went wrong. The reason we do not see the result of our tithing is because *most of us have been giving the wrong tithe*. If we give the wrong tithe, we won't receive the right result. It is like you're making the wrong payment and expecting your debtor to ease your debt. It's like making a car payment and expecting the mortgage to go down. That is ridiculous.

What do I mean by the wrong tithe? There are two tithing systems mentioned in the Bible. If we do not follow the right one, we will not receive the result we expect. Unfortunately, most believers follow the wrong system. Let me explain it a little bit more.

There were two trees in the garden of Eden, right? The Tree of Life and the Tree of the Knowledge of Good and Evil. Those trees represented two different systems. They represented two ways of life. One was God's way and the other one was of the enemy.

I believe there was a competition between God and the devil. The devil challenged God saying, "If you put my system in the garden, I am sure man will choose my way over Yours. He challenged God to see what man would do. They agreed to put two trees in the garden. One belonged to God and the other belonged to the devil. They waited to see from which tree man would choose to eat. One tree represented the way to life and the other one, death.

As you know, the devil deceived Adam and Eve; they chose from the wrong tree. As a result, man activated a fallen system, one which God never intended man would experience. We were not created to live by the knowledge of good and evil. We were created to live by the Spirit; the Bible calls it the law of the Spirit of life.

Those two trees represent those two systems. One is grace and the other one is law. One represented life and the other one, death. One represented the righteousness of God, the other one narcissistic self-righteousness. One represented the kingdom of God and the other one, religion. One represented trusting in God alone, and the other, self-reliance. One represented the way to life and the other one, the way to destruction.

One represents the children of God and the other, the children of the wicked one. One represented blessing and the other represented curse. One represents the children of light and the other the children of darkness. There are two kinds of money in this world: unrighteous mammon and righteous money.

God said that the day we ate from the Tree of the Knowledge of Good and Evil, we would *die*. That means that if there was any area dying in our life, we would be partaking in the fruit of the tree of good and evil in that area: Whether it was relationships, finances, or business, if death is at work that means we are operating under the system of good and evil or right versus wrong. We are eating of the wrong fruit and not choosing wisely.

We are supposed to partake from the Tree of Life daily. Everyone is working hard to make a better life and improve their living condition—without knowing what *life* is. We think life consists of the abundance of things we possess. So, the better material things we have, the better life we will have, right? Nope, not at all. That is a deception. Life comes only from one Person and that person is Jesus Christ. If we live with Jesus as our Source, we can live differently, eating from the Tree of Life daily.

"In Him was life, and the life was the light of men" (John 1:4). Jesus Himself is called Life. He also said, "I am the way, the truth, and the life" (John 14:6). Apart from Him there is no life. Stop chasing *a better life*, and start *chasing Life itself*, Jesus.

TWO KINDS OF TITHING

What does this have to do with tithing? Everything. There are two different tithing systems mentioned in the Bible. One is in accordance with the Tree of Life and the other one is in accordance with the Tree of the Knowledge of Good and Evil. Only if we tithe after the Tree of Life will we see the result of tithing; otherwise we will heap up curses upon ourselves instead.

Where did these two different tithing systems start? The first one started in Genesis 14 by the father of our faith, Abraham. He had a nephew called Lot, who separated from him and was living in Sodom. It was a wicked place. One day some kings came against Sodom and conquered it and took all the people captive, including Lot and his family. Someone who escaped, brought the news to Abraham and he decided to go after those kings in order to rescue his nephew and his family.

Abraham and his men fought the kings and won the battle. He brought back Lot, his family and all his possessions. On the way back from the battle, he had an unusual encounter with God. An encounter like nobody else had ever had before or after.

Melchizedek, the king of Salem, came out to meet Abraham. There is no reference to Melchizedek prior to this in the Bible. I am not sure how Abraham recognized who he was, unless he had some kind of access to the heavenlies or special discernment. Jesus mentions Abraham in John 8, saying that Abraham looked ahead to His coming and saw His day and "was glad" (John 8:56). That means he learned to access by faith what was only available to us through Jesus Christ.

> Then Melchizedek king of Salem brought out bread and wine; he was the priest of God Most High. And he blessed him and said: "Blessed be Abram of God Most High, possessor of heaven and earth; and blessed be God Most High, who has delivered your enemies into your hand." And he gave him a tithe of all (Genesis 14:18-20).

Melchizedek was a king and the priest of the Most High God. His name means "king of righteousness" after a place called "Peace" because *Salem* means "peace." Therefore it is, king of righteousness ruling over a territory called peace. That is powerful because those two attributes (righteousness and peace) are primary attributes of the kingdom of God (Romans 14:17).

Melchizedek came and brought bread and wine, which represents communion in the New Testament. They had communion together and he blessed Abraham (then called Abram). As a result, Abraham gave him a tithe of all he had. God did not ask Abraham for his tithe. There was no requirement for him to do it. Abraham gave it by faith, by the leading of the Holy Spirit, to acknowledge the One who was the Source of all his blessings.

That is the first system of tithing mentioned in the Bible. This is the one we are supposed to follow. We give tithes to acknowledge who is the

Source of all our blessings and victories. *We don't give to be blessed, we give because we are blessed.* Note that Melchizedek blessed Abraham first, before Abraham gave the tithe. That is what we should be doing.

For too long we have been tithing in the same way we use a slot machine or buy a lottery ticket. We have been giving it, hoping that someday we will be blessed, because we think someday God will open the windows of heaven and pour out some money, nice cars, or big houses into our lap, so that we could be really blessed—finally. That hasn't happened yet. Sorry to say, it will never happen, so stop waiting and wasting your life.

The first system of tithing is according to the order of Melchizedek. When we follow that system, we are tapping into the kingdom economy. One day the Holy Spirit asked me, "Abraham, do you know what Melchizedek did with the tithes he received from Abraham?"

I said, "I have no idea."

The Holy Spirit responded, "He took that tithe into heaven, into the treasury of the kingdom of heaven."

Every time you tithe according to the order of Melchizedek, you are bringing it to Him and in turn, He presents it to the treasury in heaven. You are storing your wealth where moths cannot eat, nor can thieves steal, as Jesus said in the Gospels. You are investing in the kingdom of God, just like you invest in this world's system by keeping money in a bank.

The second system of tithing was established through the Law of Moses. When the people of Israel came into the Promised Land and settled, God, through Moses, gave them instructions on every level on how to live and prosper in the land God gave them. As you know, there were twelve tribes and each one received a portion of the land as their inheritance, except the Levites. They were the priestly tribe. They did not receive an inheritance of land like the others because the Lord was their inheritance in addition to the offerings people brought.

Tithing was part of the offering they brought to the temple to give to the priests. The priests were supposed to receive it and use it to help the widows, strangers and the poor people of the land, mainly to provide them with food.

> When you have finished laying aside all the tithe of your increase in the third year—the year of tithing—and have given it to the Levite, the stranger, the fatherless, and the widow, so that they may eat within your gates and be filled, then you shall say before the Lord your God: "I have removed the holy tithe from my house, and also have given them to the Levite, the stranger, the fatherless, and the widow, according to all Your commandments which You have commanded me; I have not transgressed Your commandments, nor have I forgotten them" (Deuteronomy 26:12-13).

The people and priests stopped doing this and the priests began to misuse the tithes for their personal gain. There was no food for the widows and strangers, nor the poor (Malachi 3:8-10). The hungry began to cry out to God and He decided to have a conversation with the priests and the people of Israel. We read that conversation in the book of Malachi. This is a section in which Israel is demonstrating their disobedience; it is not a place from which we should take a doctrine for the New Testament church.

God was telling the people that they were robbing Him. He cared about the widows, strangers and the poor, but there was no food for them, so He told the people if you bring the tithes into the storehouse, there will be food in His house, He will open the 'windows' of heaven and pour out such blessing that there would not be enough room to contain it.

First of all, why would God open only the windows of heaven? I don't want Him to open just a window for me. I want to walk and live under an open heaven. You open a window to someone when you are not sure if that person is safe. You can't take much with you as you crawl through a window.

We read about windows of heaven, doors of heaven, and also an open heaven in the Bible. As a believer in Christ, we are supposed to live under an open heaven. In the New Testament we read about an open heaven, not just windows of heaven. When Jesus was baptized and came out of the water, the Bible says the heavens were opened (Matthew 3:16). From that day on, heaven never closed again; so we read about an open heaven in the rest of the New Testament.

When Jesus met Nathaniel, He told him from now on he would see heaven open and the angels of God ascending and descending on the Son of Man (John 1:51). In Revelation 4:1 we read about the door of heaven. Who is the door of heaven? Jesus said, "I am the door" (John 10:9). Jesus is the Door; we enter through Him.

If we give our tithes according to the Law, we will not receive any blessings; instead we will bring a curse upon our financial life. We do not follow the Law once we are saved by the blood of Jesus. Whenever we break a law, we become guilty and activate curses. That is the way God established the Mosaic Law in the Old Testament.

Jesus became a curse for us, to redeem us from the curse of the law (Galatians 3:13). Law represents the Tree of the Knowledge of Good and Evil. If you do good, then you will be blessed; but when you do one bad thing, everything collapses. How many of you agree that you don't want to be blessed based on your goodness? Instead, you want to be blessed based on God's goodness. As the Bible says, His goodness and mercy shall follow us all the days of our lives (Psalm 23:6).

Anytime we give tithes according to the law we are telling God, we want to be blessed based on our works, or our goodness. That is why we are fearful when we give. We are afraid that if we do not give, He is going to punish us and something bad will happen. That's what the law does: It brings fear of punishment. The law brings about the wrath of God (Romans 4:15). We tend to obey because of fear and the fear of punishment, rather than obeying God out of love.

Abraham gave tithes not because he was afraid he would lose everything if he didn't. He gave out of love, out of honor and gratitude. It was a symbol of acknowledgment of the Source of all his blessings. That's how we should be tithing. When we do that, we are partaking from the Tree of Life.

TITHING ACCORDING TO THE ORDER OF MELCHIZEDEK

When we tithe, we need to understand the order of Melchizedek. What is the order of Melchizedek? He is an eternal priest of God.

> "The Lord has sworn and will not relent, 'You are a priest forever according to the order of Melchizedek'" (Psalm 110:4).

There are two priesthood systems in the Bible. One is according to the Aaronic order and the second one is according to Melchizedek. The Aaronic priesthood ended when Jesus died on the cross and shed His blood for all humanity and the veil in the temple was torn in two. The Aaronic priesthood was set in place to foreshadow what Christ would put in place when He came through His life and His death on the cross. Once that was fulfilled, that Aaronic order become invalid.

On the other hand, the order of Melchizedek is eternal. He has no genealogy, beginning or end (Hebrews 7:3). Hebrews 6:20 says, "Where the forerunner has entered for us, even Jesus, having become High Priest forever according to the order of Melchizedek." According to the order of Melchizedek, tithing becomes an eternal principle of God. When you give with the right understanding and for the right reason, that tithe produces the right result.

Why did God allow Abraham to encounter Melchizedek when he was returning from the battle with all the spoils? There is a specific reason for that. There are two kinds of economies—the world's and the kingdom's. God orchestrated this encounter to teach Abraham about the kingdom of God's economy. God didn't want Abraham to depend on the spoils of the war, which represents this world's economy. When you return from a battle with all the spoils, there is great joy and jubilation. That's a normal response to a victory.

When he encountered Melchizedek, God revealed His kingdom, as well as its economy and culture, and the eternal priesthood of Jesus Christ to Abraham. When Abraham understood it, he gave back *all the spoils* to the king of Sodom. He did not touch even a sandal strap. That is the purpose of tithing: to acknowledge which economy we function under. Living in it and acknowledging the real Source of all our blessings is the heart of tithing.

> Now the king of Sodom said to Abram, "Give me the persons, and take the goods for yourself." But Abram said to the king of Sodom, "I have raised my hand to the Lord, God Most High, the Possessor of heaven and earth, that I will take nothing, from a thread to a sandal strap, and that I will not take anything that is yours, lest you should say, "I have made Abram rich"— except only what the young men have eaten, and the portion of the men who went with me: Aner, Eshcol, and Mamre; let them take their portion (Genesis 14:21-24).

We, as a family, tithed our entire life. We did not see much change in our financial life. We were scraping the bottom to survive from month to month. I was disappointed; and my wife was very stressed out about paying bills and buying food for the household. Though our income increased every year, there was no financial freedom. We were tithing according to the law and it did not bring the breakthrough we expected.

For a while I did not believe in tithing at all. We stopped giving tithes because it did not work for us. Instead I started to give offerings, and ended up giving more than ten percent. We started facing financial challenges as never before. For the first time in my life, my personal bank account went negative one month. I began to wonder what was going on. I asked all of our prayers partners to pray for us.

That's when the Holy Spirit began to open my understanding about Melchizedek and his life. Then, I received the revelation about the order of Melchizedek. One day I had only eighty dollars in my bank account. That was not enough to pay the bills at the end of the month nor to buy food. I was on a three day fast. On the evening of the third day, we went to church. Holy Spirit told me to give thirty dollars as a tithe, because I had received three hundred in the beginning of that month.

In obedience to the Holy Spirit, I gave that amount but I gave it differently this time. I wrote "according to the order of Melchizedek" on the offering envelope. When I prayed I said, "Lord, I bring this tithe according to the order of Melchizedek, the king and priest of the Most High God." During that time, I also read an article online about trading floors in heaven to where Melchizedek is actually in charge of the treasury room.

The next morning, I went to see one of my dear friends, who is actually a spiritual mother to me. When I was about to leave after our meeting, she said the Holy Spirit was nudging her to give me some money. I was scheduled to go to Bulgaria for a mission trip two days later.

She found her checkbook and began to write in it. She said, "This is not for ministry. I want to give it to you personally because you need money when you travel." I was curious to see the amount she was writing. It was for a thousand dollars. My heart began to rejoice. I couldn't believe what was happening. I just sowed thirty dollars the night before and within twenty-four hours I was receiving a multiplied harvest from the kingdom treasury. Thank You, Jesus!

I got in my car to drive home and I was rejoicing and crying because I couldn't believe what the Lord has done. I called my wife and said, "Tithing according to the order of Melchizedek works." I shared with her what had happened and she was in tears. I said, "Let's go and buy some food."

Thank You, Jesus for Your goodness. If you have been tithing according to the law and have not seen a financial breakthrough, I would recommend that you switch and give it according to the order of Melchizedek. It works. God will honor your giving and He will give you an abundant harvest.

I believe Abraham had a revelation from heaven when he met Melchizedek. Abraham understood that Melchizedek was the treasurer from heaven. How did he know that he was the king and priest of the Most High God is in charge of the treasury of heaven? I do not know. I believe it is by the Holy Spirit.

Tithing according to the order of Melchizedek is very sacred and honorable. We should not take it lightly. When we give, we are bringing our gift before Melchizedek in heaven; this adds seriousness and weight to the process. Tithing is not just a thoughtless ten percent off the top given to God because we have to do that. That kind of tithing is under the law. This kind of tithing requires faith and obedience.

When we give a tithe, God will pour out His ideas, insights, wisdom, favor, protection, productivity, opportunity, and divine connections from heaven. We need to put them to work or make use of them in order to prosper financially.

As a child I remember my dad talking about different ideas for business and buying cars, but He never took the steps to apply any of those ideas. I believe those ideas were given by God. Though he was a faithful tither and giver, he did not step out because of fear and other people's opinions. So, he stayed on the same financial level for a long time.

May the Lord help you receive this revelation in your spirit and practice it for the rest of your life. Everything the enemy has stolen from you and the generations before you, needs to be restored seven times. Believe and decree it by faith to make it manifest. When you give your tithe from now on, no longer do it under the law. Instead purposefully and intentionally, give it to the Lord "according to the order of Melchizedek" instead. Say this out loud, or write it on the offering envelope. You will see a definite difference.

CHAPTER - 12

SEVEN KINDS OF GIVING

There are different types of giving mentioned in the Bible and each of them bring different harvests, results and benefits. Unfortunately, most believers are not educated about this. They exercise the same type of giving all the time, expecting different harvests. It's like sowing apple seed and expecting to harvest oranges. That would never happen. Let's change that.

God instituted different types of giving in the Bible to meet different needs in our lives. Each of the types brings distinctive harvests to our lives. We are going to dig into the Word to learn more about these various types of giving and the benefits they bring.

I have mentioned seven types of giving, listed according to the order mentioned in the Bible. The first one is offerings.

1) Offerings

2) Firstfruits

3) Tithes

4) Alms

5) Vow Offerings

6) Blessings, Gifts, and Giving

7) Seed

Offerings: The Bible says in Genesis 4 that Cain and Abel each brought an offering to the Lord. Offering is a generic name for every other type of giving. This is what you give from your free will to God for His kingdom work. Offering is not the same as tithing, though that is what we usually call it. We can give offerings to special needs of ministries or individuals.

Firstfruits: The first type of giving mentioned in the Bible is firstfruits. This is not a surprise because it is literally the "first" fruit. Giving is an act of worship. God takes what we give and how we give it very seriously. That is why the Bible says God loves a cheerful giver. This means that the attitude of our hearts when we give is key to whether it will be accepted or rejected by God.

This was the case when the first two brothers brought an offering to the Lord. The Bible says Cain brought the fruit of the ground as an offering and Abel brought the firstborn of his flock and of their fat. The Lord accepted Abel's offering and rejected Cain's. Cain became jealous and angry and killed his brother. The cause of the first murder on earth was a reaction to another person's giving. There are two things that make people jealous: one is our giving and another the blessings we receive from the Lord. Not everybody is happy to see us blessed.

There is another powerful verse that talks about giving and its blessings. "Honor the Lord with your possessions, and with the firstfruits of all your increase; so your barns will be filled with plenty, and your vats will overflow with new wine" (Proverbs 3: 9-10).

When we honor the Lord with our possessions and firstfruits He has promised that He will bless our barns with plenty. This verse also shows that before we give, we need to have possessions and firstfruits. We have to have a barn used for collecting our harvest. We have to prepare the land, sow the seeds, protect it from enemies and wait for the harvest. God will then give us a bountiful harvest.

Vats are the places where the grapes are brought to make wine. We do our part by bringing in the grapes and God will bless the work of our hands—He gives us a harvest that's more than we expected. We should never wait around for a miracle; instead we should be faithful and work hard with what we have. Then God will entrust us with more. When you do a job, your first salary is your first fruit, and according to this idea, all of it belongs to God. This might not work for everyone, so it should be Spirit-led.

Tithes: The tithe is a tenth of your income, which we should now give to the order of Melchizedek. If you get ten dollars, one dollar belongs to God. *We do not give the tithe. It belongs to God* and if we do not return it to Him we are stealing from Him. Tithing was started by Abraham, the father of our faith. The tithe comes from a heart that is filled with the faith of God. It takes faith to tithe. I have written more about it in a previous chapter. See Deuteronomy 12:6; 26:12-13.

Alms: This is what we give to the poor. You give alms to store up treasures in heaven (Luke 12:33). Every believer should give to the poor. The Bible says, those who give to the poor lend to the Lord (Proverbs 19:17). Isaiah 58:10-12 speaks at length about the benefits of giving to the poor.

Vow Offerings: Many times people make a vow offering, based on what they promised to do when God met a certain condition or answered a prayer. We read about Samuel's mother Hannah making a vow to the Lord, saying that if He gave her male child (which He did), she would give that child back (which she did) to God for His service (1 Samuel 1:11). That's an example of a vow offering.

Blessings, Gifts, and Giving: We give gifts or bless people and family members on special occasions or to show our appreciation for what someone has done for us.

Seed: I have written extensively about seed in chapter 14 called "Seed and Bread." They reflect two kinds of income.

NATURAL AND SPIRITUAL GIVING

Money does not grow on trees. Money needs to be invested to grow. When you invest there is a certain amount of risk involved. In the natural, people invest in real estate, the stock market, and other kinds of investments. When you invest, there is no guarantee that you are going to make any money. It is done by faith. You can either lose all your money or make more.

That is the natural way of investing. Unfortunately, many Christians have more faith in the world and its systems than in the kingdom of God. I know many precious believers who lost their money, some of them even went bankrupt and lost everything. That is not God's will for anybody. I have not seen anyone become bankrupt because they gave to God and His work. That is the next type of giving.

Spiritual investment is the most secure investment I have ever seen. When God tells you to give something to someone, your immediate response will determine your next harvest or the next season of your financial life.

When you invest into the kingdom of God, you can be sure that you will not lose that money. The Bible says that if you cast your bread up on the waters, it will come back to you (Ecclesiastes 11.1).

> Give generously, for your gifts will return to you later. Divide your gifts among many, for in the days ahead you yourself may need much help. When the clouds are heavy, the rains come down; when a tree falls, whether south or north, the

die is cast, for there it lies. If you wait for perfect conditions, you will never get anything done. God's ways are as mysterious as the pathway of the wind and as the manner in which a human spirit is infused into the little body of a baby while it is yet in its mother's womb. Keep on sowing your seed, for you never know which will grow—perhaps it all will (Ecclesiastes11:1-6, TLB).

There is no risk involved when you invest in the kingdom. The only risk is if you do not obey when God tells you to give; that's when you lose what you have. If you hold on to what you have, God will take that and give it to someone who already has much.

Today, Christians have more faith in the system of the world than in the Word of God. They put their money in stocks and mutual funds. They lose their money and then they cry for God to help them. If they had first listened to God and given to His kingdom, they would have received a sure return.

Kingdom economy does not go through fluctuations or inflation. It stays the same from the beginning. It is secured by the Word of God which never changes.

I know ministers who used to visit our home, even before I was born and kept coming until I was thirty years old. These ministers came every month, regularly and my father blessed them financially. Some of those ministers did not have the right heart, but my father blessed them anyway. We are commanded to give, not judge.

For years it seems there was no return for all the giving he had done. His finances did not go from one level to the next. Then my mom passed away and he came to the United States. He met another woman in a church and married her. She was a U.S. citizen (originally from India), she had never married before and worked all her life and saved all her money. She had at least a million dollars in savings!

The only problem was that my dad did not know this woman had breast cancer. She passed away only a couple of years after their marriage, leaving all she had to him. Then he married yet another woman. She was a college professor; she had never been married before and was saving all her salary. They both retired and received pensions from the government. My father received social security from the U.S. government because his second wife was a U.S. citizen.

As we just read, when the clouds are filled with the water, they will empty upon the earth. Every time you give, you are filling your cloud; and when it is full, it will rain down.

> "For whoever who has will be given more, and they will have an abundance. Whoever does not have, even what they have will be taken from them" (Matthew 25:29, NIV).

There is no one who ever obeyed God in the area of giving who did not receive something in return. It may not come back in the time we expect, but when the clouds are full, they will empty their rain, and in due season you will reap.

According to the Bible, the only way to receive is to give. Jesus said, "Give, and it will be given to you" (Luke 6:38). In Acts, it says it is better to give than to receive (Acts 20:35). Giving is the nature of God. The Bible says God is love and love always gives (John 3:16).

CHAPTER - 13

SUPERNATURAL MILLIONAIRES

When you read the Bible, you notice something powerful and also very important in relation to ministers and believers and their financial lives. Ministers like Elijah, Elisha, and Paul made others rich (millionaires by today's standards) through supernatural means. There is an anointing that God is releasing upon the body of Christ now to become millionaires to fulfill kingdom purposes.

How do you supernaturally create millionaires? Of course, the secret is revealed in the Bible. You can go from rags to riches overnight when the supernatural power of God works in your life to create wealth. God said that it is He who gives power to create wealth (Deuteronomy 8:18) He blesses you, so that you can become a blessing to someone else.

There are several incidents in the Bible in which God's people went from being broke to rich in a matter of hours. This grace of God is available for you to become wealthy too. However, you have to believe it in order for this to manifest in your life. God wants to raise up super-wealthy believers in different nations for the purpose of establishing His covenant in those countries. You cannot remain poor and establish God's covenant here on earth. Without money you will only be able to talk about doing it.

How did Adam and Abraham become wealthy? Adam received the entire earth from God his Father as an inheritance. All of the wealth God created that we read about in Genesis is still on earth. Nobody has taken anything out of our planet; it only changed hands and locations. He owned all of the wealth that existed at that time. God told him about gold and precious stones. That's real wealth, and it is one of the foundations of the kingdom economy.

God called Abraham in Genesis 12. In Genesis 13, we see a wealthy Abraham. How did he become so rich in cattle, gold, silver, and servants? It was supernatural. Kings donated resources to him. The land was being overwhelmingly filled by their wealth.

When the Israelites came out of Egypt, they emerged with great riches. God told them to ask their neighbors for precious jewels and clothes, and they plundered the Egyptians. They were abused and misused for almost four hundred years. They didn't know what they were missing until the day of redemption came. Today, there are millions of believers who are not aware of what really belongs to them.

We see many people in the Bible who became supernaturally wealthy overnight: Joseph, David, the widows in Elijah's and Elisha's time, Esther, Ruth, and all of the people of Israel when they came out of Egypt. These are only some of the examples. This supernatural grace is still available in the kingdom of God to those who believe.

If our present-day ministers had empowered believers to become wealthy by training them to start businesses and engage in local politics, the United States wouldn't be in the shape it is in now. We would have had a different outcome. I believe with all my heart that it is not too late to start over.

KEY TO FINANCIAL MIRACLES

First of all, I want you to know that miracles are for those who are really hopeless and cannot help themselves. This is another reason why tithe-paying believers do not receive financial abundance. Do you remember the first time you gave your tithe? It took all the faith you had. Your hands might have been sweating when you wrote that first check. It could have been a dramatic experience. After you gave, you might have felt the peace of God flood your heart. You probably felt joy as never before. God honored your faith and blessed you. You might also have gone from one financial level to the next and experienced miracle-working power in your finances.

What happened after a while? You began to lose the fear, and the anxiety that you initially had and tithing became second nature, a sort of quick thing you did with little thought. It did not require any faith any longer, but what you did not know was this: There was no more miracle-working power of God working in your finances anymore either. When you no longer exercise faith to give your tithe, you will remain on the same financial level you were on when you first began—until you begin exercising faith again.

Until then, other than occasional bonuses or raises (those are just dimes and nickels anyway), there will be no substantial increase in your income. God wants to multiply everything we have. He is a God of multiplication (Genesis 1:28). The secret to a financial miracle is the same as in the case of any other miracle.

There is only one type of giving mentioned in the Bible that unlocks immediate financial blessings. That is when you give by faith, out of your lack, in obedience to God's direction. Sometimes it is when you give everything you have. It is difficult to understand and receive this teaching in the natural mind. That is why I asked you to receive it in your spirit. Make it a matter of prayer and let the Holy Spirit teach this to you. God will be faithful to help you understand and learn how to exercise everything you need to prosper in His kingdom.

When you tithe, God will create a situation in your life in which you will be faced with a financial challenge that you will not have enough money to meet your need. You will think: *This money is not enough to meet my need. God said if I tithed He would bless me financially. Why is this happening?* You may begin to doubt in your heart, wondering if what God said is true.

In response, God will tell you is to take some of that money, from which you do not have enough of already, and sow it as a sacrificial seed by faith. You will be worried and tense about your financial situation. Your fear will tell you, *It won't be enough for both things; don't do it.*

All of a sudden, the Spirit of the Lord will tell you to give that money away to someone, or He will ask you to sow it by faith. *Your financial breakthrough for the next season of your life depends on that single seed you sow in obedience to the voice of the Holy Spirit.*

It does not matter how much it is. It can be a penny or a million dollars. God will tell you the amount, according to your situation and circumstance.

We see an example of this in 2 Kings 4: 8-17. Here we see a woman whose was "great woman" (KJV). Every time Elisha passed through her town, she would invite him to come and have food at her house. Every time he came through the town of Shunem, Elisha went to her house, ate food, and rested.

However, this great woman had a great need. Great people have great needs. Although she was rich, the woman did not have a child. Even though she gave food and blessed others, and also gave to the man of God, nothing happened.

One day she decided to do something remarkable. She got her husband's permission to build and furnish an upper room—just to accommodate the man of God. Now, whenever Elisha came to town, he could eat and rest for a few days in a room built especially for him.

This was very unusual giving. One day Elisha came by and was staying in her house, in the newly built guest room. Suddenly something happened. The Holy Spirit dropped a thought into the prophet's heart. Elisha called her and asked her what could do for her. Think about that. Although the prophet had eaten at her house many times, he never asked her about her need before. To give some food to someone does not require much faith. If you have a family, you prepare food to eat every day; and if a guest comes, you can easily share part of your meal or prepare some extra.

This time she went the extra mile and did something that was not required of her. She allowed herself and her household to be inconvenienced by adding an extra room to her house. Construction work is not fun; it interrupts our normal routine and lifestyle. On top of that, it takes a lot of money to add an extra room to your house.

This woman took a step of faith. She did not know how long this man would keep coming by. She did not have any particular relationship with the prophet, other than that she had noticed he was a man of God in the first place. I believe the Holy Spirit put that desire in her heart to prepare a room for the prophet. God knew how He wanted to bless her, but required an act of faith from her first.

The woman sowed a seed that was big enough to be noticed by God, and her seed produced a response from the supernatural realm, which manifest itself as a desire in the heart of the man of God to ask the woman about her need. His servant told him that she had no children and her husband was old. The prophet told her that by the next year, she would embrace a son. She received a child, as promised by the man of God.

In my own life, when I sowed a particular seed into a particular ministry or person all of a sudden, I will be noticed by them. Suddenly doors will be opened for me that otherwise would never have been opened.

Although they knew me and I had known them for many years, a seed that I sowed by faith in obedience to the Holy Spirit still opened new doors of favor for me in those relationships.

How many of you have a need in your life and the money you have is not enough to meet that need?

OTHER BIBLICAL EXAMPLES

The people who received an immediate financial breakthrough or other breakthroughs were those who gave by faith out of their need, or when they did not have much at all, or were struggling to survive.

In 1 Kings 17 we read another story about a widow. The people of Israel had turned away from God; they began to worship other gods under the leadership of King Ahab. Elijah came and proclaimed a drought. As a result, there was famine in Israel; and food and water became scares.

God took care of Elijah. (God always takes care of His servants in the midst of famine or any problem.) God provided Elijah with bread and water. Elijah was staying by the Brook Cherith and ravens were bringing him food. Eventually, the brook dried up and God told him to go to Zarephath, where God commanded a widow to provide for Elijah.

We need to understand the situation this widow was in when we read this story. She had a son. When Elijah met her at the gate of the city, she was collecting sticks to make her last meal. The next step for them was death by starvation. Elijah asked her to give him a cup of water. I believe the reason he did not ask her for food might have been because he saw her impoverished condition. He might have doubted himself, thinking, *how can I ask for food from this woman when she looks like she has not eaten any in the last two months?*

But Elijah remembered the promise of God and decided to rely on it, rather than what he saw in his immediate circumstance. What he saw with his natural eyes was discouraging, but when he looked at the promises of God through his spiritual eyes, he saw abundance.

As she was going to get him some water, he asked her to bring him some food. She replied,

> "As the Lord your God lives, I do not have bread, only a handful of flour in a bin, and a little oil in a jar; and see, I am gathering a couple of sticks that I may go in and prepare it for myself and my son, that we may eat it, and die" (1 Kings 17:12).

Elijah declared to her what he saw in the spirit. He said,

> "Do not fear; go and do as you have said, but make me a small cake from it first, and bring it to me; and afterward make some for yourself and your son. For thus says the Lord God of Israel: 'The bin of flour shall not be used up, nor shall the jar of oil run dry, until the day the Lord sends rain on the earth'" (1 Kings 17:13-14).

Praise be unto the Living God! The key phrase in the above verse is "first." Elijah said if you put God first, you can have the promise. If you put God first and obey His Word, then the promise is yours.

Elijah said to make his cake "first," meaning she could not wait to see the evidence and then believe. She needed to step out in faith *first*, give him a cake *first,* and then the miracle would happen. She obeyed and brought him a cake *first.*

We need to put God and His promises first. We cannot wait to see the evidence and then obey God. That is not faith. Faith is the evidence of things not seen and the assurance of things hoped for (Hebrews 11:1).

Why did God ask such a person to provide for His man? She did not even have enough to take care of herself and her son. That is the way God works. If you need a miracle, you need to exercise your faith. *The key to a financial miracle is giving out of your need by faith.*

I believe her house became a rescue center for the community during the famine. Either that, or she might have started a pancake house. The more she used the flour and oil, the more they increased.

She went from one financial level to the next by releasing what she had in faith into the hands of God. It was not the amount she gave that determined her miracle, but the faith she had to use when she gave. In another sense, she was giving her and her son's very own life away.

The world calls it "risk-taking"; we call it operating in faith, in obedience to God's voice.

Again, *the only giving that produces a financial miracle is the seed you sow sacrificially when you do not have enough, in obedience to the voice of God.*

The only giving that will take you from one level to another is giving sacrificially. Tithing will bless and protect what you do. The person who started tithing in the Old Testament was Abraham. He was already rich before he started tithing. Many people tithe to become rich. But let me tell you, only the people who have something can tithe.

THE STORY OF ABRAHAM

The Bible says Abraham was a rich man.

> "Abram was very rich in livestock, in silver, and in gold" (Genesis 13:2).

Many think Abraham started tithing and became rich as a result. That is not true according to the Bible.

He was a rich man way before he ever started tithing. He had a habit of giving everything he had to God and helping others. *That was the secret of His wealth.* God gave him a son, after waiting for twenty-five years. God asked him to offer his son as a sacrifice. Abraham obeyed God's voice and inherited God's promise.

He gave the one son he had and now he has millions of sons. We are also called the children of Abraham. God said to him "your descendants shall possess the gate of their enemies" (Genesis 22:17b).

Sacrificial giving will create the financial miracle you need in your life. When you give sacrificially, it gets heaven's attention. It does not matter how small or large the sacrifice is. The only offering that gets registered in heaven is the offering that gets registered in your heart.

How many offerings have you given that you can remember? Not very many. I do not remember every time I tithed but I remember very clearly each time I gave out of my need because that cost me something. Remember, it is the amount of faith you needed to sow the seed, the ground, and the timing that determines the amount of harvest.

There are particular moments in your life when God will speak to you to give to someone in some way: You need to obey that immediately without any delay.

Jacob was the second son of Isaac. He inherited the promise and blessing of his father through subterfuge. He had to flee from his home for fear of his brother Esau. On the way, he had a dream in which God spoke to him about his future.

> And behold, the Lord stood above it and said: "I am the Lord God of Abraham your father and the God of Isaac; the land on which you lie I will give to you and your descendants. Also your descendants shall be as the dust of the earth; you shall spread abroad to the west and the east, to the north and the south; and in you and in your seed all the families of the earth shall be blessed. Behold, I am with you and will keep you wherever you go, and will bring you back to this land; for I will not leave you until I have done what I have spoken to you (Genesis 28:13-15).

Jacob made a commitment to God at that time, saying he would pay tithes of everything he received from God.

> Then Jacob made a vow, saying, "If God will be with me, and keep me in this way that I am going, and give me bread to eat and clothing to put on, so that I come back to my father's house in peace, then the Lord shall be my God. And this stone which I have set as a pillar shall be God's house, and of all that You give me I will surely give a tenth to You" (Genesis 28:20-22).

After a few years, God had blessed Jacob and he had become very wealthy. He had many cattle and herds. God also blessed him with a big family:

> "I am not worthy of the least of all the mercies and of all the truth which You have shown Your servant; for I crossed over this Jordan with my staff, and now I have become two companies" (Genesis 32:10).

I believe Jacob heard the idea of tithing from the story of the life of his grandfather Abraham. It took Jacob a whole of lot of faith to commit to give a tithe when he had virtually nothing in his possession. As the result of that sacrificial giving by faith, God blessed him exceedingly.

> "Thus the man (Jacob) became exceedingly prosperous, and had large flocks, female and male servants, and camels and donkeys" (Genesis 30:43).

We are familiar with the story about the boy who gave five loaves and two fish. We have heard it preached many times, but only a few of us have taken the time to think about the story from the boy's perspective. Someone told me the story about that boy from a book they read that was written by Sadhu Sunder Singh. This man lived in India many years ago. He belonged to a well-to-do Sikh family. One day out of desperation, he decided to commit suicide. Jesus appeared to him and he was miraculously converted.

After Sadhu Sunder became a believer, his family and community rejected him. This was the beginning of his lifelong walk with Jesus. No one knows how he died or where he died. He wrote many books. In one of his books, he wrote about a vision he had. In this vision, Jesus shared the story about this particular boy who gave the five loaves and the two fish.

The boy was born a paralytic, and Jesus had healed him a few days before. The boy began to follow the crowd and Jesus. His mother would pack a lunch and send it with him. They were a very poor family; that is why barley bread and fish were his lunch. When Jesus asked the disciples to feed the five thousand people, they searched frantically among the crowed, looking for food. This boy heard about it and he thought Jesus was asking for food because He was hungry.

Out of his love for Jesus and from a heart of gratitude for the healing he received, this boy gave his whole lunch to one of the disciples, believing he was giving it to Jesus. They brought it to Jesus, He took it, blessed it, and then fed the five thousand.

After feeding the multitude, Jesus asked His disciples to collect the leftovers. They filled twelve baskets with the leftover food. Jesus told the disciples to carry those twelve baskets to this boy's house to give it to his mother. The sacrificial seed he had sown to Jesus abundantly blessed the boy and his family.

THE EXODUS STORY

We all know the story of the people of Israel and how they came out of Egypt. Before God sent the tenth plague over Egypt, He commanded Moses to tell the people to prepare the Passover meal. Each family was supposed to take a lamb and kill it on the fourteenth day of the month. This lamb could not be just any lamb though; it had to have some specific qualities. It has to be a male, one year old, and without blemish.

When you are in slavery for those many years, you will not own many good things in your possession. When someone asks you to give the best lamb in your flock as an offering, it requires faith to do that. You need to keep in mind that they had never done anything like this before either. They could have grumbled and complained about it and lost their firstborn, or obey the voice of the Lord and receive the biggest breakthrough anyone had ever received.

They obeyed, killed the lamb, and applied its blood to their doorposts as they were instructed. Therefore, destroyer would not touch them nor their families. Their greatest deliverance and healing service took place that night; and finally, the people of God came out from the bondage of Egypt after 430 years.

They did according to the Word of the Lord and applied the blood to their doorposts. They were now safe from the plague; and that same night, they came out of Egypt. God had commanded them through Moses before they left Egypt to borrow gold, silver, and precious substances and to plunder them, which they did. I believe the greatest wealth transfer in the history of the world also took place that night. How would you like to receive a 400 years' worth salary in one night? In one day, the Jews received their complete wage for the entire time they had worked as slaves.

> And I will give this people favor in the sight of the Egyptians; and it shall be, when you go, that you shall not go empty-handed. But every woman shall ask of her neighbor, namely, of her who dwells near her house, articles of silver, articles of gold, and clothing; and you shall put them on your sons and on your daughters. So you shall plunder the Egyptians (Exodus 3:21-22).

In one day, some of the wealth of Egypt was transferred to the people of Israel. When they gave out of their need and gave the best that they had, they received a miracle beyond human imagination. That is why the Bible says the wealth of the sinner is laid up for the righteous (Proverbs 13:22).

Three years ago, we were living in Denver and faced with a financial challenge pertaining to our school in India. We needed close to 100,000 dollars to finish the construction of the building. We had 3,000 dollars in our bank account. One night, God spoke to me, and said, "Sow that three thousand to three different ministries." He gave us the names of the ministries.

I went to my wife and shared that with her and she agreed with me. She wrote the checks, we blessed them, prayed over them, and sent them to the three different ministries. One week later as I was getting ready to go to India, one of our friends called asked me to come by their office because they had a check for us. I drove there, and picked up the envelope, came home, and opened it. It was check for $85,000 dollars. In the end, we got all the money we needed to finish the construction.

I could share testimony after testimony. Giving has become a lifestyle for us. We live by faith and by the principle of giving found in God's economy.

HOW WE SHOULD GIVE

The Bible says God loves a cheerful giver (2 Corinthians 9:7). We should give with a joyful heart. *It is the nature of God to give.* If we give with grudges in our heart, that seed will not bring forth the fruit we expect. Jesus said when we give alms we should not let our left hand know what our right hand is doing. We should give generously. Proverbs says a person gives generously and still increases, but another person does not give, choosing to hold back what he has, and still remains in poverty (Proverbs 11:24).

It is just like the farmer who expects to receive a harvest when he sows his seed and waits for his harvest with patience. Money is a type of seed. When we sow financial seeds, we should expect a harvest. Every financially prosperous person in the kingdom could tell you that it is necessary to give with a goal in mind. *Every financial seed you sow should have an assigned harvest that you are expecting God to bring from it.*

I went to minister in a church. After the worship, it was time for the offering. The pastor went up and exhorted us to give. I had three dollars in my wallet. The Holy Spirit told me to sow that three dollars. My mind said: *That is your coffee money for tomorrow. What if you will do not receive any offering?*

I obeyed the voice of God and put the three dollars I had into the offering. The next morning, I woke up early to get ready to go to the airport. I noticed an envelope under the door. I thought it was the receipt for my room. I took it and opened it, and it was a check for $3,500 dollars from the church. Thank God I picked it up and opened it, and did not leave it, thinking it was a receipt. That pastor gave me the largest check I had ever received as an honorarium to that day.

One of verses in the New Testament that we like to quote often is Philippians 4:19, which says, "My God shall supply all your need according to His riches in glory by Christ Jesus." Very few think about how they received that promise. In verse 15, Paul shares his testimony. After Paul left Macedonia, no church gave to his ministry except the church in Philippi.

In 2 Corinthians 8:1-5 he writes about the financial condition of the Philippian church. They were in deep poverty.

> Now I want you to know, dear brothers and sisters, what God in his kindness has done through the churches in Macedonia. They are being tested by many troubles, and they are very poor. But they are also filled with abundant joy, which has overflowed in rich generosity. For I can testify that they gave not only what they could afford, but far more. And they did it of their own free will. They begged us again and again for the privilege of sharing in the gift for the believers in Jerusalem. They even did more than we had hoped, for their first action was to give themselves to the Lord and to us, just as God wanted them to do (2 Corinthians 8:1-5, NLT).

They gave out of their lack and received an unusual promise from God, the one we still hold on to today: God promised to supply all their needs.

TO WHOM WE SHOULD GIVE

We should give our tithe to the spiritual storehouse that feeds you spiritually. In the New Testament that would be a local church or a ministry through which you are spiritually fed. In the Old Testament, it was commanded to bring all the tithes to the priests, the Levites in the temple. The tithe was their possession and inheritance.

In the Old Testament, there was only one temple and one group of priests, who were spiritual leaders. Today, we have millions of small temples (church buildings), denominations, and leaders. Most people are fed by more than one spiritual leader, and I don't think there is anything wrong with splitting your tithe and giving it to more than one person or ministry. However, if your church is the primary place in which you are being spiritually fed, you should tithe to that church.

Make sure your church takes care of the poor and widows and provides food to the hungry. God wants His house to be a place of resource for every need a human has on this earth. That includes physical, spiritual and emotional needs. Many times, churches focus only on giving a good sermon on Sunday morning, while many physically, emotionally, and spiritually wounded people sit in their pews. Even if they do have a ministry to meet those needs, it is often very small compared to the need. Too often everything is poured into preaching alone.

God said to bring the tithe to the storehouse that there might be food in His house. Why is there a need for food in His house? To feed the hungry and the widows. Because churches are not doing what they are supposed to be doing, people have started private ministries apart from the local church (they are called parachurch ministries). God never intended for needs to be met that way. He wants His church to administer His kingdom to the local community, not like-minded people who have to gather on the outskirts of His body to accomplish their mission. That is out of order.

Because the church does not train its people, we have seminaries and Bible colleges. All of these works are supposed to be done *through a local church*. You may be thinking this: *If the church uses the tithe to feed the hungry and take care of the widows, then how would they be able to pay their pastors and other staff?* There is a provision made for that in the Bible.

> "Do I say these things as a mere man? Or does not the law say the same also? For it is written in the law of Moses, 'You shall not muzzle an ox while it treads out the grain.' Is it oxen God is concerned about? Or does He say it altogether for our sakes? For our sakes, no doubt, this is written, that he who plows should plow in hope, and he who threshes in hope should be partaker of his hope. If we have sown spiritual things for you, is it a great thing if we reap your material things? If others are partakers of this right over you, are we not even more? Nevertheless we have not used this right, but endure all things lest we hinder the gospel of Christ. Do you not know that those who minister the holy things eat of the things of the temple, and those who serve at the altar partake of the offerings of the altar? *Even so the Lord has commanded that those who preach the gospel should live from the gospel*" (1 Corinthians 9:8-14).

The question is what does it mean "to live from the gospel"? It does not say those who preach the gospel should live by the tithe of the people, but *from the gospel*.

> "Those who are taught the word of God should provide for their teachers, sharing all good things with them" (Galatians 6:6, NLT)

> "Remember your leaders who taught you the word of God. Think of all the good that has come from their lives, and

follow the example of their faith…And don't forget to do good and to share with those in need. These are the sacrifices that please God" (Hebrews 13:7,16).

When the people are blessed by the preaching of the gospel and understand the meaning of the true gospel, it is a natural response for people to give. When they understand that God gave His Son for their salvation, healing, and deliverance, and they receive the message, then they want to give to those who are preaching the gospel. When people are taught the Word in a local church, they are commanded to take care of those who teach them. If they do not take care of them, the Word they hear will not profit them.

HOW MUCH WE SHOULD GIVE

The tithe is a tenth of your income and an Old Testament principle. A believer should at *least* give his tithe back to God and His work. The more we give, the more we receive. We cannot out-give God. The tithe belongs to Him; it is not ours.

The same measure we use to give will be measured back to us. This means, the amount we receive is proportionately connected to how much we give. God has not put any limit on how much we receive. Instead, He left it up to us to decide the limit. The same measure *you* use will be measured back to you.

> "Give, and it will be given to you: good measure, pressed down, shaken together, and running over will be put into your bosom. For with the same measure that you use, it will be measured back to you" (Luke 6:38).

In another translation it reads,

> "Give, and you will receive. Your gift will return to you in full—pressed down, shaken together to make room for more,

running over, and poured into your lap. The amount you give will determine the amount you get back" (Luke 6:38, NLT).

That means if you give in the denomination of tens you will receive in the multiplication of tens. If your giving limit is in hundreds, your income will be in the multiplication of hundreds. If you give in the level of thousands, you will receive in the multiplication of thousands. All of us start somewhere down in the lower scale and grow higher in our giving level. I started in the ten level and am now in the thousands. It took me a while to get there. I remember when I gave my first thousand dollars. It was not easy, but with God all things are possible. I encourage you to increase your giving level and see God open new doors for you as you do.

WHAT WE SHOULD GIVE

Unfortunately, in today's Christian circles, we have been taught to give our finances alone, but giving is not limited to the financial area alone. *The principle of giving is applicable in all areas of life.* Why do we give money to God or His ministry? God does not need our money. He owns it all. All the wealth and glory in heaven and earth belong to Him. Then, why do we need to give? We give because it is a spiritual law that was set in motion by God in the earth. *If we need to receive anything, we have to give first.*

We give our tithes and offerings to God because we believe that we will receive a harvest. When Jesus said, "give and it will be given to you," He did not limit giving to money. First you give to God whatever you need in life, and you will receive it multiplied.

The Bible asks us to give to God more than our money. The scripture says, "Give unto the Lord strength" (Psalm 29:1). How do we give strength to God and why do we give Him strength. He is all powerful and His name is Almighty. God does not need strength from us, just like He does not need any money from us. We, on the other hand, do need strength from Him. To receive it, we need to give Him our small strength first. If you are weak in your body, say this out loud, "Lord, I give You all my strength."

One day while I was in India, I went to a bakery to buy something for the kids in our orphanage. It was about six-thirty in the evening. Most of the stores are owned by Hindu people, and every morning and evening they play religious music in their stores that praises and worships their gods. It was at this time when I went into this bakery. As I stood there listening to the songs, it grieved my spirit. They were singing about a particular god that was being worshiped in Kottarakara (my town).

The song went something like this: This god is the only owner of this town, he is the only ruler of this town, he is the only lord of this town, and so on. They kept on singing like that for a few minutes. One of the reasons Hinduism is so strong in India is because the people in India sing and give strength, wealth, honor, respect and reign to the demons they worship.

Every year there is a special season of Hindu celebrations in most of the temples. During this time, *all day and all night, they sing*, praising and exalting that demon *for ten days nonstop*. Imagine the power of darkness in some of these areas! They have been doing this for hundreds of years. Meanwhile Christians go to church on Sunday morning, do their religious thing for an hour and a half, get tired, run out to their favorite buffet to find some juicy pork chops, and that's it! Lord, have mercy.

We need to learn to give God what we desire from Him. Whatever you desire God to do in your area, get some saints and give Him what you are believing for first. Remember the golden rule; do unto others as you would have them do unto you. Then you will see change take place slowly. God will answer you as you sow seed over your geographical area. He wants people to come to know Him. If we want to see Him lifted high in our area, we should begin by doing that very thing. In turn, God will give us ideas about how to see Him made manifest in a deeper way in our culture.

There are times I get tired in my body and have no more strength. When those times come, I start praising Him, saying, "Lord, I ascribe to You strength and power!" Wherever I go, God always strengthens me to do what He has called me to do.

FAITH, THE NEEDED INGREDIENT

The Bible says it is impossible to please God without faith. When you come before great kings and dignitaries, you bring a gift to gain their favor. When you come before God, the best gift you can bring to get His favor is faith. Faith is the key to the miraculous. Faith unlocks the supernatural world to you. Faith opens the treasure house of the kingdom of God.

If you want to enter into financial abundance, you need faith. Many people ask God for many things. What they actually need is faith. In the Gospels, we see that every time the disciples could not do something, Jesus would do it. He asked them why they didn't have enough faith.

> "Now if God so clothes the grass of the field, which today is, and tomorrow is thrown into the oven, will He not much more clothe you, O you of little faith?" (Matthew 6:30).

There are different kinds of faith. This refers to the kind of faith for food and clothing.

> "Then His disciples came to Him and awoke Him, saying, 'Lord, save us! We are perishing!' But He said to them, 'Why are you fearful, O you of little faith?' Then He arose and rebuked the winds and the sea, and there was a great calm" (Matthew 8:25-26).

This speaks of the kind of faith for power over nature and fear.

> "And immediately Jesus stretched out His hand and caught him, and said to him, 'O you of little faith, why did you doubt?' And when they got into the boat, the wind ceased" (Matthew 14:31-32).

This is about faith to do the impossible and extraordinary things.

> Now when His disciples had come to the other side, they had forgotten to take bread. Then Jesus said to them, "Take heed

and beware of the leaven of the Pharisees and the Sadducees." And they reasoned among themselves, saying, "It is because we have taken no bread." But Jesus, being aware of it, said to them, "O you of little faith, why do you reason among yourselves because you have brought no bread? Do you not yet understand, or remember the five loaves of the five thousand and how many baskets you took up? Nor the seven loaves of the four thousand and how many large baskets you took up? How is it you do not understand that I did not speak to you concerning bread?—but to beware of the leaven of the Pharisees and Sadducees." Then they understood that He did not tell them to beware of the leaven of bread, but of the doctrine of the Pharisees and Sadducees (Matthew 16:5-12).

These verses are about the kind of faith we need to believe in sound doctrine. It takes faith to believe in sound doctrine. One of the reasons the Pharisees erred was because they did not believe unless they could see with their own eyes.

And Jesus answered and said, "O faithless and perverse generation, how long shall I be with you? how long shall I bear with you? bring him hither to me." And Jesus rebuked him; and the demon went out of him; and the boy was cured from that hour (Matthew 17:17-18, ASV).

This refers to the faith we need for deliverance from demonic bondage.

"And His name, through faith in His name, has made this man strong, whom you see and know. Yes, the faith which comes through Him has given him this perfect soundness in the presence of you all" (Acts 3:16).

This verse talks about the kind of faith that brings healing to physical bodies. It was actually faith that healed the lame man. Peter said it was the faith that comes through Him, meaning faith that came through Jesus had healed him completely.

When we need a financial breakthrough, healing or deliverance, we should not petition God for the need. Instead, we should ask Him for the kind of faith we need for that particular miracle to face that need.

What is faith? Hebrews says,

> "Now faith is the substance of things hoped for, the evidence of things not seen" (Hebrews 11:1).

Faith is the substance of things. This means that if you are hoping to have some "things" (money, house, healing, anointing, or anything else) in your life, you need faith. The world was created by faith. God knew exactly what would appear when He spoke the Word.

We need to ask God for the substance of things we are hoping for, which is faith itself. By faith, the world was created. We know the world is made of substance, and faith created that substance. I would rather have the substance of things instead of the things. I would rather ask God to give me the substance of things. I can have anything I believe for. Substance creates things. Things do not come first; substance makes things come.

> "What is faith? It is the confident assurance that something we want is going to happen. It is the certainty that what we hope for is waiting for us, even though we cannot see it up ahead" (Hebrews 11:1, TLB).

It is possible to have little faith and great faith.

> When they came to the crowd, a man approached Jesus and knelt before him. "Lord, have mercy on my son," he said. "He has seizures and is suffering greatly. He often falls into the fire or into the water. I brought him to your disciples, but they could not heal him." "You unbelieving and perverse generation," Jesus replied, "how long shall I stay with you? How long shall I put up with you? Bring the boy here to me." Jesus rebuked the demon, and it came out of the boy, and he was healed at that moment.

Then the disciples came to Jesus in private and asked, "Why couldn't we drive it out?" He replied, "Because you have so little faith. Truly I tell you, if you have faith as small as a mustard seed, you can say to this mountain, 'Move from here to there,' and it will move. Nothing will be impossible for you" (Matthew 17:14-20, NIV).

This story is about a man who brought his son to the disciples for deliverance, but they could not cast the demon out of him. They asked Jesus why they could not cast the demon out, and Jesus' reply was that they did not have enough faith (verse 20) or no faith at all (see Matthew 17:17 quoted above).

The gospel of Mark shares the unbelief of the father.

"Jesus said to him, 'If you can believe, all things are possible to him who believes.' Immediately the father of the child cried out and said with tears, 'Lord, I believe; help my unbelief!'" (Mark 9:23-24).

Jesus also talked about having great faith. One particular centurion came to Jesus for the healing of his servant. Jesus told him that He would come and heal his servant. The centurion told Jesus that it was not necessary for Him to come into his house. Instead all Jesus needed to do was speak a word, and he had faith that his servant would be healed.

"When Jesus heard this, he was amazed and said to those following him, 'I tell you the truth, I have not found anyone in Israel with such great faith'" (Matthew 8:10, NIV).

WHY DO THE UNGODLY PROSPER?

Unfortunately, the ungodly people are more prosperous financially than the people of the kingdom. You might have wondered why these people prosper more than believers. Jesus said the children of the world are more shrewd (or wise) than the children of the light.

> "So the master commended the unjust steward because he had dealt shrewdly. For the sons of this world are more shrewd in their generation than the sons of light" (Luke 16:8).

God has set principles and laws in the earthly realm. Whoever, regardless of their religious background, utilizes those principles and laws *will benefit from them*. The law of gravity works the same for everyone. There are laws of prosperity mentioned in the Bible. I will mention a few in this book. Whoever practices those laws will prosper financially, regardless of their religious background.

CHAPTER - 14

TWO KINDS OF INCOME: THE SEED AND THE BREAD

Remember, there is no one-size-fits-all formula in the Bible. The reason I believe the Holy Spirit is allowing me to share different aspects and types of giving is because you will need to find out from Him which one fits and will work for you.

If you do not practice this type of giving, you will not tap into the supernatural resources God has for you. If you and I are going to fulfill the purpose God has for us, we need to know how to tap into the unlimited resources God has for us. If we depend on the natural to fulfill the spiritual task God has entrusted to us, we are not going to be successful.

How do we tap into the riches God has? Is there a heavenly bank somewhere on earth where we can go withdraw some money? God has mentioned a type of giving in His Word called *seed*. The word *seed* has different meanings in the Scriptures. *We* are called the seed of Abraham. We have been born-again by the seed of *the Word of God*. The *preaching* of the Word is compared to sowing seeds. Lastly, *money* is compared to a seed; and that is what this chapter is all about.

The Philippian church supported Paul and his ministry from its inception. He commended them for their giving in Philippians. He boasted to the Macedonian church about the Corinthians, that they were willing to give and that they were so generous (2 Corinthians 9:1-4). The Macedonians took it as a challenge and wanted to beat the Corinthians in their giving.

Though the Macedonians gave, the Corinthians did not fulfill their commitment, so Paul wrote to them to remind them of their willingness to give. He was telling them to get it ready before he came. Both chapters 8 and 9 in 2 Corinthians were committed to this one truth that Paul was trying to communicate to the believers in Corinth.

The particular collection they were taking was not to support Paul or his missionary work. It was to minister to the needs of the saints in the church, especially the poor. The early church not only ministered to the spiritual need of the people, but the needs of their soul and body too. So the churches grew, not only in numbers, but they were healthy churches in every aspect too.

Most of the unbelievers today talk about the church as though it were something despicable. The media does not have much good to say about the church. They look at some rich or wayward preachers who used the power and authority in the gospel to make themselves rich, and judge the whole church by their ministries. Meanwhile, many poor believers suffer; some even go without food for themselves and their children.

As we have learned earlier, one of the purposes of tithing was to have enough food in the storehouse so that widows, strangers, and the poor could come and receive what they needed. Many churches have food banks, filled with canned food not even good to feed animals. That food was not usually provided through tithing either. In most churches, the food they have in their food bank was given to the church from what was left over in the homes of the parishioners. They did not want it, so they thought they'd donate it for a good cause and brought it to the church. Does that sound familiar?

Paul wanted equality among believers within the church and between churches (2 Corinthians 8:13-15). James said the same thing in his letter. If someone came to church hungry and naked, we shouldn't just say, "God bless you, my brother, go in peace. " Instead we should give them something to eat as well as clothing to cover their nakedness (James 2:16).

2 Corinthians 9:6-15 teaches about the sevenfold blessings for those who sow the seed:

> But this I say: He who sows sparingly will also reap sparingly, and he who sows bountifully will also reap bountifully. So let each one give as he purposes in his heart, not grudgingly or of necessity; for God loves a cheerful giver. And God is able to make all grace abound toward you, that you, always having all sufficiency in all things, may have an abundance for every good work. As it is written: "He has dispersed abroad, He has given to the poor; His righteousness endures forever."

> Now may He who supplies seed to the sower, and bread for food, supply and multiply the seed you have sown and increase the fruits of your righteousness, while you are enriched in everything for all liberality, which causes thanksgiving through us to God. For the administration of this service not only supplies the needs of the saints, but also is abounding through many thanksgivings to God, while, through the proof of this ministry, they glorify God for the obedience of your confession to the gospel of Christ, and for your liberal sharing with them and all men, and by their prayer for you, who long for you because of the exceeding grace of God in you. Thanks be to God for His indescribable gift!

THE BLESSING OF ISAAC

Many times, people use Isaac as an example for tithing and receiving a hundredfold blessing, but that is not correct. As the son of Abraham, I believe Isaac practiced the principle of tithing, but that did not stop him from experiencing famine. Everyone in the land was going through a season of famine. In modern terminology I would call it a recession. Both Christians and non-Christians are experiencing a recession and many believers are facing financial crisis just like everyone else. There is no difference, but there has to be a difference. That was the case with Isaac.

When all the people around him were facing the famine, in Isaac's household there was plenty and abundance. There was great harvest and singing and dancing in his house that comes with harvest times. Isaac knew a secret that the people of the land did not know—that principle was sowing the seed during famine. The Bible specifically says that Isaac sowed in the land and received in the same year a hundredfold.

> "Then Isaac sowed in that land, and reaped in the same year a hundredfold; and the Lord blessed him. The man began to prosper, and continued prospering until he became very prosperous; for he had possessions of flocks and possessions of herds and a great number of servants. So the Philistines envied him" (Genesis 26:12-14).

Isaac did not prosper by giving tithes. Do not misunderstand me. If tithing would have prospered the people in the church, people would stand in line to give tithes; you wouldn't need to compel or persuade them. If tithing had prospered Isaac, he would not have been affected by the famine and would not have needed to sow seed.

When he was going through a season of famine he did not eat the seed, he sowed it instead. He prospered when he began to sow seeds. It says he sowed; you too can sow seeds. You can sow your seed during famine and it will give you a harvest. I believe there is only one way to overcome the recession that the world is experiencing, and it is through sowing seeds.

You can bounce back from any setback or economic turmoil if you learn to sow seeds. Sometimes, sowing the seed has to be strategic and timely. A strategic and timely seed will break the backbone of the demon of lack and poverty, and release divine favor and prosperity upon you. People will begin to envy you when they see the blessings God bestows on you; they will come and ask you for help.

Famine and recession are opportunities for God to show His faithfulness on our behalf. Believers needs to learn how to tap into the kingdom economy and not live based on the world's economy. Then they need to become a blessing to the people around them, and not wait for those people to give to them. The church is waiting for the wealth of the world to come to them, while they are not practicing the kingdom principles that create wealth. God said He is the One that gives *power* to get wealth.

God did not say we should wait for the world to bring their wealth to us. He said He would give us power to create wealth. What is this power He is talking about? Military power? No. He is talking about creating businesses, inventing, manufacturing and the distribution of products. God also gives us ideas and intellectual knowledge. Believers need to move into these arenas if they want to see the prosperity God has promised.

SIX KINDS OF WEALTH MENTIONED IN THE BIBLE

Jesus preached about six levels of financial investment. Most of the parables Jesus shared had more than one meaning, so it depends on how you interpret them. Though He used parables relating to money, estates and investments, the main purpose was to communicate spiritual truths about the kingdom in a language people understood.

Below are examples of the areas of investments that Jesus spoke about in His parables.

1) Inheritance: An inheritance is something that is left to you from your family or others. It can be money, land, houses, or any kind of wealth that parents or relatives leave behind or give. The parable of the prodigal son is an example of an inheritance. He asked his father to give him the inheritance which was supposed to be his only *after the death* of his father (Luke 15:11). In eastern culture the family inheritance goes to the children. In my culture in India, the youngest son inherits the family house and the parents till they die.

WHAT THE BIBLE SAYS ABOUT INHERITANCE

In the New King James Version, the words *inheritance, inheritances, possession,* and *possessions* appear 398 times. God put a great deal of importance on inheritance in His Word. The father's blessings were supposed to go to his children. The firstborn inherited a double portion. If there were no sons, the daughters inherited the blessing. If there were no children, the closest relative received the inheritance. Someone got the inheritance. When the people of Israel reached the Promised Land, God gave them their inheritance according to the size of their families.

> "And you shall divide the land by lot as an inheritance among your families; to the larger you shall give a larger inheritance, and to the smaller you shall give a smaller inheritance; there everyone's inheritance shall be whatever falls to him by lot. You shall inherit according to the tribes of your fathers" (Numbers 33:54).

In Proverbs we read that a good man leaves an inheritance to his children's children.

> "A good man leaves an inheritance to his children's children, but the wealth of the sinner is stored up for the righteous" (Proverbs 13:22).

An inheritance is something you receive from your previous generation; it is money or wealth that has been passed on to you.

> "Houses and riches are an inheritance from fathers, but a prudent wife is from the Lord" (Proverbs 19:14).

TWO KINDS OF INCOME: THE SEED AND THE BREAD

In the Old Testament people inherited their families' wealth.

> "The lines have fallen to me in pleasant places; yes, I have a good inheritance" (Psalms 16:6).

In the Old Testament the Levites did not receive an inheritance from among their brethren. The Lord was their inheritance. Every tithe and first fruit offering that the people gave to the Lord belonged to the Levites.

> Then the Lord said to Aaron: "You shall have no inheritance in their land, nor shall you have any portion among them; I am your portion and your inheritance among the children of Israel. Behold, I have given the children of Levi all the tithes in Israel as an inheritance in return for the work which they perform, the work of the tabernacle of meeting. Hereafter the children of Israel shall not come near the tabernacle of meeting, lest they bear sin and die. But the Levites shall perform the work of the tabernacle of meeting, and they shall bear their iniquity; it shall be a statute forever, throughout your generations, that among the children of Israel they shall have no inheritance. For the tithes of the children of Israel, which they offer up as a heave offering to the Lord, I have given to the Levites as an inheritance; therefore I have said to them, 'Among the children of Israel they shall have no inheritance'" (Numbers 18:20-24).

The New Testament also talks about inheritance.

> "So now, brethren, I commend you to God and to the word of His grace, which is able to build you up and give you an inheritance among all those who are sanctified" (Acts 20:32).

> "In Him also we have obtained an inheritance, being predestined according to the purpose of Him who works all things according to the counsel of His will" (Ephesians 1:11).

"That the God of our Lord Jesus Christ, the Father of glory, may give to you the spirit of wisdom and revelation in the knowledge of Him, the eyes of your understanding being enlightened; that you may know what is the hope of His calling, what are the riches of the glory of His inheritance in the saints" (Ephesians 1:17-18).

I will share more about our inheritance later in this book. *Each believer has received an inheritance from God.* And that inheritance includes everything we need to fulfill His purpose on earth.

2) Real Estate: Real estate includes lands, houses or buildings that you own. Jesus talked about a man who saw a precious treasure in a field. He hid the treasure in the field and went and sold everything he had and bought that field (Matthew 13:44).

The words *land, lands, country, countries, nation, nations, house,* and *houses* appear 4,624 times in the New Kings James Version. Whenever God promised someone something or made a covenant, it always involved land. It is God's will for you to own land for His glory. When the righteous own much land, it gives that much more spiritual jurisdiction for the kingdom of God to operate on this earth.

"So it shall be, when the Lord your God brings you into the land of which He swore to your fathers, to Abraham, Isaac, and Jacob, to give you large and beautiful cities which you did not build, houses full of all good things, which you did not fill, hewn-out wells which you did not dig, vineyards and olive trees which you did not plant" (Deuteronomy 6:10-11).

"Lest—when you have eaten and are full, and have built beautiful houses and dwell in them; and when your herds and your flocks multiply, and your silver and your gold are multiplied, and all that you have is multiplied" (Deuteronomy 8:12-13).

3) **Precious Metals:** Another area of investment is precious metals like gold, silver, platinum, or precious stones. The words *precious stones, jewelry, gold, silver, gems, rubies* and *ornaments* appear 890 times in the Bible. People buy them and store them as part of their investment.

God created all the precious metals and stones. They are part of God's blessings to His children. As mentioned before, Genesis begins by talking about gold as good (Genesis 2:12). The Bible ends by talking about gold as well.

> "The construction of its wall was of jasper; and the city was pure gold, like clear glass. The foundations of the wall of the city were adorned with all kinds of precious stones: the first foundation was jasper, the second sapphire, the third chalcedony, the fourth emerald, the fifth sardonyx, the sixth sardius, the seventh chrysolite, the eighth beryl, the ninth topaz, the tenth chrysoprase, the eleventh jacinth, and the twelfth amethyst. The twelve gates were twelve pearls: each individual gate was of one pearl. And the street of the city was pure gold, like transparent glass" (Revelation 21:18-21).

Deuteronomy 8:13, which we just read, also referred to the multiplication of silver and gold. And we already looked at how Abraham was rich in these metals as well (Genesis 13:2) God never said gold or silver was evil. If we know how to manage it and use it well, both would be a blessing to the kingdom.

4) **Cash:** The words *money, wealth, wealthy, rich,* and *riches* appear 429 times in the NKJV. This refers to the cash that is invested in businesses, long term deposits, insurance, stocks, and more. Jesus told a parable about the talents. He gave one person five talents, another two talents, and another one talent. He told them to invest the money until He returns (Matthew 25:15, 27).

5) **Estates/Agriculture:** The words *vineyards, cattle, livestock, herds,* and *olive groves* appear 578 times collectively in the Bible. (These refer to

when you invest money into agricultural pursuits, like planting estates of various crops). Jesus told different parables about men planting vineyards and appointing people to take care of them.

In the times of the Old Testament, cattle, sheep, herds or livestock were considered investments. A person's wealth was measured by the number of domestic animals servants, and land they possessed.

6) Wisdom: God considers having wisdom as more valuable than gold or riches. When compared to wealth and riches, wisdom is superior in quality and in value. The Bible says,

> "Wisdom is the principal thing; therefore get wisdom" (Proverbs 4:7).

You can lose all the money and wealth you have; but if you have wisdom, you can gain it back in a matter of time. We should strive to have more wisdom and understanding in our life.

Wisdom is more precious than gold or silver (Proverbs 16:16).

> "The fear of the Lord is the beginning of wisdom, and the knowledge of the Holy One is understanding" (Proverbs 9:10).

> "There was a man in the land of Uz, whose name was Job; and that man was blameless and upright, and one who feared God and shunned evil. And seven sons and three daughters were born to him. Also, his possessions were seven thousand sheep, three thousand camels, five hundred yoke of oxen, five hundred female donkeys, and a very large household, so that this man was the greatest of all the people of the East" (Job 1:1-3).

CHAPTER - 15

UNDERSTANDING YOUR INHERITANCE

"In Him also we have obtained an inheritance, being predestined according to the purpose of Him who works all things according to the counsel of His will"
(Ephesians 1:11).

The final revelation you need to understand in order to prosper and meet all your needs is a revelation of the inheritance God has given you. When you become a child of God through faith in Jesus Christ, you become His heir, a joint heir with Christ (Romans 8:17). This means that *when God wrote the final will of all that He owned*, all His riches, all His wisdom, wealth and power, *He included your name* in it. Now, whatever God owns you have the right to receive a portion of because you are His son or daughter. This is based on your need to accomplish His purpose on earth.

Imagine that you were born into the richest family on this earth: How will you think of yourself? How will you behave and live? That should be the way we live. If you study the lives of the apostles in the New Testament, we do not see them running around having no money to pay their bills, or their travel and ministry expenses. We do not see Paul stopping his journey for a few weeks because he did not have enough money to cover his expenses for his next mission trip. Never.

Though Paul might not have owned a mansion nor a fleet of ships, he was not living as a poor man. He lived like a person who owned the whole world. Listen to his own testimony: "As unknown, and yet well known; as dying, and behold we live; as chastened, and yet not killed; as sorrowful, yet always rejoicing; as poor, yet making many rich; as having nothing, *and yet possessing all things*" (2 Corinthians 6:9-10).

Paul lived like he possessed all things. A person looking from the outside at Paul's life might have thought he was a poor man, but he knew in his spirit that he possessed all things and people did not understand that. Every time a need arose he just made a withdrawal from what he possessed in the Spirit. That is the way we should be living too.

Everything in the world was at Paul's disposal. It is not easy to reach this place in the spirit; in fact, most do not. A person will need to die a million deaths before he can attain it. That means you will have to die to every passion and ambition to reach this place and until only Christ is left. Paul wrote that he died daily (1 Corinthians 15:31).

That is the same thing Peter said too!

> As His *divine power* has *given to us all things* that pertain to life and godliness, through the knowledge of Him who called us by glory and virtue, by which have been given to us exceedingly great and precious promises, that through these you may be partakers of the divine nature, having escaped the corruption that is in the world through lust (2 Peter 1:3-4).

Peter wrote that God's divine power has given us *all things* that pertain to life and godliness. The phrase, "divine power" is another term for *grace*.

When you see the words *gift, blessings,* or *power* in the New Testament, they are all related to grace. That means *everything we need to live our life and fulfill our purpose has already been given to us by God.* He is not withholding anything from us. Then why do many precious saints act like they do not have enough money to survive or to pay their bills? They do not have a revelation of this truth. Their trust is in their job, their checkbook, or in what they can do with their hands or the system of this world.

> "He who did not spare His own Son, but delivered Him up for us all, how shall He not with Him also freely give us all things?" (Romans 8:32).

WHERE IS YOUR INHERITANCE?

So you may ask, "If God has given me an inheritance, where is it now? How do I tap into it?" Your inheritance is in heaven, meaning it is in the heavenly realm or in the spirit world. You cannot see it with your natural eyes. You need to believe what the Bible says and tap into your inheritance by faith.

> "Blessed be the God and Father of our Lord Jesus Christ, who has blessed us with every spiritual blessing in the heavenly places in Christ" (Ephesians 1:3).

This says that God has already blessed you with all spiritual blessings and they are in the heavenly places in Christ. That means they are in the unseen realm in Christ Jesus. Paul prayed for the church in Ephesus that they might receive a revelation of this inheritance. In order for us to receive a revelation of this inheritance, we need to receive the Spirit of wisdom and revelation and the eyes of our understanding need to open, meaning God needs to open the eyes of our spirit.

> "That the God of our Lord Jesus Christ, the Father of glory, may give to you the spirit of wisdom and revelation in the knowledge of Him, the eyes of your understanding being

enlightened; that you may know what is the hope of His calling, *what are the riches of the glory of His inheritance in the saints"* (Ephesians 1:17-18).

Many saints are waiting to get to heaven to receive and enjoy their inheritance. That is good, but in heaven you do not have any need of anything. You will not need to bless anyone; there will be no poor people nor any expenses there. You will not need to build a house or pay for your child's college tuition. All our needs are here on the earth. You will not need to support any ministry in heaven. We need the resources now, right here on this earth. This is why God is telling us He has given us an inheritance.

Unfortunately, many do not tap into it. It is as though someone told you they had deposited a trillion dollars into your bank account; and instead of getting anything out of the account, you decided to walk around and sing and shout about it, without ever making a withdrawal. How does it benefit you or anyone else? You know that the money is yours, but you cannot even afford to pay for a meal. That is the way most Christians live. They have this inheritance God has given them, but they are waiting to die to receive it, without realizing the Person who wrote the will already died for them so they can receive their inheritance.

When someone gives you an inheritance, you do not need to die to enjoy it. If you did, you'd leave the inheritance for someone else and it would be wasted. The person who bequeathed their inheritance to you had to die so you could get it. That is what happened exactly. When Jesus died, that will became active and you can now withdraw from it anytime you want, by faith.

> "The Spirit Himself bears witness with our spirit that we are children of God, and if children, then heirs—heirs of God and joint heirs with Christ, if indeed we suffer with Him, that we may also be glorified together" (Romans 8:16-17).

Another reason many believers do not enjoy the inheritance God has given them is because they are not mature yet. They are still acting and living like babies. In the natural even though a person received an inheritance, they have to reach eighteen years old to personally enjoy it. Until then it is managed by trustees. The trustees decide how much the minor should have and for what purpose. But when they reach the age of maturity, they can decide for themselves, and have full access to their inheritance. That is what the Bible says. Please read and meditate on the following verses.

> "Now I say that the heir, as long as he is a child, does not differ at all from a slave, though he is master of all, but is under guardians and stewards until the time appointed by the father. Even so we, when we were children, were in bondage under the elements of the world. But when the fullness of the time had come, God sent forth His Son, born of a woman, born under the law, to redeem those who were under the law, that we might receive the adoption as sons. And because you are sons, God has sent forth the Spirit of His Son into your hearts, crying out, "Abba, Father!" Therefore you are no longer a slave but a son, and if a son, then an *heir of God through Christ*" (Galatians 4:1-7).

Your inheritance has everything you need to fulfill your calling here on earth right now in this life. God knew your calling and what it takes to fulfill it, so when He decided your inheritance He included more than enough to meet all those needs. There is no one in the Bible who did not do what God called them to do because they did not have money. Such a thing did not happen. However, we see a majority of people who are not doing what God called them to do today because they do not have money. It should not be that way.

The reason we became like that is because most churches told their people only about tithing. They said that if we pay tithes, God will bless us. Many Christians are paying their tithes, but their financial situation is not improving. First, you need to have a revelation of the kingdom of

God. Second, you need to have a revelation that you are a child of God. Thirdly, you need to have a revelation of your calling and then about your inheritance. Unless we walk in this revelation knowledge, we will live like others, and die with very few people knowing that we existed.

HOW DO WE TAP INTO OUR INHERITANCE?

There were saints in the Old Testament who foresaw the time of Christ in the Spirit and tapped into the blessings that we enjoy today. The first person who did that was Abraham. Though he lived thousands of years before Christ, he saw the day of Christ and enjoyed the benefits of a believer in Christ (John 8:56). He is the first New Testament believer who ever lived on this earth. The gospel was preached to him beforehand (Galatians 3:8). How did he do that? By faith. If the father of our faith can do it, we certainly can tap into the blessings now, which God has prepared for us in heaven. All we need is faith. David was another person who lived like that.

May the Lord open our eyes to see the glorious riches of His inheritance that God has bestowed upon us through Christ Jesus.

> "To them God willed to make known what are the *riches* of the glory of this mystery among the Gentiles: which is Christ in you, the hope of glory" (Colossians 1:27).

ABUNDANT SUPPLY

> "Therefore, having been justified by faith, we have peace with God through our Lord Jesus Christ, *through whom also we have access by faith into this grace in which we stand,* and rejoice in hope of the glory of God" (Romans 5:1-2).

We have sung many times that all wisdom, power, wealth, riches, honor, glory and strength belong to Jesus. We read that in the book of Revelation too (Revelation 5:12). Do you really believe that in your heart? If everything belongs to Him, and the Bible says He lives in you, that means you are walking around carrying a person who owns the whole universe. The person who created the whole universe is living in you! Have you ever cared to ask Him why He made all these things and for whom?

If the above statement is true (and in fact, it is true)—if all the glory, power, strength, honor, riches, wisdom and wealth belongs to Christ—and He lives in you—and you are in Him, does that mean you own all that glory, power, strength, honor, riches, wisdom and wealth too? I believe that is why Paul said he lived like he possessed all things. The problem with us is that when the Bible says words like *all* and *nothing*, we do not really believe it; we just read through it without understanding it. Read this verse and see if you believe it.

> "Therefore let no one boast in men. *For all things are yours:* whether Paul or Apollos or Cephas, or the world or life or death, or *things present or things to come—all are yours.* And you are Christ's, and Christ is God's" (1 Corinthians 3:21-23).

Do you know that you have access to the throne room of God? Do you believe that you can enter into His presence anytime you want? You are not required to sing three fast songs and two slow songs to enter there! Why did He give you that permission? To worship Him? That is what many believe. That is not what it says in the New Testament though.

> "Let us therefore come boldly to the *throne of grace*, that we may *obtain mercy* and *find grace* to *help in time of need*" (Hebrews 4:16).

> "In whom we have *boldness* and *access* with *confidence* through faith in Him" (Ephesians 3:12).

This verse says that God has given us access to His throne for our benefit, not to worship Him: to obtain mercy, to find grace to help in time of need. Did you ever have a need or go through a time when you needed help from God? We all have had numerous times when we needed God's help.

Unfortunately too many of us have never made an attempt to go to His throne and present our need in order to receive help. Of course we've prayed piously, thinking, *God is up there in heaven*, but we are not always sure whether He has heard our prayers or not. That is why we do not receive the answers to our prayers. Next time when you pray, pray with this revelation: that you are standing in the throne room of God; God is sitting on His throne and you are standing in front of Him to present your need.

You are not standing there shaking and shivering with fear, because the Bible says to come to the throne of grace boldly and not fearfully. If you are afraid, you do not have a revelation of His grace. Do you know what grace means? The above verse says to come before the throne of grace to find grace to help in time of need. Grace means that whatever you do not have and need, or unable to do, God will help you with. He will step in to cover or meet that need for you.

When you are weak in strength, He says, "My *grace* is sufficient for you, for My strength is made perfect in weakness" (2 Corinthians 12:9a).

When you need salvation, He says, "For by *grace* you have been saved through faith" (Ephesians 2:8a).

When you are poor, He says, "And God is able to make all *grace* abound toward you, that you, always having all sufficiency in all things, may have an abundance for every good work" (2 Corinthians 9:8).

And He says, "For you know the *grace* of our Lord Jesus Christ, that though He was rich, yet for your sakes He became poor, that you through His poverty might become rich" (2 Corinthians 8:9).

If sin abounds, He says, "*grace* abounded much more" (Romans 5:20).

When you need forgiveness He says, "In Him we have redemption through His blood, the forgiveness of sins, according to the riches of His *grace*" (Ephesians 1:7).

That means whatever need you have, there is the grace of God to meet that need. He has provided everything we need through His grace. His grace never runs out, so you do not need to worry about exhausting His grace. Now, He is saying to us to come to His throne of grace in time of need to find help. Can He make it any easier than that, my brothers and sisters? Grace is whatever you want it to be. In truth, it is the revelation of God's name, "I am that I am." Whatever you need, He is that to you at that moment. He never changes.

We knew grace only as it related to salvation. We say carelessly when people ask, "How are you doing?" We respond, "By the grace of God, I am fine." Do you really mean that? The grace of God is multifaceted and multidimensional. It will fit anyone for any situation. The Bible calls it the manifold grace of God.

> "As each one has received a gift, minister it to one another, as good stewards of the *manifold grace* of God" (1 Peter 4:10).

Your provision to fulfill your calling will not come from your job; it does not matter how many jobs you have. You will kill yourself if you try to fulfill your calling on your own. What you need is a revelation of God's grace—which He has made available to you and me through Jesus Christ. He has reconciled all things in heaven and on earth. That means there is a peace treaty between heaven and earth now. The trade route has been opened because of what Jesus did on the cross (Ephesians 1:10; Colossians 1:19). People on earth can access the things in heaven and people (God and angels) in heaven can access things on earth.

> "For through Him we both have *access* by one Spirit to the Father" (Ephesians 2:18).

I grew up in India. Ever since I can remember, there has been a border dispute between India and Pakistan. They fought over it for years but could not come to a permanent solution. When there was no peace between the two countries, they closed all the trade routes between them. No one in Pakistan could bring any goods to India and no Indian could take any goods to Pakistan. Recently, there has been less tension between the two countries and they opened up trade again.

That is what Jesus did for us. Through His blood we have been justified by faith and as a result, we have peace with God (Romans 5:1). The trade route between heaven and earth has been opened wide for anyone who can access it by faith.

> "And of His fullness we have all received, and *grace* for *grace*" (John 1:16).

I did not understand this until I was writing this book. It says of His fullness we have all received grace *for* grace. What does that mean? The first grace is what qualifies us to receive the second grace. The first grace is for salvation, which qualifies us to become a child of God. The second grace is the grace that covers all our needs. That is why the verse in Hebrews says that we should come to the throne of His grace, to find grace. There we see grace used two times again. First, we're given grace is to come His throne. Next, we're given grace to cover our needs. Thank You, Jesus!

> "For all things are for your sakes, that *grace*, having spread through the many, may cause thanksgiving to abound to the glory of God" (2 Corinthians 4:15).

We see the phrase "all things" repeated here. There is grace available to cover it whatever you need. There is nothing the grace of God cannot meet or afford. That is why the Bible says, "According to the riches of His grace" (Ephesians 1:7). Christians say things like, "We cannot afford it, or it is too expensive."

That is an insult to our heavenly Father. We say that because we do not have the revelation of the second grace. We believe we are saved by grace, then we live like the grace has ended there, and we have to figure out the rest. No. Please change your vocabulary; speak in alignment with the Word of God.

> "And God is able to make *all grace* abound toward you, that you, always having *all sufficiency in all things*, may have an *abundance for every good work*" (2 Corinthians 9:8).

This is one of my favorite verses. God has made all grace available, so that you always have all sufficiency in all things. Again, notice the word *all* in the verse. Whatever your need, there is grace available to cover that need. Thank Him for His grace. We need to talk and face life from a place of sufficiency, and not with an attitude of lack and shortage. We need to talk *abundance* and not just *enough*. The New Testament begins with grace and ends with grace.

> "And of His fullness we have all received, and *grace* for *grace*" (John 1:16).

> "But may the God of all *grace*, who called us to His eternal glory by Christ Jesus, after you have suffered a while, perfect, establish, strengthen, and settle you" (1 Peter 5:10).

> "But grow in the *grace* and knowledge of our Lord and Savior Jesus Christ. To Him be the glory both now and forever. Amen" (2 Peter 3:18).

> "The *grace* of our Lord Jesus Christ be with you all. Amen" (Revelation 22:21).

- Salvation is part of His grace.
- Spiritual gifts are His grace.
- Forgiveness of sin is a grace.
- Strength is a grace.
- Financial needs being met is a grace.
- The gospel is a gospel of grace.
- We receive the Word of His grace.
- Power of God is His grace.

- Healing is His grace.
- Walking in victory is His grace.
- Relationship with God is a grace.
- Escape from judgment is a grace.
- Access to His presence is a grace.
- Giving is a grace.

GRACE IS A SPIRIT

"Of how much worse punishment, do you suppose, will he be thought worthy who has trampled the Son of God underfoot, counted the blood of the covenant by which he was sanctified a common thing, and insulted the *Spirit of grace*?" (Hebrews 10:29).

"And I will pour on the house of David and on the inhabitants of Jerusalem the *Spirit of grace* and supplication; then they will look on Me whom they pierced. Yes, they will mourn for Him as one mourns for his only son, and grieve for Him as one grieves for a firstborn" (Zachariah 12:10).

WE ARE LIVING IN THE DISPENSATION OF GRACE

"If indeed you have heard of the dispensation of the grace of God which was given to me for you" (Ephesians 3:2). Whenever you read the Bible and see the word *grace*, I would encourage you to mark it and see what type of grace is being spoken of,

EACH OF US RECEIVED A MEASURE OF GRACE

"But to each one of us grace was given according to the measure of Christ's gift" (Ephesians 4:7).

That means each of us has received sufficient grace to meet every need we will ever have. Whenever you read the word *grace* in the Bible from now on, read it with this understanding: God has made available everything He has to you and me to meet our every need. There is sufficient grace; it never run short, so we will have no excuse on the day of judgment.

When you see someone in financial need, you have the grace of God to meet that need. When you see someone sick in their body, you have the grace to release their healing.

When you see someone in need of forgiveness or salvation, you have the word of His grace in you. When you see something happening that is not God's will, you have the grace of God to stop it. Memorize and keep speaking the verse below until it becomes your reality.

> "And God is able to make *all grace* abound toward you, that you, always having all sufficiency in all things, may have an abundance for every good work" (2 Corinthians 9:8). Amen.

THE UNSEARCHABLE RICHES OF CHRIST

Do you know who arranged the longest feast on this earth? I believe it was King Ahasuerus of Persia. He reigned over one hundred and twenty-seven provinces from India to Ethiopia. One day he decided to throw a feast for all his officials and governors across his vast domain. The feast he arranged lasted a hundred and eighty days. That means it lasted six months. Can you imagine the preparation, expenses, and management required to arrange such a feast? We struggle to arrange one meal (forget about a feast) for five people!

> That in the third year of his reign he made a feast for all his officials and servants—the powers of Persia and Media, the nobles, and the princes of the provinces being before him—when he showed the riches of his glorious kingdom and the splendor of his excellent majesty for many days, one hundred

and eighty days in all. And when these days were completed, the king made a feast lasting seven days for all the people who were present in Shushan the citadel, from great to small, in the court of the garden of the king's palace (Esther 1:3-5).

When those 180 days were over, he held an additional seven days of feasts for all the people in the capital. However, the Bible says King Solomon's riches and wisdom exceeded that of other kings on the earth. That means that compared to Solomon, King Ahasuerus was a junior, or a joke. Can you imagine that?

"So King Solomon surpassed all the kings of the earth in *riches* and wisdom" (1 Kings 10:23).

The reason I am writing about these kings is this: If the king of an earthly nation has such an abundance of riches and wisdom, how much more does our King Jesus possess? He is not just a king of one nation. He is the King of the whole universe. He is the King of all kings. He owns the cattle on a thousand hills. He lives in you. King Ahasuerus held that extravagant feast to show the riches of his glorious kingdom and the splendor of his excellent majesty. It took one hundred and eighty days to show it all to the people. Our God has been feeding the whole creation since the earth began, and His resources have not diminished any from what He had when it all began. He never had to borrow from anyone. His kingdom never had to borrow from another kingdom.

Do you know why God decided to save a bunch of sinners like us? He wanted to show off the riches of His grace to the devil and his kingdom. He has been showing that for more than two thousand years and has not run out yet—and never will. There is sufficient grace for whatever you are going through.

"But God, who is rich in mercy, because of His great love with which He loved us…that in the ages to come He might show the exceeding riches of His grace in His kindness toward us in Christ Jesus" (Ephesians 2:4,7).

Read the following verses and meditate on the riches of Christ.

God blesses us according to the riches of His goodness.

> "Or do you despise the *riches of His goodness*, forbearance, and longsuffering, not knowing that the goodness of God leads you to repentance?" (Romans 2:4).

God chose the Gentiles to show the riches of His glory.

> "And that He might make known the *riches of His glory* on the vessels of mercy, which He had prepared beforehand for glory" (Romans 9:23).

God forgives our sins according to the riches of His grace.

> "In Him we have redemption through His blood, the forgiveness of sins, according to the *riches of His grace*" (Ephesians 1:7).

We should preach the unsearchable riches of Christ.

> "To me, who am less than the least of all the saints, this grace was given, that I should preach among the Gentiles *the unsearchable riches of Christ*" (Ephesians 3:8).

God meets our needs according to His riches in glory.

> "And my God shall supply all your need according to *His riches in glory by Christ Jesus*" (Philippians 4:19).

God wants us to walk in the revelation of these truths. When you think about the riches of Christ, consider how much greater His riches are in comparison to that of any other king or wealthy person on earth. We spend most of our life asking for things which God has already given to us. There is no prayer request in the New Testament for material needs. Paul never prayed for any of the members of the churches to receive a bigger house or a new donkey! God has made everything that He has and everything He owns available to us. It is up to us how much we will believe, and appropriate, God's grace in our lives.

What would happen if all the believers stopped praying (begging God) for their material needs, but began to thank God for providing all their needs according to the riches of His grace? What if believers began to pray the purposes of God into existence? This world would never be the same. May the Lord cause that to happen before He comes. Amen

What is included in our inheritance?

> "Ask of Me, and I will give You the nations for Your *inheritance*, and the ends of the earth for Your possession" (Psalm 2:8).

> "O Lord, You are the portion of my inheritance and my cup; You maintain my lot. The lines have fallen to me in pleasant places; yes, I have a good inheritance" (Psalm 16:5-6).

> "No weapon formed against you shall prosper, and every tongue which rises against you in judgment you shall condemn. This is the heritage of the servants of the Lord, and their righteousness is from Me," says the Lord" (Isaiah 54:17).

> "Blessed are the meek, for they shall inherit the earth" (Matthew 5:5).

REASONS PEOPLE ARE NOT BLESSED

When God blesses you, He wants you to be a blessing to others. He wants to bless others through you. Many people are not blessed because they do not allow God to let His blessings flow through them. Instead, those blessings get stuck with them. The moment you hesitate to give away what He tells you to give the flow of blessing will stop. It requires our immediate obedience. Two of the blessings of Abraham are: He will make him a blessing and all the families of the earth shall be blessed through him. The reason God chose Israel was for them to be a blessing to others. Unfortunately, they were not willing to do that, so God took away their blessings.

God will test you on this. He will ask you give away the most precious thing you have. Sometimes He will tell you to give away all your savings. Your willingness to obey or disobey will show where your trust is and who your real source is. I have failed a couple of times on this test and passed at other times. God wants you to increase your level of giving with each season. Abraham gave the tithe to Melchizedek, but that was just the beginning of his giving. Eventually God asked him to give away his son, the most precious thing he had; he obeyed and received an eternal blessing.

God wants you to be a conduit of His grace and blessings.

> "Let him who stole steal no longer, but rather let him labor, working with his hands what is good, that *he may have something to give him who has need*" (Ephesians 4:28).

This verse also explains why we should work. It is so we have something to give to those in need. That should be our motivation for living. When you live like that, you will not lack anything. You will always have abundance in all things.

LET US RECEIVE ALL HIS GRACE

Some believers do not receive all of God's grace; they only receive some. Some receive saving grace; some receive healing grace; others receive going to heaven grace. There is a different grace for different needs, as I mentioned earlier. God has made all His grace available to us by Christ. Do not misunderstand me; there are not ten different kinds of grace: There is one grace that is sufficient for all things, but we understand it differently. Just like the Bible says God has seven Spirits, but there is only one Holy Spirit. Please receive with wisdom what I am trying to communicate.

The apostle Paul taught the believers in Corinth about giving by mentioning the example of the churches in Macedonia? The Macedonian believers were very poor. They did not have much to give, but they had received a grace. In the midst of their lack and poverty, they gave liberally.

If they had not received that grace, they would not have given because poor people are afraid to give.

> "Moreover, brethren, we make known to you the *grace of God* bestowed on the churches of Macedonia: that in a great trial of affliction the abundance of their joy and their *deep poverty* abounded in the riches of their liberality" (2 Corinthians 8:1-2).

When they gave, the bondage of poverty was broken off their lives and they received a revelation to tap into the riches of God, the riches of His glory. They were ignorant of God's riches in glory prior to this. They would not have received that revelation if they had not received the grace to give from their poverty. They were the only church that participated in giving to his ministry.

> "Now you Philippians know also that in the beginning of the gospel, when I departed from Macedonia, no church shared with me concerning giving and receiving but you only" (Philippians 4:15).

SPIRITUAL INHERITANCE

Here's another secret I found in Scripture: The responsibility of a truly anointed servant of God is to cause others to possess what really belongs to them in the Spirit. Moses and Joshua helped the entire people of Israel possess their spiritual inheritance. We need ministers like that in our day. Unfortunately, many ministers steal from their people instead of empowering them. These are not true minsters of the gospel. They are wolves in sheep's clothing. A true minister of the gospel will empower others to tap into their spiritual inheritance for the benefit of the kingdom, rather than focus on personal gain. Paul said that he had made many rich (2 Corinthians 6:10).

If you study the lives of these people you will see that they all have something in common. Their intention was to help others discover and fulfill their purpose. This is why Abraham gave Lot the first choice of the land. He also let Lot choose where he wanted to live when they were forced to separate. He fought against enemies to rescue Lot and his family. Abraham had the grace of God upon him to turn a desert into a garden, but Lot didn't. Moses, Elijah, and Elisha also created instant millionaires by supernatural grace.

Elijah and Elisha helped start businesses. When the widow's oil was multiplied, it was an instant miracle of supernatural wealth. She went from being poor to wealthy, in a matter of a few hours. In all of these instances, those involved had to do something. It was not free money transferred into their account. They were given a business idea or an opportunity, which they had to put to work and develop.

The church in Corinth was a very special church. Though they had many moral issues, they were one of the most powerful churches in the Spirit that Paul established. He said they became instantly wealthy. They began to reign in life. That is what God intends for every church in every nation.

Paul said that even though he seemed to be poor in the natural, he possessed all things. That meant he had the power to release anything to anyone at any time. This is true apostolic grace and authority. Paul could make a person rich instantly.

The best example of all is our Lord Jesus. He became poor for our sake, so that through His poverty we can become rich (2 Corinthians 8:9). Why did the Creator of the universe and the greatest King of all time choose to be born poor on this earth? It was not an accident, but a deliberate choice for the sake of the many who were oppressed by the curse of poverty.

The saddest thing that has happened with the modern prosperity movement is that instead of empowering believers to become what God created them to be, many ministers have empowered themselves and taken advantage of ignorant believers to become individually wealthy, while the majority of the believers remain living hand-to-mouth or in survival mode.

CHAPTER - 16

THE TWELVE LAWS OF KINGDOM ECONOMY

Every successful leadership or financial principle that works is based on the Bible. Prosperity comes when we practice the principles that are mentioned in it. Many read the Bible to learn about sin, salvation and the Holy Spirit, but few study the financial principles in it and the laws that govern the natural and spiritual worlds.

The ungodly people prosper because they practice biblical principles without even believing in the God of the Bible. God established laws and principles that work the same for the believer and the unbeliever, just as the law of gravity works the same for everyone regardless of their faith. The sun rises and rain falls on both the wicked and the righteous.

God is not partial to anyone. When we put to practice the following principles, we will prosper in what we do. They are not exclusive laws, but they are the basic laws that govern prosperity.

1. THE LAW OF DILIGENCE

Diligence is a work ethic. Being diligent is not just working hard, but working smart. Diligence is a combination of hard work, perseverance, knowledge, and excellence. God expects us to give Him our best. When we work well and with a spirit of excellence, He rewards us with success.

> "The lazy man does not roast what he took in hunting, but diligence is man's precious possession" (Proverbs 12:27).

> "He who has a slack hand becomes poor, but the hand of the diligent makes rich" (Proverbs 10:4).

> "The soul of a lazy man desires, and has nothing; but the soul of the diligent shall be made rich" (Proverbs 13:4).

> "The plans of the diligent lead surely to plenty, but those of everyone who is hasty, surely to poverty" (Proverbs 21:5).

> "Be diligent to know the state of your flocks, and attend to your herds; for riches are not forever, nor does a crown endure to all generations. When the hay is removed, and the tender grass shows itself, and the herbs of the mountains are gathered in, the lambs will provide your clothing, and the goats the price of a field; you shall have enough goats' milk for your food, for the food of your household, and the nourishment of your maidservants" (Proverbs 27:23-27).

> "Whatever your hand finds to do, do it with all our might" (Ecclesiastes 9:10, NIV).

2. THE LAW OF INVESTING/SAVING

Money does not grow on trees. But money does have the capacity to grow if it finds the right environment. It grows as we invest in businesses, real estate, or other institutions. It takes time to grow money, and there is nothing wrong with investing it. God likes and appreciates it when we invest and make more than we had when we started.

The parable of the talents is a perfect example of financial investment. It was the last parable Jesus told before He went to Jerusalem for His crucifixion. Many believers in Third World countries misunderstand investing. Some of them believe that banks, real estate and precious metals all belong to the devil and the world, so they try to stay away from those things. That is not what Jesus taught.

In the parable of the talents, the master told the people to whom he gave the talents, "Do business till I come" (Luke 19:13).

When you get a hundred dollars you pay the tithe, which is ten percent and save five percent for the future. Do not spend all the money you get. Most people spend more than what they earn. When you get a hundred dollars you should spend only 85 dollars. This is a discipline that needs to be developed over time. Believers should be saving money regularly.

3. THE LAW OF SOWING AND REAPING

I have explained this principle in detail in one of the earlier chapters of this book.

4. THE LAW OF COMMITMENT

Whatever we do in life requires commitment to stay on course and finish the task. There is a honeymoon season that will last six months to a year in every new endeavor we enter in life: marriage, new business, church, and so on. Only committed people will finish worthy goals.

When the going gets tough, the tough get going. Just because things are challenging or hard does not mean we need to quit, or that what we are doing is not God's will. Whenever we step out to do God's will, *we will face hardships and go through some turmoil. That is to test our commitment.*

Whatever you do in life will be tested beyond description. There is a law of resistance that you will need to overcome to move forward in life. The best advice I remember receiving from people when I was growing up was, "Never give up!" When things get difficult, you need to stay in the game long enough to receive victory. You need to know from God when it is time to move on or stay in the game.

5. THE LAW OF DREAMS AND DESIRE

God communicates His purpose for us through dreams and desires. That is why the Lord tells us to guard our hearts with all diligence for out it flows the issues of life. God-given desires do not go away. They do not leave our hearts. We are not commanded to suppress our desires. We need to guard our heart from evil desires. All desires are not evil. God put desires in our heart to believe and achieve them for His glory.

God will put a dream in our heart and we need to pursue it with all our heart. Many times, believers are not in a position of influence because inwardly they believe they are supposed to be poor and separated from the world. We need to be sure we are fulfilling the purposes God has for us here on earth instead.

> "Guard your heart above all else, for it determines the course of your life" (Proverbs 4:23 NLT).

6. THE LAW OF INTEGRITY

Integrity should be the foundation of our character. Many times when we get blessed, we tend to lose our integrity. Money and influence have spoiled many great leaders and their focus. It is difficult to stay true to our original purpose when we receive unprecedented amounts of blessings.

We have to watch our hearts and our intentions. Stay close to God and close to the original vision God gave you. Many multi-billion-dollar businesses have crumbled overnight because they had no integrity in their financial dealings. Whatever is not built on integrity, whether in business or ministry, will fall eventually (Proverbs 28:6).

7. THE LAW OF TEAMWORK

It takes more than one person to achieve anything of quality, that's valuable and enduring. One of the things that surprises me is the large crew that it takes to produce movies or videos. If you watch the end of the production, you will see the names of people who were part of making that movie. There will be hundreds of people who were part of making that movie! Each one had a unique and valuable role in it. They bring their expertise and talents together to achieve a common goal.

They work as a team. I cry sometimes, and ask God, "Lord, why don't I see that in the church?" Everyone is trying to achieve their own little goals and build their own little kingdoms. If someone is talented and able, they will not help someone else; instead they will go out and start their own so-called "ministry." One of the reasons the church is not effective is because we have been fragmented into hundreds of ineffective pieces, and are not working as a team.

8. THE LAW OF PLANNING AND BUDGETING

Knowing what God wants you to do is a small thing compared to how to do what He wants you to do. Many fail, not because they do not know what God wants them to do, but because they do not ask God for His plan (His way) to fulfill His purpose. Ninety eight out of one hundred new ventures fail for lack of planning and poor budgeting. What is a budget? A budget is the amount of money that is available for, required for, or assigned to a particular project.

Before we step out to do anything, we need to sit back and consider whether we have the needed resources to complete that project. Someone once said: "A vision without a plan is wishful thinking."

Many step out to do things "by faith" but it is not faith; its presumption, and they end up in financial calamity. I have done that myself and learned valuable lessons. It does not matter how much I feel in my heart that I should do something; I must step back and consider whether I am prepared to endure whatever it takes to complete it. Jesus said anyone who is planning to build a tower needs to plan whether he has enough resources to finish the task.

> "For which of you, intending to build a tower, does not sit down first and count the cost, whether he has enough to finish it—lest, after he has laid the foundation, and is not able to finish, all who see it begin to mock him, saying, 'This man began to build and was not able to finish'" (Luke 14:28-30).

Then Jesus tells the story about the king who goes off to fight against his enemy. He must decide whether he has enough power to defeat the enemy. Otherwise, he needs to make peace before he goes to battle. That means he needs to call off his project until he is ready to finish it.

> "Or what king, going to make war against another king, does not sit down first and consider whether he is able with ten thousand to meet him who comes against him with twenty thousand? Or else, while the other is still a great way off, he sends a delegation and asks conditions of peace" (Luke 14:31-32).

We cannot substitute planning for spirituality, nor prayer and faith for budgeting. We need to pray, plan and budget according to the leading of the Spirit. You might be speaking in tongues and fasting three days a week, but these good practices should not replace planning and financial budgeting.

Natural and spiritual things go hand in hand. They are the two rails of the same railway track. Trains cannot run on a single rail. It needs two properly arranged and balanced rails for a smooth ride. What happens if we try to run the train on a single rail? There will be an accident.

We should not minimize the importance of the spiritual nor the natural side of our Christian life. We need both to live properly on this earth. Without the one, the other would derail. God is the Master Planner. He has planned the earth from beginning to end, before the He laid its foundation. "Just as He chose us in Him before the foundation of the world, that we should be holy and without blame before Him in love" (Ephesians 1:4).

What does that mean? It means He has chosen us in Christ before the foundation of the earth. He finished all the work concerning earth before He laid its foundation. He is not sitting up in heaven worried about how He is going to finish what He started.

> "For we are God's masterpiece. He has created us anew in Christ Jesus, so we can do the good things he planned for us long ago" (Ephesians 2:10, NLT).

Any significant work that was done in the Bible was done with proper planning and budgeting. Whether it was building the ark, the tabernacle, or the temple—all were done with extensive planning and budgeting.

> "Where there is no counsel, the people fall; but in the multitude of counselors there is safety" (Proverbs 11:14).

> "Plans go wrong for lack of advice; many advisers bring success" (Proverbs 15:22, NLT).

> "Plans succeed through good counsel; don't go to war without wise advice" (Proverbs 20:18, NLT).

> "The plans of the diligent *lead* surely to plenty, but *those of* everyone *who is* hasty, surely to poverty" (Proverbs 25:1).

One of the enemy's tactics against God's servants is that he will push them to start new ventures and projects without proper planning and counsel. They blindly believe God will help them and give them success.

The enemy laughs at them when they cannot finish the project and run away from it.

9. THE LAW OF FIRSTFRUITS

The law of firstfruits is one of the primary laws of prosperity. When we study the Bible, we see a powerful principle established by God in the area of giving—the law of firstfruits. *God wants to be first* in every area of our life. People in biblical times understood this powerful principle.

> "Honor the Lord with your possessions, and with the firstfruits of all your increase; so your barns will be filled with plenty, and your vats will overflow with new wine" (Proverbs 3:9-10).

Firstfruit means you give God *the first and the best portion* of your income, time, and whatever you possess. When you get your salary, before you pay your bills and expenses, write a check or separate the tithe first, then use the remainder of the money for whatever you need.

If a servant of God comes to your house to stay, give him the best room you have in your house. When you feed someone, give him the best portion of food that you have. When you do that you are honoring the Lord.

Another reason why tithe-paying believers do not receive a financial miracle is because they do not put God first. They spend money on themselves when they get paid and bring to the Lord what is left over. That is backwards. God is not pleased with that.

> "You shall not delay to offer the first of your ripe produce and your juices. The firstborn of your sons you shall give to Me. Likewise you shall do with your oxen and your sheep. It shall be with its mother seven days; on the eighth day you shall give it to Me" (Exodus 22:29-30).

In the Old Testament times, people's primary source of income was agriculture and livestock. They were commanded to bring the firstfruits of all their increase and the firstborn of their children as an offering to the Lord.

> "For all the firstborn among the children of Israel are Mine, both man and beast" (Numbers 8:17).

The first recorded offering in the Bible was the offering, which Cain and Abel offered to God. God was pleased with Abel's offering and rejected Cain's. Genesis 4 says Abel brought from the firstborn from his flock, but Cain brought what he could find.

> "And in the process of time it came to pass that Cain brought an offering of the fruit of the ground to the Lord. Abel also brought of the *firstborn* of his flock and of their fat. And the Lord respected Abel and his offering, but He did not respect Cain and his offering. And Cain was very angry, and his countenance fell" (Genesis 4:3-5).

After the flood, when Noah and his family came out of the ark, the first thing Noah did was not to build a house for himself or a garden. Instead, he took the best that he had and offered it as a sacrifice to the Lord.

> "Then Noah built an altar to the Lord, and took of every clean animal and of every clean bird, and offered burnt offerings on the altar. And the Lord smelled a soothing aroma. Then the Lord said in His heart, "I will never again curse the ground for man's sake, although the imagination of man's heart is evil from his youth; nor will I again destroy every living thing as I have done" (Genesis 8:20-21).

When the people of Israel reached the Promised Land, the first city they occupied was Jericho. God specifically told them that all the silver and gold and all other precious metals must be brought to the treasury of the Lord.

"But all the silver and gold, and vessels of bronze and iron, are consecrated to the Lord; they shall come into the treasury of the Lord" (Joshua 6:19).

But one of the Israelites brought a curse upon the whole nation and they were defeated before the people of Ai. Why? Because Jericho was the firstfruit of the blessings God gave to His people. They did not honor Him with their firstfruit. God takes our giving very seriously. There are many other examples.

10. THE LAW OF PRODUCTIVITY

The first commandment in the Bible is to be fruitful (Genesis 1:27). God expects fruitfulness from us. If something is not producing the fruit He is expecting; either He will remove it or take it and give it to someone else who will put it to better use. Being barren or unfruitful is considered a curse in the Bible. I have explained this in detail in a previous chapter, so please refer to it.

11. THE LAW OF PREPARATION

Do you know why most Charismatics and Pentecostals do not excel in any area? They do not believe in the law of preparation. They want God to do everything for them and they call that believing God for a miracle. I haven't heard of anyone winning an Olympic medal unless they prepared for it. Why? Preparation is necessary for success in most worthwhile pursuits. You have to study for the test that takes you to the next level, or gives you the certificate that enables you to practice your craft. This is true on all levels of society. From the hairdresser to the lawyer to the judge to the doctor: They must all pass tests to be able to practice. Each one must prepare to have success.

The Bible talks about the law of preparation a lot. Moses was in preparation for forty years before God released him into the ministry he was called to do. Jesus prepared for thirty years. Paul spent fourteen years in the wilderness, receiving revelation from God. There is no shortcut to success.

We are always looking something for a quick fix. We have abused God's miracle-working power with our laziness and excuses. That is why God is not manifesting His power as He would like. Miracles are for the most hopeless and helpless cases—for people who are at the end of their rope. In church, everyone runs to receive a miracle. We have made spiritual crutches to support our inability to prepare or persevere. *Success is preparation meeting an opportunity.* When the opportunity shows up; if you are not prepared, you will miss your chance.

12. THE LAW OF STEWARDSHIP

Whatever you have right now is a gift from God which He has given you to manage. The Bible says, a man can receive nothing unless it is given to him from above (John 3:27). We may have worked or received what we have by different means, but it all comes from Him. We need to have an attitude of gratitude—thinking that anything we have could be demanded by its original owner. Everything we are is His and at his disposal.

Stewardship is an important subject in the Bible and in the kingdom. If we are not faithful with what we have, it will be taken from us and given to someone who will be faithful. Faithful means more than just protecting something we have received. It also speaks of multiplying what we received. If there is no multiplication, then there is no growth and eventually, no faithfulness.

Many believers think if they just protect themselves and make few mistakes by the time they reach their deathbed, then they have lived a faithful life. Not according to the Bible. In the Bible, God expects everything that has life to grow and expand. That has been His will and pattern from the beginning.

> "Moreover it is required in stewards that one be found faithful" (1 Corinthians 4:2).

> "As each one has received a gift, minister it to one another, as good stewards of the manifold grace of God" (1 Peter 4:10).

TWELVE KEYS FOR PROSPERING AT YOUR WORKPLACE

If you are working for a company, I would like to give you some advice. If you practice what I'm going to share with you, you will prosper and be promoted within no time.

Consider your workplace as though it were your own company: What would you do differently if you owned that company? How would your performance and attitude change? Do exactly that. You will be amazed where you will end up.

Most people work for a salary. Their stomach and personal needs are their priorities. When a company hires you, they did not hire you because of your need. They wanted someone to help them achieve their goals. Make their goals your priority and adjust your attitude when you are at your workplace. There has to be a balance, of course. I am not suggesting you should put your job before your family or your own health. You should not become a slave or be abused by the system.

If you notice something that needs to be done, take the initiative and get it done: If you see something out of place or that someone messed something up in the common area, take care of it. Put things in the right place; clean up the mess someone else made. Don't complain. Your actions will be noticed sooner or later and you will be rewarded.

Offer suggestions and solutions to improve the company or your department: If you get an excellent idea to solve a problem that your company or department is facing, share it with the responsible people. Even if your idea is stolen and others get the credit for it, eventually you will receive your just reward. Don't just think about yourself. If you do not have any ideas, ask the Holy Spirit to give you ideas and solutions to be a blessing to the company.

If you are in a meeting, take notes: When your department is having their weekly or monthly planning meeting, make sure you are taking notes. If you are running a meeting and if you expect others to take notes, make sure you do the same. When you are in your weekly meetings, have a pen and notebook at hand. Be a resource and an asset to others in the company.

Ask questions about where your company is going and what their needs and goals are: Remember the Golden Rule? Do to others what you expect them to do for you! (Matthew 7:12). Don't wait for your boss to come and ask you about your struggles and needs. Have a heart to care for the company. Treat it as if it were your own. Take ownership.

Report illegal activities: If you notice someone misusing the company's resources or doing anything illegal, report it to the appropriate authority. You might become the enemy of some; but if you are doing it for the common good, you are helping yourself.

Be willing to learn new things: Managers and leaders love people who are hungry to learn. They are looking for people who have potential and a heart to grow. If you foresee where your company is going and its future need, offer to help and start learning now.

Have an abundant mindset, not a scarcity mindset: Mindset is very important. Your mindset is contagious. Many have a closed and narrow mindset based on how they were brought up and how their worldview was formed. An abundant mindset attracts growth.

Do more than what you are asked or required to do: Self-centeredness causes people to get by with doing just the bare minimum. You will not be promoted that way. Whenever you are given an assignment or project to complete, go the extra mile and do more than what you were required to do. When you do that, it reveals your heart toward the job and the company you are working for. Have a spirit of excellence.

Do not make excuses: Managers and leaders don't like excuses. Unless something tragic happened and you tried every way that is out there, making an excuse is not acceptable. There are people who made making excuses their second nature. The real problem is laziness. A lazy and unorganized person will find excuses for not doing something when they are supposed to do.

Be on time: Being on time is not enough, you need to be early. People who are productive like to do things as early as possible. When you come to work, be at least five minutes early. Don't think in your heart, *They are not paying me for that five minutes so why should I spend it for the company?* If you value your work and the company you are working for, eventually you will be paid more for your time. If you were late for the last three out of five appointments, know that you have a problem with being late.

Know that it's always teamwork: You can't succeed alone. God created us to live in communities. Whether families, governments, companies, or church, there are communities everywhere. However, we live in a culture where individualism is glorified. We need to learn to live as an individual in a community. Both are important.

What I find lately is that wealth and success is an attitude. If you have the right attitude, you can achieve the impossible. In the same way, if you have the wrong attitude, you will fail in life. Your attitude creates an atmosphere for success or failure. The good news is that your attitude can be adjusted or fine-tuned. Your attitude is an invisible compass to where you are going and how far you will go in life. It happens without your knowledge or awareness. You are governed by your attitude.

You will be surrounded with hostile circumstances, but if you have the right attitude you can find favor and the way out easily. *God allows negative circumstances, not to destroy you, but to strengthen your character and faith.* The struggles you overcome in life determine how well you do in life. In this way, your *attitude* determines your *altitude*. Just like the test you take determines your grade. How well you respond to your circumstances determines what is in you. How you face challenges in life shows what you are made of.

Remember *like* produces *like*. Men and women in the Bible are remembered for the struggle they overcame, the battle they won, and the enemies they put to flight. They were not staying in their entertainment rooms watching the sports channel. The spirit of entertainment has bound more people in America than any other principality. Everywhere people go they are looking for entertainment (people call it fun). In school they are looking for entertainment. When they go to church, they want to be entertained. They go out and buy special furniture for all their entertainment devices. I am not against entertainment, but that should not consume how I spend most of my time.

Many are deceived by the devil, thinking if God wants them to do something, He will make them do it. And if it is God's purpose, He will make it happen. No! He is looking for people whose hearts are perfect toward Him (2 Chronicles 16:9). Open your eyes! Whenever God picked someone to use, He always picked people who were busy with their lives. He went to the place of their work, like when He called Moses or the twelve disciples.

CHAPTER - 17

PROSPERITY AND SUFFERING

Why should I talk about suffering in a book about economy? There is a misconception in some circles of the body of Christ that if we are really prosperous, we will not have to go through any suffering or struggles in this life and if you do, then there is something wrong with your faith. They teach that God does not want us to suffer, but to be wealthy and prosperous. That is far from the truth. As long as we live here, we will suffer in one way or other. Whether you are a billionaire or in financial debt, we all suffer.

In some of the eastern parts of world, people have equated poverty with suffering. They glorify their poverty by saying they are suffering for Christ and they are rich spiritually. Being poor is not suffering for Christ. The Bible does not teach that. It is important for us as Christians to have a proper understanding about what the Bible teaches about suffering.

Blessing and suffering go hand in hand. We should expect to have both in our lives.

> "Yes, and all who desire to live godly in Christ Jesus will suffer persecution" (2 Timothy 3:12).

This scripture does not exclude anyone.

Instead it exhorts us to do the following:

> "Therefore let those who suffer according to the will of God commit their souls to Him in doing good, as to a faithful Creator" (1 Peter 4:19).

> "God blesses those who patiently endure testing and temptation. Afterward they will receive the crown of life that God has promised to those who love him" (James 1:12, NLT).

Suffering is the will of God (1 Peter 3:17). Paul exhorted the believers in Ephesus in Acts 14:22, saying that they would have to suffer, but that they should strengthen one another and continue in their faith.

There are two types of sufferings. One is for righteousness sake.

> "For what credit is it if, when you are beaten for your faults, you take it patiently? But when you do good and suffer, if you take it patiently, this is commendable before God. For to this you were called, because Christ also suffered for us, leaving us an example, that you should follow His steps" (1 Peter 2:20-21).

Human life is a battle between good and evil. Spiritual life is a battle between spirit and flesh. In our mind, there is a battle between the voice of our spirit and voice of our flesh (1 Peter 3:14-17).

The other kind of suffering is punishment for doing evil. Peter exhorts us to live lives of holiness, no longer conforming to our flesh, but living according to our spirit (1 Peter 1:12-16). The Bible discusses suffering because we are being punished for our rebellion against God's authority or governmental authority, or reaping our own bad habits.

What type of suffering is it?

The suffering we go through in our Christian life is not sickness or poverty. Neither sickness nor poverty comes from God. They come from the devil, and we need to resist and fight against them. The suffering we go through in our Christian life is the affliction we face from other people.

Jesus said if anyone forsakes father, mother, land or possession and follows Him, that person shall receive hundredfold with persecution and life eternal in the world to come. That persecution comes from people who are jealous, ignorant, or envious about our walk with the Lord. So basically, people will hate us for our faith and blessings. Both Christians and non-Christians will persecute us for our faith in Christ.

> "For to you it has been granted on behalf of Christ, not only to believe in Him, but also to suffer for His sake" (Philippians 1:29).

We are "partakers of Christ's suffering" according to 1 Peter 4:13-19. 1 Peter 2:22-23 speaks of the type of suffering Christ went through. Christ did not get sick nor was He a beggar. He experienced sickness and poverty only for us. He allowed Himself to come under the curse we were also under to deliver us from it.

> "Who comforts us in all our tribulation, that we may be able to comfort those who are in any trouble, with the comfort with which we ourselves are comforted by God. For as the sufferings of Christ abound in us, so our consolation also abounds through Christ. Now if we are afflicted, it is for your consolation and salvation, which is effective for enduring the same sufferings which we also suffer. Or if we are comforted, it is for your consolation and salvation. And our hope for you is steadfast, because we know that as you are partakers of the sufferings, so also you will partake of the consolation" (2 Corinthians 1:4-7).

How long will the sufferings of God remain in our life? 1 Peter says a little while:

> "Resist him, steadfast in the faith, knowing that the same sufferings are experienced by your brotherhood in the world. But may the God of all grace, who called us to His eternal glory by Christ Jesus, after you have suffered a while, perfect, establish, strengthen, and settle you. To Him be the glory and the dominion forever and ever. Amen" (1 Peter 5:9-11).

> "For our light affliction, which is but for a moment, is working for us a far more exceeding and eternal weight of glory, while we do not look at the things which are seen, but at the things which are not seen. For the things which are seen are temporary, but the things which are not seen are eternal" (2 Corinthians 4:17-18).

THE PURPOSE OF SUFFERINGS

- We suffer to make us perfect (1 Peter 5:10).

    > "God, for whom and through whom everything was made, chose to bring many children into glory. And it was only right that he should make Jesus, through his suffering, a perfect leader, fit to bring them into their salvation" (Hebrews 2:10, NLT).

In Matthew it says, be perfect as your Father in heaven is perfect. God lets us go through things in our lives to perfect our character. To become perfect in our character, we need to be perfected in patience and long-suffering.

- We suffer to teach us obedience (Hebrews 5:8).

Jesus was the Son of God, but He needed to learn obedience through the things He suffered. It took thirty years for Jesus to learn obedience.

- We suffer to cease from sin (1 Peter 4:1-2).

- We suffer to be glorified with Him (Romans 8:17-18; 1 Peter 5:9-10).
- We suffer to learn to comfort others (2 Corinthians 1:3-7).
- We suffer to partake of His holiness (Hebrews 12:10).
- We suffer to manifest God's wisdom. There are people like Job whom God chose to go through afflictions to prove to the enemy, man's faithfulness to God. Most people will not go through such trials and remain faithful to God. Job was an example of such a person to whom God could trust to remain faithful, no matter what they went through.

DIFFERENT KINDS OF SUFFERING

TEMPTATION

Jesus was tempted in every way, yet without sin. We will be tempted in different areas of our lives by the enemy. This is one form of suffering. As long we live we will be tempted in the areas of lust of the flesh, lust of the eye, and the pride of life.

PERSECUTION

Persecution is the hostility we face because of our faith in Jesus Christ. In many parts of the world, Christians are persecuted because of their faith in Christ. When a person comes to Christ from a Hindu background in India, sometimes all hell breaks loose. His or her own family will disown them and forsake them.

TRIBULATION

Tribulation is from the world system. As a Christian, when we step out to do something, we experience opposition because the world governments and their systems are not set up to assist Christians. Most of the governments are corrupt in some way. When we get out there with our good intentions, the people in the world will fight against us.

Jesus said, "In the world you will have tribulation" (John 16:33).

SUFFERING

Hebrews 11:13 says that the Old Testament saints were pilgrims and strangers here. Some ministers teach that they were all nomads, homeless, and poor. That is not true. Some of the Old Testament saints were wealthy, and some of them were *the* wealthiest people of that time, namely Abraham, Isaac, and Jacob. Some of them lived like nomads (Hebrews 11:36-38).

"Lord remember David and all his afflictions" (Psalm 132:1).

In some translations, it renders this word *sufferings*. 1 Chronicles 22 gives an account of the wealth David collected to build the temple. This is one man's donation to the work of God. He was not poor nor sick. However, we read about the afflictions David went through in his life because of his enemies in his psalms. He went through depression, discouragement and betrayals several times in his life. Many were through people in his own family.

> "For it is not an enemy who reproaches me; then I could bear it. Nor is it one who hates me who has exalted himself against me; then I could hide from him. But it was you, a man my equal, my companion and my acquaintance. We took sweet counsel together, and walked to the house of God in the throng" (Psalm 55:12-14).

Moses went through sufferings too. When the Bible talks about suffering, it is not talking about poverty or sickness. Most of the time, the Bible refers to suffering because of problems caused by other people.

CHASTENING OF THE LORD

There is another kind of suffering that the Bible speaks of that we go through as Christians. God is our Father and we are His sons and daughters.

Every parent who loves their children disciplines them. The reason we discipline our children is to develop their character and help them mature.

Parents who are nice to their children all the time, and never correct them, will have unruly children who will take advantage of their parents. Our children won't do what they are supposed to do or respect us as they ought if we do not discipline them. When children disobey their parents, they need to be corrected and disciplined, even though it is painful to them at the time. As parents, we know it is for their good that we discipline them.

This same principle applies in the Spirit. God is our Father and He corrects us and disciplines us for our good.

> "If you endure chastening, God deals with you as with sons; for what son is there whom a father does not chasten? But if you are without chastening, of which all have become partakers, then you are illegitimate and not sons" (Hebrews 12:7-8).

Some children test their parent's patience; they will not respond or do something when they are told the first time. Others rebel against their parents and need to be corrected. There are three words used in the Bible in relation to God's disciplinary actions toward His children. God disciplines us in three stages. First, He gives instruction and if we do not listen, then He will rebuke us. If we do not listen to that rebuke, He will scourge us.

> "My son, do not despise the chastening of the Lord, nor be discouraged when you are rebuked by Him; for whom the Lord loves He chastens, and scourges every son whom He receives" (Hebrews 12:5-6).

The three words used above are chastening, rebuking, and scourging. We see a progressive increase in the intensity of the correction. We are going to look at the Greek to find what each of these words specifically mean.

The word for "chastening" is *paideia*[27] which means "the whole training and education of children, including mind and morals"; and "instruction which aims at increasing virtue." God starts with giving instruction and then if we do not listen He will go to the next step and rebuke us.

The word for "rebuke" in the Greek is *elegcho*[28] which means to convict, refute, or confute, generally with a suggestion of conviction. It also means "to find fault with, correct by word, to reprehend severely, chide, admonish, and reprove."

If we do not pay attention again, He will go to the next step, which is scourging. The word used in Greek is *mastigoo*[29] from the root word *mastix*[30] which means "to whip" or "a calamity" or a "misfortune sent by God to discipline or punish."

Unfortunately, most of us pay attention to God only after a scourging. We will keep going until something tragic happens. That is not God's perfect will for us. Others, because of a lack of understanding, get bitter toward people and God. One of the most difficult things to know is the purpose of pain when you are in the middle of it. Others hold on to their bitterness and grudges, which often manifests as sickness and disease later in their lives. Some believe that more than seventy-five percent of people in hospitals with physical illnesses have sicknesses that are rooted in emotional causes.

---

27 James Strong, "3809. Paideia," Biblehub.com, accessed January 12, 2019, https://biblehub.com/greek/3809.htm.

28 James Strong, "1651. Elegchó," Biblehub.com, accessed January 12, 2019, https://biblehub.com/greek/1651.htm.

29 James Strong, "3146. Mastigoó," Biblehub.com, accessed January 12, 2019, https://biblehub.com/greek/3146.htm.

30 James Strong, "3148. Mastix," Biblehub.com, accessed January 12, 2019, https://biblehub.com/greek/3148.htm.

CHAPTER - 18

MAMMON AND GOD

Mammon is a word used by Jesus for money in the Bible. Actually, mammon is a demonic entity that controls the financial system of the world. Money has power because of this evil spirit that works behind it. The demonic entity that is using that power to control lives, corporations, ministries, churches and nations through greed and covetousness is called mammon.

Only a fraction of the world's wealth is needed to alleviate the poverty that is in the earth. The people who own the wealth are not willing to share because of selfishness and greed. The wealthy have put their trust in their riches, as if it is their god. God is sending a shaking across the economies of the world to communicate a message to them.

It does not matter how much money you have; do not put your trust in it. Do not depend on it as if it was your source of joy and fulfillment. The money you have today, you may not have tomorrow.

> "Do not overwork to be rich; because of your own understanding, cease! Will you set your eyes on that which is not? For riches certainly make themselves wings; they fly away like an eagle toward heaven" (Proverbs 23:4-5).

Let me be frank with you. The goal of Christian life is not to be materially wealthy. *There is a difference between using the wealth you have to serve God and using God to get wealthy.* Many in the church today are trying to use God and His principles to make money for themselves. In the end, they all end up with the same result: shame and grief. If you are making money to serve God it is OK, but if you live with the sole intention of making money to be wealthy, it is wrong and you are heading for danger.

The goal of Christian life is not to be rich, famous, and materially prosperous. We do not see anyone testifying about financial miracles in the early church. We've lost the proper focus of our faith for at least the last 150 years. Jesus said a man's life does not consist of the material abundance he possesses (Luke 12:15). That means whether you have little or a lot does not determine how spiritual you are.

Jesus said to love our enemies. We cannot even love our own family members! Divorce is as rampant in the church as it is in the world. It is time to practice what we preach. Jesus said He left His peace with us, but most people in the church have no peace. Why? Because we are too busy worrying about material stuff which Jesus said we should not worry about. We worry about the house, car, stocks, bank balance, money and things we would like to have. We are not supposed to worry about these things. Most of the worry we have is money related.

I would rather live in a cave like Elijah and have the power of God on my life than live in a three million dollar house with a cabinet full of medicine bottles. The love for the world has infiltrated the church with all the prosperity preaching. The Bible says, "Adulterers and adulteresses! Do you not know that friendship with the world is enmity with God? Whoever therefore wants to be a friend of the world makes himself an enemy of God" (James 4:4). The world and its lust will pass away, but those who do the will of God will remain.

We can be ensnared by money and become a slave to money. God warns us in His Word about the danger of having riches and wealth. There will come a time when we have to choose: Either we are going to serve God or the money He gave us. We can use our money to serve God, but we cannot serve money and God at the same time.

Many in the world and in the church are ensnared by the spirit of mammon—with greed and covetousness. All they desire is more money, and then a little more money. They are never satisfied. They live and die for money. In the Old Testament, again and again God told His people not to forget the purpose and the source of their blessing.

> "Beware that you do not forget the Lord your God by not keeping His commandments, His judgments, and His statutes which I command you today, lest—when you have eaten and are full, and have built beautiful houses and dwell in them; and when your herds and your flocks multiply, and your silver and your gold are multiplied, and all that you have is multiplied; when your heart is lifted up, and you forget the Lord your God who brought you out of the land of Egypt, from the house of bondage; who led you through that great and terrible wilderness, in which were fiery serpents and scorpions and thirsty land where there was no water; who brought water for you out of the flinty rock; who fed you in the wilderness with manna, which your fathers did not know, that He might humble you and that He might test you, to do you good in the end—then you say in your heart, 'My power and the might of my hand have gained me this wealth.' And you shall remember the Lord your God, for it is He who gives you power to get wealth, that He may establish His covenant which He swore to your fathers, as it is this day. Then it shall be, if you by any means forget the Lord your God, and follow other gods, and serve them and worship them, I testify against you this day that you shall surely perish. As the nations which the Lord destroys before you, so you shall perish, because you would not be obedient to the voice of the Lord your God" (Deuteronomy 8:11-20).

We cannot serve God and mammon. Jesus called money a master. He said no man can serve two masters.

> "No servant can serve two masters; for either he will hate the one and love the other, or else he will be loyal to the one and despise the other. You cannot serve God and mammon" (Luke 16:13).

We will hate one and love the other: Many believers are ensnared by the world. They are trapped by the power of money and have stopped serving God. Paul had a couple of those people in his ministry; they had lost their vision for God and left a ministry position to go after financial gain.

> "For Demas has forsaken me, having loved this present world, and has departed for Thessalonica" (2 Timothy 4:10). The Bible also says people will do ministry for the sake of gaining money" See Titus 1:11 and Romans 16:18.

Though God wants to bless us, our goal in life should not be to become rich. Making more money should never be our focus, regardless of the reason why we want to make money. Many believers come up with good business ideas and say, "After I get blessed, I will give to God's ministry." They say when they get the money, they will secure themselves first, invest money for their children, and buy properties. Whatever is left they will give to God's kingdom. That is a wrong attitude. If you have thought like that, please get on your knees and ask God to forgive you.

I have not seen anyone with that mentality prosper yet. That is not the right motive and it is the wrong order. The Bible says if we try to become rich in our own strength, we will end up in grievous trouble.

We bring curses upon ourselves by saying things like this too. That is what happened to Ananias and Sapphira in Acts 5. They kept some money for themselves first, brought the balance to God, and lied to Him. God was furious and they fell dead.

Instead of putting God and His kingdom last, live to give to God's kingdom first. Live on whatever is left over and you will see unlimited resources coming your way. I have seen people shipwreck their lives trying to be rich time and time again.

> "But those who desire to be rich fall into temptation and a snare, and into many foolish and harmful lusts which drown men in destruction and perdition. For the love of money is a root of all kinds of evil, for which some have strayed from the faith in their greediness, and pierced themselves through with many sorrows" (1 Timothy 6:9-10).

Prosperity preaching has corrupted the Christian faith. Men and women want to believe in God for the benefits they can receive. Billions of dollars have been spent on material stuff which should have been spent on winning and making disciples. One of the whoremongers of money in the church today is building programs. The greatest investment in the kingdom today is on materials that are going to be burned with fire. Then someone like me comes along, requesting money for missions, and there is little to nothing left. The missionaries receive the leftovers. Most churches spend more money on their toilet paper than they spend on supporting a missionary. They give $100 each, to fifty different missionaries and broadcast to the world that they are world changers.

The love of material things and entertainment has robbed the church of its power. People come to church, not because God is first in their lives, but because they want to become millionaires. We should learn to be content with what we have. Do not get into the race for greater and greater possessions. We should not make money our god. The goal of the Christian life should be to know God and to make Him known. Jesus is our God.

Paul wrote,

> "Yet indeed I also count all things loss for the excellence of the knowledge of Christ Jesus my Lord, for whom I have suffered the loss of all things, and count them as rubbish, that I may gain Christ" (Philippians 3:8).

Again he said, I want to know Christ and the power of His resurrection. Jesus did not come to me preaching the gospel of prosperity. He did not say to his audience, "Give $100 and then watch what I will do with that." Having a bigger house or cars (or deeper wells and larger herds) were not the subject of His messages. Instead, He taught that we were to carry our cross daily and follow Him. Nobody wants to carry the cross (it is not talking about a literal cross); everyone wants to get more money.

WARNING

The Bible warns about the improper use of money. As I mentioned earlier, money is a kind of power, like electricity. If we do not properly direct and use it, it can be dangerous. We cannot live without electricity; it has become a big part of our life. We cannot live without money either; it is also an important part of our life.

We have to be careful that we do not fall into the trap in which many mighty people have fallen and lost their destiny: Love of money, lust of the flesh, and pride are the three most dangerous weapons that we need to resist. This requires vigilance.

Because of its deceptiveness and ignorance, many have chosen the path of poverty and totally miss out on the plan God has for them. That is not God's will for any of His children. Financial riches are regarded in the Bible as neither good nor bad in themselves; what matters is whether or not they are properly or improperly used. Let's see what the Bible says about the use of material wealth.

It is temporary.

> "For riches don't last forever, and the crown might not be passed to the next generation" (Proverbs 27:24, NLT).

They are not to be trusted in (Mark 10:23; Luke 18:24; 1 Timothy 6:17); they are not to be gloried in (Jeremiah 9:23); the heart is not to be set on them (Psalm 62:10); but they are made by God (Psalm 104:24), and come from God (1 Chronicles 29:12); and they are the crown of the wise (Proverbs 14:24).

Those possessing wealth are liable to certain kinds of sins, against which they are frequently warned: high-mindedness (1 Timothy 6:17); oppression of the poor (James 2:6); selfishness (Luke 12 and 16); dishonesty (Luke 19:1-10); self-conceit (Proverbs 28:11); and self-trust (Proverbs 18:11).

It is of interest to note that in five places in the KJV of the New Testament in which the word *lucre*—as applying to wealth—is used, it is prefaced by the word *filthy* (1 Timothy 3:3,.8; Titus 1:7,11; 1 Peter 5:2); and that in four of these five places, it refers to the income of ministers of the gospel, as though they were particularly susceptible to being led away by the influences and power of money, and so needed special warning.[31]

TREASURES OF WICKEDNESS PROFIT NOTHING

Proverbs 10:2 tells us that treasures or wealth accumulated through wickedness do not profit anything. Most people are trying to make enough money to survive. They will do that through any means, including lying, cheating, stealing, and more. I recently read a news article about the biggest ATM theft in history.

It happened in Japan. In 2016, Japanese police were investigating a nationwide ATM heist after nearly £8.8 million, or 1.4 billion yen (¥), was illegally withdrawn through 14,000 cash transactions in the span of two hours.[32] Cash was withdrawn almost simultaneously across Tokyo and sixteen other prefectures using as many as 1,600 counterfeit credit cards

---

31 "International Standard Bible Encyclopaedia," Biblesoft, lucre: International Standard Bible Encyclopaedia Electronic Database © 1996, 2003, 2006. All rights reserved.

32 "Convenience Store ATM Heist Sees ¥1.4 Billion Stolen in Two Hours across Japan," The Japan Times, May 22, 2016, accessed January 13, 2019, https://www.japantimes.co.jp/news/2016/05/22/national/crime-legal/convenience-store-atm-heist-sees-¥1-4-billion-stolen-two-hours-across-japan/#.XDrDFlxKjBU.

containing account information stolen from the South African institution, Standard Bank! This is just one example of people obtaining the treasures of wickedness.

> "He who has a slack hand becomes poor, but the hand of the diligent makes rich" (Proverbs 10:4).

This verse reveals one of the secrets to why some people remain poor and others become rich. He who has a slack hand becomes poor. You can sit and complain about your poverty and your misfortune all day long. That is not going to change anything. It will only lead to more poverty.

This verse describes two types of hands: the slack hand and the diligent hand. It tells us that poverty and riches depend on the hands of people. *Hands* refers to what we do with our life, our work. Some people are born without hands. Others find it hard to move their hand to do anything. They will find an excuse for everything. In the morning they will say it's too early and they will do it in the evening. When the evening comes, they will postpone it to the next day because it's too late. Months and years go by and they never accomplish anything. Having a slack hand does not mean they are not doing anything. Slack hands can be busy or seem busier than productive people, *but they have no goals and therefore produce no fruit.* They lack discipline and diligence.

> "He who gathers in summer is a wise son; he who sleeps in harvest is a son who causes shame" (Proverbs 10:5).

Summer has different meanings in the Bible. It means the hot season in the natural. But it also means the prime of our life. There is a season in each person's life in which they need to be working hard. If they miss that season it will be very difficult for them to catch up later. "He who gathers in summer" is a picture of someone who saves and invests in the prime of their life. They will be safe when they get old or when hard times come.

I believe you have been tremendously blessed by this book. I recommend you read it more than once and study it until it becomes part of your life. Obtain more copies and use them for Bible study groups. I also recommend getting other volumes in the Kingdom Awareness Series. I encourage you to pray the Lord's Prayer whenever you can. If you are part of an *ekklesia*, when you come together, pray this prayer as a group. I have paraphrased it for you below. Feel free to personalize it as the Holy Spirit leads you.

> *Our Father in heaven, hallowed be Your name.*
> *Let Your name be made holy in our nation, in my family, and in the whole earth.*
> *Thank You for giving us Your kingdom.*
> *Help us to administer it effectively according to Your will.*
> *Teach us how to tap into Your kingdom resources to solve problems here on earth.*
> *Let Your kingdom rule and dominion come into my life, family, and nation.*
> *Let Your kingdom government, family, economy, culture, education, and health come to this earth, in my life, nation, and family.*
> *Let Your will be done on earth as it is in heaven.*
> *Give us this day our daily, physical, financial, spiritual, and emotional bread (ideas, solutions, favor, wisdom, grace, and connections).*
> *And forgive us our debts as we forgive our debtors.*
> *(If there is anyone you need to forgive, say their name and release forgiveness from your heart now.)*
> *And do not lead us into temptation, but deliver us from the evil one and his works.*
> *Thank You for delivering us from evil, curses, offenses, jealousy, strife, sickness, ignorance, fear, deception, lies, debt, lack, and poverty,*
> *For Yours is the kingdom and the power and the glory forever.*
> *Amen.*

More Books & Resources

DISCIPLING NATIONS SERIES

Kingdom Mandate (for any donation)
Discovering the Lost Kingdom (Volume 1) $14.00
Purpose, Calling, and Gifts (Volume 2) $15.00
God's Original Design (Volume 3) $20.00
Seeing, Entering, and Manifesting the Kingdom of God (Volume 4) $20.00
The Ekklesia (Volume 5) $30.00
The Gospel of the Kingdom (Volume 6) $20.00
Power and Authority of the Church (Volume 7) $15.00
Kingdom Family (Volume 8) $15.00
The Birthing of a kingdom nation (Volume 9) $20.00
What happened to God? (Volume 10) $20.00
7 Dimensions and Operations of the Kingdom of God (Volume 11) $15.00
Kingdom Economy (Volume 12) $15.00
Kingdom Government (Volume 13) $15.00
Releasing Kings and Queens to their Original Intent (Volume 14) $10.00
Kingdom Secrets to Restoring Nations Back to God (Volume 15) $20.00
Keys to Fulfilling Your Kingdom Assignment (Volume 16) $15.00

KINGDOM LIVING SERIES

The Three Most Important Decisions of Your Life $15.00
Recognizing God's Timing for Your Life $12.00
Overcoming the Spirit of Poverty $10.00
Seven Kinds of Believers $10.00
7 Dimensions of God's Glory $5.00
7 Dimensions of God's Grace $10.00
7 Kinds of Faith $7.00

KINGDOM BOOKS FOR KIDS

Genesis 126 Three Volume Book set for boys $25.00

TO PLACE AN ORDER:

www.TheKingdomNetwork.org
Phone: 1-800-558-5020
Email: info@TheKingdomNetwork.org

THE KINGDOM UNIVERSITY

Are you struggling to discover your **PURPOSE ?**
You are not supposed to fit in but stand out !

Sign up today for the upcoming
FREE Online Kingdom Course

DISCOVERING
THE LOST KINGDOM

In this course you'll DISCOVER:

>> Your true identity and purpose
>> What God is doing on the earth and how you can partner with Him in it
>> Why God created the earth and put us on this planet
   And much more ...

Why are people becoming more and more disinterested in **church and religion** globally?
Join the course, and discover what your soul has been searching for all along.

FREE BOOK AND STUDY GUIDE

other courses available
>> DISCOVERING PURPOSE, CALLING AND GIFTS
>> SEEING, ENTERING AND MANIFESTING THE KINGDOM
>> GOD'S ORIGINAL DESIGN | FEBRUARY 2024
>> The Ekklesia
>> The Next move of GOD
   And more ...

Register Now @ **www.TheKingdomUniversity.org**

Welcome to

KINGDOM DELIVERANCE
— WORKSHOP —

Are you tired of waiting and looking for breakthroughs? Kingdom of God has the answer.

This kingdom deconstruct workshop is divided into EIGHT major categories which deal with the seven major areas of our life. Each one is connected to the next, and so if one of these areas dysfunctions, it will affect all other areas of your life.

1. Relationship with the Father
2. Spiritual Healing
3. Emotional Healing
4. Recognizing Purpose and Calling
5. Identifying and Mastering Natural and Spiritual Gifts
6. Finances—Learning to Live in Kingdom Economy
7. Healing Relationships
8. Physical Health

Take action now. Order all 8 workshop manuals today !

Thank you so much for taking the courses from The Kingdom University. Taking a course is only the first step. We are pleased to present you with the next step—that of going through the process to get rid of all the extra weights that have been slowing and hindering you from fully living out your kingdom assignment.

Call 1 800 558 5020   www.TheKingdomNetwork.org

www.ingramcontent.com/pod-product-compliance
Lightning Source LLC
Chambersburg PA
CBHW070051080526
44586CB00013B/1002